1991

*Soundings in Critical Theory*

*Emile Durkheim: Sociologist and Philosopher*
*A Preface to Sartre*
Madame Bovary *on Trial*
*Rethinking Intellectual History: Texts, Contexts, Language*
*History & Criticism*
*History, Politics, and the Novel*

CO-EDITOR

*Modern European Intellectual History:*
*Reappraisals and New Perspectives*

# Soundings in Critical Theory

Dominick LaCapra

*Cornell University Press*

ITHACA AND LONDON

First published 1989 by Cornell University Press.

International Standard Book Number 0-8014-2322-8 (cloth)
International Standard Book Number 0-8014-9572-5 (paper)
Library of Congress Catalog Card Number 89-30080

Printed in the United States of America

*Librarians: Library of Congress cataloging information
appears on the last page of the book.*

*The paper in this book is acid-free and meets the guidelines for permanence
and durability of the Committee on Production Guidelines for Book
Longevity of the Council on Library Resources.*

For Beau, Ratsie, and
the memory of Bamse

# Contents

# Acknowledgments

Portions of the Introduction appeared in *The Journal of The History of Ideas* 49 (1988). Other chapters, or versions of them, appeared in the following places: Chapter 1 in Murray Krieger, ed., *The Aims of Representation* (New York: Columbia University Press, 1987) © 1987, Columbia University Press; Chapter 2 as The University of Minnesota Center for Humanistic Studies Occasional Paper Number 5 (1985) © University of Minnesota Press; also in *Critical Inquiry* 13 (1987), © 1987 The University of Chicago Press, and reprinted in Françoise Meltzer, ed., *The Trial(s) of Psychoanalysis* (Chicago: University of Chicago Press, 1988); Chapter 3 in *The Journal of Modern History* 60 (1988) © 1988 The University of Chicago Press; Chapter 5 in *Poetics Today* 9 (1988) © 1988 Duke University Press. Chapters 4, 6, and 7 are published here for the first time.

I thank Jane Pedersen for reading the manuscript and offering many fruitful suggestions.

DOMINICK LACAPRA

*Ithaca, New York*

*Soundings in Critical Theory*

And as regards the sounding-out of idols . . . which are here touched with the hammer as with a tuning fork.

—Friedrich Nietzsche, Foreword to *The Twilight of Idols*

Your objections as to phraseology and style have good grounds to stand on; many of them indeed are considerations to which I myself was not blind; which there (unluckily) were no means of doing more than nodding to as one passed. A man has but a certain strength; imperfections cling to him, which if he wait till he have brushed off entirely, he will spin forever on his axis, advancing nowhither.

—Thomas Carlyle, letter of June 4, 1835, to John Sterling concerning *Sartor Resartus*

# Introduction

This book addresses some general issues in contemporary thought through the medium of dialogic exchanges with other critics. This situated notion of critical theory tends to reverse the more conventional format in works that approximate the status of a treatise on method or a theoretical system. Conceptual problems are here approached through—or at least introduced by—specific arguments with significant contemporary theorists. And what is often relegated to footnotes is here embodied and interrogated in the principal text. These procedures attest to my attempt to leave certain traces of production evident in my own writing. The larger incentive in this approach is to enact within my own "textual" practice an open dialectical interaction both between concrete interlocutors and between thematic unification and those challenges to it that may prove to be provocative in carrying critical reflection further. My conviction is that the critique of totalization that has been so prominent in recent thought should not devolve into an indiscriminate reliance on techniques of fragmentation, decentering, and associative "play." It should be conjoined with a critical and self-critical attempt to elicit the actual and desirable articulations among aspects of culture and society—articulations open to forces that contest and displace but do not simply eliminate them. One such articulation joins three important intellectual tendencies: Marxism, psychoanalysis, and poststructuralism. The elaboration of connections among this trio of critical theories has been a primary preoccupation of intellectual life in the modern context. I try to put forth some reasons why this has been the case—and in a transformed fashion should continue to be. I also indicate ways in which this preoccupation may be inflected in directions more pertinent for a critical and self-critical historiography.

Ideally these chapters should be read as dialogic interventions in an ongoing debate. They do not attempt to be the last word in, or a judicious summary of, that debate. They are essayistic interventions precisely to the extent that they try to address and counteract either a hypertrophic or a stunted development and to prepare the way for a more desirable interaction of discursive and institutional forces. Nonetheless I at times defend the provocative role of hyperbole in a larger discursive network of forces. I also try to distinguish the person from the idea or argument, however difficult this distinction may be to establish or maintain. Proper names in these pages should be taken as shorthand for positions or perspectives, and I hope that argumentative exchange, even when it turns polemical, may remain good-spirited while not abandoning either commitment or wit.

In the recent past, two tendencies have been prominent in the work of some influential historians and literary critics: the interpretation of "low" or popular culture (often conflated with mass or commodified culture) as bearing an oppositional charge and a utopian potential, and the understanding of "high" or elite culture as typically—or even by definition—functioning to reinforce a structure of dominance in society and politics.[1] Because I take issue with this combination of interpretive tendencies in its marked form, I have at times tried to compensate for its excesses by stressing what it tends to obscure or misconstrue. But this corrective strategy should not be confused with the defense of the polar opposition between "high" and "low" culture. Nor should this strategy be seen as leading to the idea of a separate aesthetic realm or a discrete sphere of canonized artifacts that should be the elitist object of displaced religious devotion and detached contemplation. By contrast I am stressing the need to analyze and criticize the constitution and functioning of "high," "low," and commodified culture and to explicate in detail how specific texts or artifacts relate to a larger

[1] See, for example, Fredric Jameson, *The Political Unconscious* (Ithaca, N.Y., 1981); idem, "Reification and Utopia in Mass Culture," *Social Text* 1 (1979), 130-48; Carlo Ginzburg, *The Cheese and the Worms*, trans. John and Anne Tedesci (1976; Baltimore, 1980); and Peter Stallybrass and Allon White, *The Politics & Poetics of Transgression* (Ithaca, N.Y., 1986).

sociocultural configuration in ideologically reinforcing, critical, and potentially transformative ways.

One crucial problem that has become increasingly insistent, particularly in Western industrialized countries, is the role of a commodity system in assimilating and affecting the qualitative character of various areas of culture. "Mass" culture tends to be commodified culture, and it is open to question not because it appeals to many people but because of its commodified character. The controversial issue is to what extent mass culture reinforces a commodity system and to what extent it harbors a viably critical or even a transformative or "utopian" charge. It is difficult to avoid the general conclusion that the level of commodification and capital investment in mass culture is so high that ideologically reinforcing or adaptive forces tend to be marked or even preponderant and that "utopian" elements tend to be restricted to contained fantasy and wishful thinking. But only the "close reading" of artifacts and their relation to institutional settings and pressures can address these issues with the required specificity.

One should of course elicit and try to build upon any critical currents that do indeed exist in artifacts of mass culture. Still, it is dubious simply to conflate mass culture with popular culture and to ascribe to it the characteristics—especially those of resistance and legitimate utopian potential—that have often been attributed (accurately or not) to popular culture. How mass culture assimilates and modifies elements of popular and high culture is as intricate a problem as that posed by the interaction of high culture with both popular and mass culture.

To the extent that certain segments of high culture (particularly print culture)—while never transcending a more or less unconscious participation in existing ideologies—contain a relatively pronounced critical force, it may be because they are objects of relatively small capital investment and not central to the functioning of a commodity system. But this marginal status itself lessens the social and political role they can play. The ineffectiveness of marginalization is exacerbated by the compulsion toward, or cultivation of, hermetic inaccessibility in artifacts of high culture. The monumental difficulty in both the creation and the reception of these artifacts—a difficulty confronting intellectual and cultural history itself—is how to render their critical and transformative potential more accessible without either domesticating or sacralizing them. One dimension of this problem is simply put but not simply addressed: how should one read and interpret texts and other artifacts?

A specific object of criticism in these chapters is the meagre status accorded to the problem of textuality within professional history. When one raises the problem of reading texts and of conceptualizing their relations to inferential reconstructions of other activities, including their contexts of production and reading, one still tends to meet with two responses from professional historians. The first is the belief that a close interest in problems of textuality leads to the end of historiography. The second is the view that historians have in fact been interested in these problems all along and that criticism of reductive forms of contextualism, historicism, and neopositivism trades in caricatures, beats dead horses, and fabricates straw men. These mutually contradictory (and metaphorically mixed) responses are, in psychoanalytic terms, themselves evidence that criticism in this area still has a point. I try to offer some additional evidence for its continued pertinence in the course of this book.

There are, however, signs that some historians are indeed becoming interested in an approach to texts that does not reduce them to simple documentary indexes of a hypostatized reality and that even poses differently the very problem of reading and using documents.[2] And the inevitable traces of interpretation, "transference," and dialogic exchange in research are beginning to be thematized as problems in the self-understanding of historians. It would be premature to refer to a "new history" or even to a "new intellectual history." But the problem of how to read texts or documents and how to relate them to processes of contextual understanding and the inferential reconstruction of other sociocultural activities is finding a place on the agenda of historical studies today. To aid in formulating a better notion of what that place should be is one major purpose of this book.

[2] See, for example, the lucid and informative discussion in John Toews, "Intellectual History after the Linguistic Turn: The Autonomy of Meaning and the Irreducibility of Experience," *American Historical Review* 92 (1987), 879-907.

It should be evident, in reading these chapters, that I do not reject social history, eliminate the referent, or defend an intellectual history fixated on canonical artifacts and "great books." Canonicity is an important issue but not because it provides an exclusive list of great thinkers and artists for quasi-transcendental humanistic education. Nor does it simply serve as the occasion to display cultural snobbery by adorning texts with learned allusions. A canon has intellectually ambivalent functions, and it is related to institutional and disciplinary problems. On the one hand, it is a source of authority, and it often functions to legitimate hegemonic class, gender, and racial elites. On the other hand, canonical artifacts themselves have complex, internally divided relations to their contexts of creation and use. These relations may be better investigated if we reopen the question of the canon by reformulating the text/context problem as crucial for intellectual and, to some extent, social history and by examining closely the precise way given texts come to terms with their contexts, including their canonical status. I have intimated that the objective of a more or less noncanonical reading of them is to bring out critical and possibly transformative potentials ignored or repressed in canonical uses. But in the course of my argument I add two further points. Certain anticanonical readings (such as those fostered by the appeal to Foucault in the so-called New Historicism) may focus exclusively on the symptomatic role of texts and their function in reinforcing canonicity and other dimensions of a "power structure." And the desire to stress the critical or even potentially transformative implications of texts should not induce presentism or procedures of forced interpretation and projective reprocessing of the past.

Given its role in this book and elsewhere in my publications, it may be useful if I turn explicitly to my relation to the work of Jacques Derrida, a relation I characterize as one of highly selective "appropriation." I do not attempt to emulate Derrida's "style"—his extravagantly playful enactment of a disseminatory, nonproductive movement of the signifier that supplements his rigorous deconstruction of traditional metaphysics. I make the admittedly problematic attempt to elaborate a critical and self-critical historiography that remains open to the risks Derrida explores but also insists

5

upon certain constraints in a manner that engages the disciplinary conventions of professional historians.

The notion of "appropriation" may, however, be inadequate to characterize my relation to Derrida's texts or, for that matter, to account for the relationship between any interpreter and an object of inquiry or selective use. In this book and elsewhere, I attempt to conceive of the relation between the historian or critic and the "other" on the model of transference in Freud. In a transferential relation one tends to repeat in a displaced way the very processes that are active (at times uncritically) in one's object of inquiry. The point, however, is not simply to indulge in transferential relations or to deny them. It is to "work through" them in a "dialogic" (or openly "dialectical") fashion that strives for empirically and critically controlled reciprocity in an exchange.

I find a questionable reprocessing of the past to be characteristic of important dimensions of Derrida's own recent essay on Paul de Man.[3] (This tendency may of course be induced by strong transferential relations attendant upon close friendship and a degree of intellectual identification.) Particularly in Derrida's analysis of "Les juifs dans la littérature actuelle," an article published by the young de Man in 1941, strained interpretation is abetted by a process of analytic dismemberment that eliminates the argumentative direction and thrust of de Man's appalling article. This interpretative procedure culminates in an extremely implausible attempt to transform what is manifestly anti-Semitic into an anticonformist critique of anti-Semitism—an attempt that in my judgment receives little or no support in de Man's text. This is not the place for an extended critical reading of Derrida's essay; let me simply say that certain proclivities evident in this essay do not represent the dimensions of Derrida's work that I defend. My basic point in this context—with reference both to Derrida's reading of de Man and to my reaction to it—is that one has to refer to texts in making arguments about them, and one must be open to the possibility that the text may indeed resist one's interpretations. Of course the arguments of other interpreters are crucial in helping one to detect one's

[3] See "Like the Sound of the Deep within a Shell: Paul de Man's War," *Critical Inquiry* 14 (1988), 590-652.

shortcomings, but these arguments are convincing insofar as they appeal to the textual evidence and enable one to see things one did not see at first.

One dimension of Derrida's work I have found quite fruitful is his sustained undoing of binary oppositions that are themselves crucial for a scapegoat mechanism. Among the binaries deconstructed by Derrida is that between continuity and discontinuity in the understanding of time. In complex fashion, Derrida connects with both Heidegger and Freud in rethinking temporality in terms of interacting processes of repetition and change—change that may be traumatically disruptive. I also consider deconstruction important both as a strategy of reversal of the dominant hierarchies in which binaries are organized and as an attendant and equally necessary method of displacing and rearticulating relations. The undoing of binary oppositions does not, however, eliminate the need to investigate carefully their actual role in intellectual, social, and political relations where they may be quite constraining intellectually and have strong institutional support. Nor should the undoing of binaries eventuate in the obliteration of distinctions. Instead it leads to the problem of rearticulating distinctions and attendant relations in a larger, transformed field or network.

This larger field or network of relations is precisely what Derrida refers to as the "general text." Derrida could not be more consistent and insistent in stressing that he is not using "text" in the ordinary sense but in a different or "infrastructural" sense to refer to relational networks of "instituted traces" in general. I take this view in the direction of a reconceptualization of the relation between texts and contexts in historical interpretation. I argue that in intellectual history one should not take "context" as a simple explanatory concept; rather one should pose as an explicit problem the question of how texts come to terms with contexts and vice versa. But this does not imply a conventional "intratextual" perspective or a so-called linguistic turn. One respect in which I very much agree with Mikhail Bakhtin is in his departure from a narrowly linguistic perspective and in his insistence upon an investigation of language in use as a historical issue. In the chapters that follow, I often attempt to supplement Derrida with Bakhtinian perspectives, particularly in the investigation of specific historical or institutional matters and in the combination of empirical-analytic techniques of research with a dialogic exchange vis-à-vis the object of inquiry.

In specific terms, this book makes a qualified defense of intellectual history as a disciplined but self-questioning attempt to read and interpret artifacts in context. But it also indicates the need to arrive at a better understanding of contexts themselves in terms of an informed conception of modern culture and society. In this sense, intellectual history is both constituted and deconstituted in the course of the argument. It is constituted and defended—at times polemically—against dubious conceptions of it or attacks upon it. But it is simultaneously deconstituted with reference to a larger critical and historical conception of culture and society to which intellectual history must contribute and into which it may enter in still unpredictable ways. The broadest ambition of the book is to further a process of self-criticism and reconstitution in historical studies, a process that is intimately bound up both with the understanding of the past and with sociocultural and political critique bearing on the present and future. Thus the essential tension between the professional status of the historian and the paraprofessional status of the critic must not only be tolerated but actively affirmed as a crucial index of one's place in the contemporary conflict of interpretations. In entering this conflict, one need not abandon all hope of common ground or consensus. But achieving common ground should not be confused with settling into the benevolent intolerance of a commonsense hermeneutics, and it cannot result from unearned declarations of interdisciplinary convergence. Consensus itself is at best a problematic, limited component of the present and a figure for a more desirable future that can never entirely transcend the scarred imprint of the past. It should also go without saying that, even in the most ideal and genuinely cooperative of futures, agreement must be open to criticism and to more engaging, self-critical modes of difference or radical questioning.

The reader may find it useful if I provide a brief indication of the contents of the following chapters. "Criticism Today" offers a general assessment of the problems and the prospects of criticism as a contemporary genre that questions its own limits, crosses disciplinary boundaries, and raises issues relevant to a variety of fields. It refers specifically to the roles of Jacques Derrida, Michel Foucault,

Jean-François Lyotard, and Mikhail Bakhtin as important reference points in contemporary criticism.

"History and Psychoanalysis" assesses the implications of Freud's thought for the writing of history. It departs from the more common historiographic practices of explaining psychoanalysis through the attempt to place Freud in fin-de-siècle Vienna and of employing psychoanalysis to account for the life and work of historical figures or the nature of movements. Instead it turns the question of psychoanalysis back on historiography itself in order to explore the extent to which the attempt to come to terms with Freud may transform the manner in which we both understand history and practice historiography.

"Chartier, Darnton, and the Great Symbol Massacre" treats the recent debate between two important historians, Roger Chartier and Robert Darnton—a debate whose occasion was Darnton's book *The Great Cat Massacre*. Here the focus is on the question of reading texts and documents in historiography. To test Darnton's use of texts in his acclaimed book, the chapter concludes with a reading of Jean-Jacques Rousseau's prefaces to *La nouvelle Hélöise*.

"The Temporality of Rhetoric" was originally planned as an inquiry into the problem of temporality in history and, more particularly, into the interpretation of Romanticism through a comparison of M. H. Abrams's *Natural Supernaturalism* and Paul de Man's "Rhetoric of Temporality," and critical analysis still constitutes the major part of the chapter. Like many others who had written about de Man just before the discovery of his early World War II articles, I was placed in the double bind of either not addressing the problems they posed or adding something, however premature and partial, about them. I decided upon the latter course, but I stress that my discussion is based on limited information and that it is quite possible that further disclosures may affect my response in positive, negative, or more complex and even ambiguous ways. My discussion of "Les juifs dans la littérature actuelle" is in good part motivated by my critical reaction to Derrida's treatment of it in "Like the Sound of the Deep within a Shell: Paul de Man's War." The body of the chapter was already written in substantially the form in which it appears before I learned of the wartime articles and wrote the postscript.

"Culture and Ideology: From Geertz to Marx" acknowledges Clifford Geertz's important contribution to the understanding and use of a protean concept, but it attempts to argue for a qualified return to Marx's conception of ideology. The chapter tends to assume a point that may deserve explicit treatment: the concept of ideology itself raises the intricate issue of the "displacement" of religious categories into secular forms of interpretation and justification. The concept of ideology arises in the context of the secularization of culture, and it requires the elucidation of the relation between religious and secular forms in terms of involved processes of recurrence and transformation. Thus the chapter's topic is closely related to the issues treated in the two chapters that precede it.

"Up against the Ear of the Other: Marx after Derrida" begins with the question of the implications of deconstruction for the reading of Marx. One of the most important of these is the need to attend to heterogeneous tendencies that challenge the coherence and unity of a corpus of writing. The essay offers a general schema for reading Marx in terms of Hegelian-utopian, positivistic, and more openly dialectical (or dialogic) voices or forces that run through his work and provide bases for often contradictory interpretations of it. It also defends the third of these "voices" as the most fruitful and deserving of further development.

"Intellectual History and Critical Theory" tries to explicate and explore the project of establishing a link between intellectual history and critical theory. In the process it reviews the contributions of deconstruction and the New Historicism, and it discusses one of John Pocock's recent essays as a statement of an important and influential tendency in the historical reconstruction of the past. It also inquires into the interaction between historical reconstruction and dialogic exchange, and it is premised on the basic point that we should neither disavow nor freely act out a transferential relation to the other but rather attempt to work critically through it.

# 1

## Criticism Today

James looked at the Lighthouse. He could see the whitewashed
rocks; the tower, stark and straight; [. . .] he could see that it
was barred with black and white; he could see windows in it;
he could even see washing spread on the rocks to dry. So that
was the Lighthouse, was it?

No, the other was also the Lighthouse. For nothing was
simply one thing.

—Virginia Woolf, *To the Lighthouse*

How can one try to account for critical discourses today? At
best one acknowledges that any attempt to do justice to them can
never attain metanarrative or megatheoretical mastery and must
by contrast accept, indeed actively affirm, its own status as one discursive venture engaging in dialogue with heterogeneous others.
One also begins with a brief and inadequate evocation of the problematic nature—the frustrations and the hopes—of contemporary
criticism.

Any assembly of "critics" today will have representatives of various established departments who are uneasy with their own representative function and may find more to say, listen to, or at least
argue about with other critics than with more securely "representative" members of their own department or field. Indeed contemporary critics are no longer content with interdisciplinary
efforts that simply combine, compare, or synthetically unify the
methods of existing academic disciplines. Their questioning of
established disciplines both raises doubts about internal criteria of
purity or autonomy and unsettles the boundaries and protocols of
given fields. Criticism in this sense is a discursive agitation running

across a variety of disciplines and having an uneasy relation to its own institutionalization. It seeks out threshold positions that cannot securely locate their own theoretical grounds, and it may even cultivate the risks of insistently hybridized discourses—discourses that may breed fruitful variants but may also prove to be sterile if not monstrous. At least in terms of academic politics, the strategy of criticism is thus transgressive, and it demands not a quarantined place in the margins of established discourses or disciplines but a generalized displacement and rearticulation of them.

Yet it is also the case that disconcertingly liminal criticism has proved more compelling in certain established fields than in others: in literary criticism, Continental philosophy, interpretive social theory, and intellectual history, say, than in literary history, analytic philosophy, positivistic social science, and conventional historiography. And within the fields or disciplines in which it has made a difference, it has been most pronounced in already marginalized areas of the university, even if mainstream thought has subsequently accommodated it in more or less naturalized form. Hence it has appeared first in French or comparative literature before making significant inroads in English departments, and it has had a sporadic, uneven role in intellectual history, sensitive to the exceptional voices and counterdiscourses of the past, before affecting social history, attuned to representative discourses and collective mentalities. Elsewhere criticism in the sense I have evoked makes its mark at best through the active resistance or renewed stimulus for self-definition it provokes as well as through the convenient image of the "radically other" it provides for those seeking a reaffirmation of their identity.

In these respects, criticism is itself a paradoxical genre that contests the limits of generic classification. It brings down on itself the ire and the irony of those with an interest in reasserting the conceptual and institutional integrity of realms of discourse and disciplines. The very discourses of critics speaking in hybridized or "undecidable" voices are difficult to classify, and they at most bear the marks of certain disciplinary inflections which give them a relative specificity. Yet signs of internal strain also appear; for disciplinary and professional bonds have their hold even on those who grow restive with their constraints, and one may tire of the repeated sounds of the new or the predictable discovery of the uncanny in every discursive nook and cranny. This strain may help to explain the reversions to type and the "god-that-failed" reactions of some critics who become disenchanted with their earlier "experimental" selves; but it may also induce reflection about what specifically ought to be changed and what preserved in a discipline one questions. It may also induce one to confront the general problem of how the relations among disciplines or fields should be rearticulated.

Especially for those critics who see Continental thought as a reference point, the most imposing tradition of critical theory is represented by Marxism. And one of the tasks of recent criticism has been to try to sort out the elements of the Marxist tradition in order to discern what is still relevant to contemporary sociopolitical and interpretive issues. One current in Marx's texts that was further codified by Engels and the theorists of the Second International is, of course, positivism, and it has been subjected to a far-reaching attack in the recent past. One might define positivism as the isolation and autonomization of the constative dimension of discourse. It fosters a narrowly "social-scientific" delimitation of research in empirical and analytic terms, and it avoids or occludes the very problem of a critical theory of society and culture. Jürgen Habermas has been a foremost critic of Marx in this respect, and he has attempted to recast critical theory in a complex manner that includes a relativized "constative" dimension in a more complex hermeneutic and emancipatory paradigm for social research.[1] In Louis Althusser's powerful rereading of Marx, however, one may perhaps detect tendencies that lend themselves to a subtle rehabilitation of positivism. Althusser's important conception of ideology as centered on the subject seems to obviate the possibility of an objectivist or scientistic ideology, notably one that privileges science by presenting it as a "subjectless" discourse. Science seems to become a "realm of discourse" that unproblematically transcends ideology, and the very role of a "scientific" subject in constituting an object realm is itself occulted. Yet other aspects of Althusser's

---

[1] See esp. *Knowledge and Human Interests*, trans. Jeremy J. Shapiro (Boston, 1971).

conception of ideology would imply that its wiles are many-sided, and the recurrent displacement of the necessary blindnesses it brings is a sign of the necessity of recurrent critique.[2]

A second tendency in Marx's texts has had remarkable staying power in modern thought despite the criticism of Althusser and many others. I am of course referring to Hegelianism. At times in Marx, for example, in the afterword to the second German edition of *Capital*, it is amalgamated with positivism in a composite image of a positivist dialectic that is revealed as the inverted Hegelian "rational kernel in the mystic shell" of speculative idealism. But, whatever the precise form it takes, Hegelian Marxism provides the basis for a metanarrative or "dialectic" in which the proletariat becomes the "materialist" surrogate for *Geist* as the redemptive subject of history. Hegelian Marxism has recently received a new lease on life in Fredric Jameson's theory of the political unconscious, which, through a disarming ruse, construes the vast metanarrative of class struggle leading to redemptive emancipation as itself the repressed content of contemporary thought.[3]

My condensed and truncated account thus far should at least indicate that I stress in Marx's texts the heterogeneous forces that help to account for the divergences and inner strains in subsequent Marxism. Two further aspects of Marx's thought remain, I think, highly relevant today—aspects that deserve to be defended, if need be, against other aspects of Marx's thought itself. One of them is general: it is the very understanding of critical theory in contrast to both narrowly positivistic and expansively metanarrative inclinations. The problem is of course that of the nature of the critical theory one would defend. I argue for a displacement of totalizing dialectics in the direction of supplementarity and dialogism that raise the issue of articulating the relations between contestatory, indeed incommensurable, forces in thought and practice. This displacement requires an investigation of language, and of signifying practices in general, that Marx never provided and even tended to

[2] Compare *For Marx*, trans. Ben Brewster (1965; London, 1979); *Reading Capital*, trans. Ben Brewster (1968; London, 1979); *Lenin and Philosophy*, trans. Ben Brewster (New York, 1971); and *Essays in Self-Criticism*, trans. Grahame Lock (London, 1976).

[3] *The Political Unconscious* (Ithaca, N.Y., 1981).

obscure in his binary opposition between base and superstructure.

Another aspect of Marx's thought is more specific. It is his critique of a commodity system, much of which remains applicable even to a transformed capitalism and may, furthermore, furnish a model for the critique of other developments in modern history. Crucial to Marx's analysis of the commodity form is his delineation of the process of reductive equalization or commensuration whereby qualitative differences are bracketed in the constitution of exchange value. A commodity as an exchange value can replace or be substituted for another commodity. Substitution implies that commodities have something in common beneath their appearances in phenomenal form. (Marx is here rendering and developing the metaphysical assumptions of classical economics in free indirect style.) This principle of identity is asserted by Marx to be abstract labor power—an identity implicit in the theories of classical economists but never made explicit by them. Abstract labor power is itself produced through a reduction of qualitatively different modes of living labor to a commensurable, equalized, homogeneous form— human labor in the abstract—which is then employed as a means in the production of exchange values. The process of equalization or commensuration reaches its reductive apogee in the designation of one commodity, ultimately in the money form, as universal equivalent.

Marx's crucial analysis of the commodity harbors internal difficulties. The very voice in which it is formulated is divided: it is both positivistic and critical. The analysis, even in its critical dimension, seems to accept the binary opposition between exchange and use value. Use value is related to qualitative differences between commodities and seems entirely transparent in nature. The culminating account of "commodity fetishism" itself seems to trace the mystified, fetishized character of the commodity to a simple reversal: "A commodity is therefore a mysterious thing, simply because in it the social character of men's labor appears to them as an objective character stamped upon the product of that labor." This statement has the virtue of calling into question the process of naturalization or normalization essential to ideological mystification. Yet the difficulty is that the strategy of simple reversal invests the social with foundational powers, and it readily accords both with a redemptive rendition of class struggle and with a productivist image of the revolutionary goal. The unproblematic notion of the transparency of use value, moreover, obscures the more basic issue of the very opposition between use and exchange value as well as the implication of use value in utilitarian norms that are operative in the reduction of living labor to instrumentalized labor power. (But does "use value" also evoke an older idea of usufruct as well as function in a newer, utopian register?) The more forceful dimension of Marx's account, I think, lies in the critical delineation of the mechanism of equalization involving a reduction of labor to "the same unsubstantial reality in each [exchange value], a mere congelation of homogeneous labor power." This critique enables one to question the very division between instrumentalized labor and autonomized symbolic meaning in the fetishized commodity, and it may be extrapolated into a more general displacement of what Marx saw as the "absurd" forms of relationship in a commodity system.

Equalization is itself a normalizing device, and it is crucial in the formation of pure binary oppositions insofar as each opposite is fully homogeneous, identical, or equal to itself and totally different from its other. The critique of normalization and of pure binary opposites has, of course, been pronounced in so-called poststructuralism, and it signals a way in which the critique of language and of signifying practices in general finds a point of contact with a critique of the commodity system as a crucial signifying practice in modern society. Here the investigation of processes of signification may be seen as a necessary supplement to Marxism understood as a critical theory of society and culture, but of course it is a supplement that takes Marxism in certain directions rather than others.

The three "poststructural" figures to whom I shall briefly allude in the attempt to indicate the relation of a critique of signifying practices to a critical theory of society are Jacques Derrida, Michel Foucault, and Jean-François Lyotard. Except for certain facets of Foucault's work, all three may be seen as engaging in a critique of positivism—positivism which is characterized by a reductive equalization of all texts and artifacts into a homogeneous body of documentary "information" or constative statements as well as by a disavowal of any transferential relation to the object of inquiry. All three also elude the familiar charge that poststructuralism is a neoformalism, especially in its manifest avoidance of political and historical issues and its autonomization of texts as scenes for the narcissistic play of liberated (or what Derrida would call transcendental) signifiers. In addition, I contend that their work suggests the project of a critical genealogy of both positivism and formalism as complementary, fetishized enterprises: one reducing texts or artifacts to their narrowly constative dimension as documents in the reconstitution of "contexts" or "social realities," while the other becomes fixated on the internal play of the performative dimension of texts isolated from the "external" (or externalized) contexts of their writing, reception, and critical reading.

In different ways, Derrida, Foucault, and Lyotard attempt to intensify a legitimation crisis in modern society as well as to suggest antidotes to it. Their variable modes of writing are strategic interventions in the linguistic institution that has often been taken as the bedrock of communication and community. At times they almost seem to engage in stylistic guerrilla warfare waged under a black sun. They may even carry to an explosion point the crisis of representation that artistic and intellectual elites have confronted at least since the end of the nineteenth century. Indeed, the stylistic experimentation and "alienation effects" in the writing of modern cultural elites may be interpreted as a complex response to disorder and alienation in the larger society—a response that resists, however problematically, symbolic and contemplative solutions to these problems in either analytic or narrative form.

One of the recurrent motifs of social theorists such as Marx or Durkheim is that the established modern order is in fundamental ways an established disorder. For Nietzsche the established disorder is both the scene of nihilistic decadence that had to be worked through and the setting for unheard-of creativity, at times played out on the edge of madness. The most potent modes of thought had to be the most radically ambivalent and dangerous, open both to the best uses and the worst abuses. One point on which Durkheim and Nietzsche, who are so different in many respects, might nonetheless agree is that modern society and culture posed with special urgency the problem of the relation between the exception and the rule or, in other terms, the relation between transgression and normative commitment. They both also advocated the careful study of mores, routines, and practices in everyday life.

It may well be true that a desirable goal of sociocultural life is to provide the institutional and ethical basis for strong commitment to practices and routines in daily life that create trust among members of society. This context might both lessen the prevalence or the need of routine transgression and make "sublime" or "uncanny" overtures more engaging and less banalized. It may also be the case that certain tacit ties and practical commitments have retained greater resiliency in areas of everyday life, and it would be foolhardy to root them out on the pretext that a cultural revolution must be furthered in every conceivable manner. But it is, I think, self-deceptive to point to everyday practice and routine or to identify face-to-face conversation (in contrast with the written text) as a pragmatic origin or source for the generation of meaning and thus the answer to doubt and criticism. This gesture is suspiciously ideological in a number of ways. It is altogether unspecific in its characterization of routine and the everyday "life world," thereby generalizing and normalizing what may well be only partial realities. It also ignores the problem of the extent to which a legitimation crisis has affected the level of everyday routine itself, turning routine into empty ritual and making cliché the linguistic definition of ordinary social reality. (One need not recount the familiar catalog of daily mishaps and routine horrors that have helped to make the sitcom and the disaster movie two of the most "representative" documents of contemporary life.) Indeed in proposing everyday *phronesis* or practical consciousness as the "meaningful" way out, one occults the very role of ideology in creating routine complacency, and one threatens to replicate its role in one's own analysis. One also transfers to a commonsense level the metaphysic of origins and of presence one believes one has transcended, and one may even further a methodological populism that in recent sociology and social history has at times taken a decidedly anti-intellectual turn.[4]

It should no longer be necessary to observe that Derrida does not privilege writing in the ordinary sense and that his notion of the

---

[4] On these issues, see my *History & Criticism* (Ithaca, N.Y., 1985).

text is not to be identified with the discrete written artifact (and certainly not with codes). The very propensity, despite all evidence to the contrary, to see his work in this light is instructive, however, for it testifies to the deep-seated nature of the metaphysical desires Derrida deconstructs. Derrida has insisted that philosophy, despite its own desire for totality and closure, is not a separate realm and that the "logocentric" metaphysic of presence, which significant philosophical texts stage in a powerful *Darstellung*, may be operative in a more offhand and routine manner in everyday life as well as in the social sciences that study it. Derrida has also recently stressed the need to rethink the very notion of the institution, and he has made some attempt to connect his readings of written texts with a critique of institutions and forms of everyday life, notably in the cases of education, technology, mass media, and nuclear power.[5] But it is initially plausible to argue that the effects of Derrida's intervention have been most evident in the rereading and rewriting of written texts and that the implications of his work for institutional formations and everyday life need to be further developed and made more convincing in sociopolitical terms. What should be apparent, however, is that the oft-quoted maxim *"il n'y a pas de hors-texte"* (there is no outside-the-text) is not a charter for formalism, an invitation to intratextual narcissism, or an endorsement of the free play of liberated signifiers. It is a critique of the attempt to ground the work and play of textuality in some totally extratextual foundation or "context" that itself would escape involvement in a relational network or field. And the very strategy of "deconstruction" requires that one assume a necessary complicity with dubious discourses and attempt to work through them in the articulation of significantly different possibilities. The implication is that there is no "inside-the-text" either—no autonomous realm of signification of either literary or documentary language. In brief, formalism is as questionable as positivism. One has here, I think, an invitation to reformulate the entire problem of the relation between "texts"

---

[5] See, for example, GREPH, *Qui a peur de la philosophie* (Paris, 1977); "Entre crochets," *Digraphe* 8 (1976); *La carte postale: De Socrate à Freud et au-delà* (Paris, 1981); "Philosophie des Etats Généraux," in *Etats Généraux de la philosophie* (Paris, 1979); and "No Apocalypse, Not Now," *Diacritics* 14 (1984).

and "contexts" in terms that may take one further in directions Derrida has, however unevenly, at least traced.

The interest of Foucault, as well as the inducement not to make too much of his polemic with Derrida, is that he has ostensibly gone further in precisely these directions. He has investigated discursive and social practices as they bear on the "mad," the imprisoned, and various other social groups, and he has construed the treatment of "transgressive" minorities as indicative of the processes operating in society at large. More generally, he has forged an alliance between history and criticism that poses a stylistic and substantive challenge to standard procedures in both conventional historiography and literary criticism. Indeed a closer articulation of the initiatives of Foucault and Derrida might reveal a way to work through certain limitations of established disciplines.

Yet, at least on a thematic level, Foucault has often treated specific texts as mere tokens or symptoms of larger epistemic or discursive structures rather than explicitly posing in a more complex and problematic way the issue of symptomatic, critical, and possibly transformative relations between texts and their contexts of writing and reception. (There is a parallel, allusive use of artifacts in the more lyrical dimension of Foucault's writing.) In addition, he has often created the impression of offering a massively totalizing account, one that paradoxically eliminates or plays down the forces of resistance in the past analogous to those Foucault would like to further in the present. Thus in his influential *Discipline and Punish* (*Surveiller et punir*), Foucault—especially toward the end of the book — provides the image of a "carceral archipelago" or a panoptic society that conjures up the fantasia of a totalitarian organization of societies in the nineteenth century that is beyond the dreams of even recent regimes.[6] (In his contribution to *L'impossible prison*, Foucault specifies that his object of analysis in *Discipline and Punish* was a normative paradigm cutting across a number of institutions — one that motivated thought and action but was not fully realized in existing society.[7] This retrospective self-interpretation is pertinent and fruitful, but much in the book exceeds its modest claim.)

[6] *Discipline and Punish*, trans. Alan Sheridan (1977; New York, 1979).
[7] Michelle Perrot, ed. (Paris, 1980).

Foucault has also proposed a concept of power-knowledge that is critical in revealing the complicity of forces that are often neatly separated, especially in defense of a value-neutral, unworldly, contemplative idea of research. He has thus elicited the multiple ways idle curiosity is not simply gratuitous but directly or indirectly implicated in a regime from which its advocates would like to disinculpate themselves. But, in the guise of a kind of black functionalism, the form Foucault's notion of power-knowledge has taken threatens to revive an indiscriminate, late 1960s idea of "the system" or "the dominant ideology" that necessarily "co-opts" everything it touches, including all forms of resistance. This all-consuming idea offers too simple a shortcut in interpretation, and it may even be politically self-defeating. It does, however, accord with another questionable feature of some of Foucault's writing—a feature that is perhaps most pronounced in his famous "principal" texts. It is the comprehensive delegitimation of existing phenomena as hopelessly complicit with the dominant "system" of power-knowledge and the confinement of political response to faint apocalyptic tremors on the other side of disaster.

This entire frame of reference not only provides little space for the "punctual" political interventions Foucault defends in his occasional pieces. It also obscures the workings of hegemony. Hegemony cannot be identified with power in that it articulates power and authority in a manner that is at least partially internalized, even by critics of a "system" or an "ideology." Moreover, to present hegemony in overly hegemonic terms is to pave over the fissures, heterogeneities, and uncertainties in the dominant system where forces of resistance may appear. Forces of resistance do face the threat of co-optation or recycling, which is quite pervasive in a commodity system, but this threat should not be automatically transformed into a foregone conclusion (for example, by reifying "the system" and attributing to it all sorts of mysterious powers). The various tendencies in Foucault I have briefly evoked may help to account for his seeming evasiveness or at least his hesitancy to propose alternatives, especially in terms of institutional practices. The question with which Foucault leaves us, I suggest, is not the traditional one of reform or revolution but rather that of the way a necessarily delegitimating critique should proceed if it is sensitive to the problem of alternative institutions.

In discussing recent French thinkers, it is difficult not to suc-
cumb to the "star" (if not the Caliban) syndrome and to herald
the advent of the latest—or at least the most recently discovered—virtuoso from Paris. Jean-François Lyotard has been around
for a long time, but he has recently attained a rather distinctive voice
among contemporary critics. His is an especially attractive voice since
it seems to convey the best of recent French thought but to transcend
its internecine contentiousness. Instead polemic is directed at more
clearly differentiated opponents, such as Jürgen Habermas in his
rather dismissive reaction to recent French criticism.

Lyotard's emphases may justifiably be seen as converging with
those of another recently discovered theorist of language and culture, Mikhail Bakhtin, and as providing the occasion for a critique
of some of the arrested developments of Bakhtin's own work (its
occasional myth of populist origins and its phonocentric metaphysic, for example). I would like simply to focus on a few features
of Lyotard's thought that I find particularly suggestive or controversial, and I shall extend the discussion into areas that border on
Bakhtin's concerns. In this manner, I shall be able to return to more
general problems in criticism that I touched upon at the beginning
of this chapter.

The political and social import of Lyotard's work is immediately
apparent in his attempt to conjoin the motif of difference or heterogeneity with his insistence upon justice. He has associated a passion-
ate *plaidoyer* for postmodern experimentalism with a critique of
metanarratives that totalize their objects. His emphasis upon
"difference" has taken two more or less related forms. One is the
partial return to Kant, notably to the implications of an incommensurable gap between the "Idea" and its embodiment or exemplifica-
tion. Not only does the Idea remain "unpresentable" in that it cannot be fully realized, for example, in institutions. The Idea cannot
even be adequately conceptualized, and it cannot be figured in the
form of totality. It remains a critical fiction or regulative idea that
is contestable and open to the future. Thus any claim to have realized the just society, either in thought or in practice, is necessarily
mystified. Here one has a rebuke to both Hegelian and Marxist
totalization—to conceptual Absolute Knowledge as well as the
redemptive dictatorship of the proletariat. In line with his

22

critique of totalization and metanarrative, Lyotard has defended the importance of "little stories" and of the right to a narrative voice as itself a significant political right. Any account is a supplement to existing accounts, and it cannot claim full authority (or authorship) in appropriating or totalizing the others. The roles of speaker and listener, as well as those of writer and reader, become reversible, and the "just" context is an openly dialogized one in which obligations are mutual.

Even this brief sketch of Lyotard's recent views is enough to bring out their significance and appeal. I want, however, to raise certain questions about the implications of these views. Lyotard is convincing in his argument that any Idea—let us say, any utopia or sovereign, indeed "sublime" principle—cannot be fully conceptualized much less realized in institutional practice. But this convincing argument about the nature and role of critical fictions or regulative ideas does not obviate the need for critical thought about institutions or the possible duality of certain notions as both critical fictions and institutional options. (Bakhtin's "carnivalization" is, I think, one of these dual, ambivalent, or catachretic notions.) In fact one might insist that Lyotard's concerns require the rethinking of institutions in terms that resist the inclination of modern intellectuals to align themselves exclusively with the Idea and to relegate the institution to the sublunary realm of the hopelessly degraded or fallen. This inclination relies on a binary opposition between realms or spheres, and it may return criticism to an unworldly, noumenal realm of detached Ideas or perhaps of blind faith. The problem, as I intimated earlier, would rather be to displace the concept of totalization in the direction of a notion of articulation between *différends* or even incommensurables such as the critical fiction and the institution—an articulation that might allow for the spanning of gaps that cannot be closed. Here one need not assume that institutional proposals are necessarily dogmatic. On the contrary, if attempts to formulate a regulative idea are contestable, institutional proposals are doubly contestable in that they attempt to trace the import of a regulative idea for sociocultural life. But they are also necessary, for if one takes leave of this obligation, one can be reasonably certain that others will all-too-readily take it up.

The very desire to relate the themes of difference and justice would itself seem to require a reopening of thought about institutions. While justice may require the respect for certain differences, not all differences are just and worthy of respect. The difficulty is in thinking through and creating institutions that articulate "just" differences in sociocultural life. This difficulty is great, and it requires inquiry into the relation of hierarchy and equality. A total egalitarianism does not pose the problem of justice; it eliminates it. And it is dubious as a simple reversal of hierarchy. Indeed in the contemporary political and academic context, it readily becomes subservient to populistic modes of scapegoating and intolerance for exceptions.

One of the most potent institutional implications of the poststructuralist critique of binary oppositions is a critique of the scapegoat mechanism. Scapegoating on a discursive level is itself essential to the constitution of pure oppositions insofar as internal alterity, perceived as guilty or fallen, is purged, and all "otherness" is projected onto the discrete other. In social life, scapegoating provides instant purification and the ability to localize the source of contamination in an individual or group bearing the most recognizable differences from the ingroup. It is also operative in the crucial conversion of absence into loss—in the assumption that what is missing in the present (identity, totality, plenitude) must have existed in the past and must be recaptured in the future. Scapegoating has of course had a blatant historical role in generating solidarity and sociocultural identity. It has also had more subtle connections with the complex of metaphorical identity, narrative closure, and dialectical synthesis (all of which require the expulsion or reduction of heterogeneities and remainders). The critical task is to work out alternatives to it. A different understanding of institutions as settings for the interaction of social individuals, marked by internal alterity yet committed or obligated to one another, is a necessary step in this respect. The very oxymoronic notion of a social individual reveals how the individual is "altered" from the beginning of anything that may be called cultural life by social relations; but it also counters a simplistic social metaphysic that postulates "society" (collective routines or mentalities) as the origin of all meaning and value.

Institutions require limiting norms, but these norms need not stipulate a rigid definition of class, status, and power or demarcate unbreachable boundaries between groups or individuals. The axial opposition between hierarchy and equality should itself be displaced in the direction of a finer network of similarities and differences in terms of which the exception need not be scapegoated and the less able seen as mere refuse of the system. And boundaries should be rethought as a function of problematic distinctions instead of hard-and-fast dichotomies. I am of course merely gesturing toward a range of difficult problems, but, without an awareness that these problems exist, there is the danger that the defense of the Idea may become escapist, and the advocacy of little heterogeneous stories may turn into a narrativist rendition of *On Liberty* with a comparable blindness to the institutional and "material" correlates of free speech or the right to narrate. In fact, in certain fields, such as historiography, the right to tell stories is quite secure. But they often take the form of ingratiating anecdotes that void historiography of a critical impetus and induce premature "anecdotage."

I have intimated that Bakhtin's notion of carnivalization—the high point of dialogism—is best interpreted as a liminal or threshold term that connects, and perforce transgresses the opposition between, the regulative idea and the institution. It is indeed a critical fiction, but it would lose its critical force if it had no institutional import. Carnival is a social institution, although carnivalization would be mystifyingly reified if it were simply identified or conflated with an institutional embodiment.

Bakhtin's argument (as I read it) is that the interaction between carnival as a social institution and carnivalization as a critical force in art and literature is itself a vital component of a viable society and culture. For him the decline or disfigurement of carnival as a social institution affects both art and the nature of social life. In modern culture, it may induce a hermetic appropriation of carnivalesque forces in artifacts of high culture that are used to protest the nature of the dominant society but that confront the problem of their own distance from popular culture and their co-optation by elites as status symbols or signs of membership in a *cénacle*.[8]

---

[8] The hermetic appropriation of the carnivalesque and the process of commodification pose problems for the contact between high and popular culture that are elided in Gregory Ulmer's recent appeal for a postdeconstructive pedagogy in *Applied Grammatology* (Baltimore, 1985). I must confess that I was seized by a perverse image in reading this thought-provoking book. It involved a massive movement to rechristen the Arts and Sciences Quad as the AG ("Applied Grammatology") Quad.

25

The larger issue in the modern Western context is the relation among elite, popular, and mass or commodified cultures. In this context work tends to be effectively cut off from play on the level of production, thus eliminating any alternation of labor and carnivalesque activity in the general "economy" of social life. But play is recuperated on the level of consumption and confined within "leisure" or "free" time. In this reduced state, it may be serviced by culture industries that have their share in the system of production. Or it may be restricted to the nuclear family as the domestic, privatized space for the celebration of holidays or the enactment of the "sitcoms" of everyday, routine life. Mass or commodified culture affects both elite and popular culture. Indeed, in the modern West, popular culture is to a significant extent assimilated or appropriated by commodified culture, and this development is one reason for the heightened "alienation" of segments of elite culture. (How much wishful thinking is there in the emphasis upon the critical force of commodified culture?) But elite culture itself of course does not escape the "star" syndrome, the talk-show variant of dialogism, or the temptation of cultural despair and apocalyptic exaltation.

Bakhtin himself did not view the carnivalesque as a total answer to modern problems. But this was not because the notion had no institutional bearing for him. It was rather because it referred to a dimension of sociocultural activity that had to be related to other activities in the more general movement of social life. One of these other activities was of course work. Bakhtin did not envision a simple suspension of work in a totally carnivalized utopia. Instead he tried to rethink the relations of work and play, for example, by seeing the carnivalesque consumption of food as the culmination of the labor process.

Carnival itself for Bakhtin is on the borderline between life and art: it is neither a purely social nor a purely aesthetic institution. One might invoke other theorists to suggest that craft is also on the borderline between life and art—the "missing link" between them. The articulation of work and play might in this sense be understood in terms of the relation between craft and carnival, and the enormous problem in modern society would be how to make all jobs crafts and simultaneously to introduce carnival-type institutions that would interact with work in a viable rhythm of social life.

One may note that for Bakhtin narrowly functional analyses of carnival were misguided because they ignored the philosophical and existential significance of carnival itself. Indeed, the turn to narrowly functional analysis may be taken as a sign of one's distance from the "carnival spirit." In any event, it is worth noting that the function of carnival varies. It has neither a universally conservative nor a universally revolutionary role. It does convey at least the possibility of change and in this sense has a contestatory potential, but this potential is actualized in different forms from the relatively harmless safety-valve to highly disruptive insurgence. For Bakhtin, however, carnival is best when its function is itself deeply ambivalent—when it demonstrates that one can legitimately take seriously and joke about one's basic commitments.

With penultimate concision that scarcely serves to broach an important set of problems, I shall raise an issue that deserves further reflection. Bakhtin approached the festive through carnival and tended to play down the element of scapegoating that might appear in carnival itself. More generally, he turned his eyes from bloodletting and acknowledged the ambivalence of the carnivalesque in a manner that affirmed its joyful, life-enhancing side. He did not raise the question of the relation of the feast to tragedy, which is perhaps epitomized in sacrifice. The approach to festivity through a notion of ambivalence that stresses the tragic and sacrifice was developed of course by Georges Bataille, and it has been taken to an extreme pitch by René Girard. Bataille saw sacrifice as a ritualized form of violence that enabled a momentary collective outlet for the excess everyone harbors and must control in daily life. He thus situated sacrifice within a "general" economy open to deep play between life and death. The festive consumption of a surplus in this economy, which at its limit involved the sacrifice of life itself, countered the instrumental, profit-maximizing norms of a "restricted" economy such as capitalism where a surplus is continually reinvested. Implicit in my own account is a desire to distance carnival from scapegoating and to align it with a critique of the scapegoat mechanism that would also be a critique of sacrifice insofar as it resorts to scapegoating. Here one may perhaps distin-

27

guish between the "sacrifice" or gift of self that Bataille saw as essential to social life, on the one hand, and the victimization of others that depends upon a denial of internal alterity, on the other. Insofar as sacrifice relies on victimization and the achievement of purity for the self through a projection of guilt onto a separate "other," it should, I think, itself be seen as a type of restricted economy and related to the series I mentioned earlier: metaphoric identification, narrative closure, and dialectical synthesis. The critique of scapegoating and of totalization would not deny the significance of other dimensions of Bataille's understanding of festive *dépense*, notably his insistence on the risk of extreme loss in nonacquisitive expenditure or his specific sense of "totality" in existential commitment to a group or a way of being that is not subordinated in instrumental fashion to some delimited end. It might also reinforce Bataille's attempt to distinguish his views from those put forth by fascist ideologists. But it would leave open the difficult questions of the relation between the "elective" groups Bataille defended and egalitarian, democratic values as well as the interaction between tragic and carnivalesque *dépense*. (At least indirectly, *dépense* in Bataille's sense might in addition serve to bring up the issue of liberality or generosity beyond delimited forms of "justice.")

I shall conclude with a few brief remarks about "criticism" in the academic institution—remarks that may help to specify the institutional implications of my opening words. In terms of a minimal program, what I have said would imply the need for greater diversity in basic perspective among those housed in the same department. A department should be a place where fundamental issues in interpretation can be argued—hence a significantly contested place. In addition, any university should have a somewhat decentered center where critics who are seeking their way can encounter others with comparable concerns.[9] These two rather minimal institutional

---

[9] In the very recent past there has been an increase in the number of centers for the humanities, cultural studies, or critical theory—centers that are manifestly interdisciplinary or transdisciplinary in nature. But it is unclear whether they bear witness to newer intellectual and institutional formations or are little more than sops to humanists at a time when most of the perquisites are still flowing in the direction of the natural sciences. These centers are often underfunded, exist on soft or grant money, rarely have permanent faculty lines or provisions for the education

proposals—which in the existing academic context might well appear to be enormities if not howlers—would at least be initial steps in the attempt to rethink the articulation of the university. "Articulation" is after all not totalization but the (often problematic) joining of differences, and it becomes effective in culture when the differences engage one another in controversy and play—indeed when difference is itself linked to obligation and solidarity.

---

and support of graduate students, and are usually the temporary perches for visiting *oiseaux de passage*—all of which limits their long-term effect as both stimulant and exemplary model for newer tendencies in the university. To play even the limited role suggested in this chapter, such centers would have to acquire greater significance.

# 2

## *History and Psychoanalysis*

It may thus be said that the theory of psycho-analysis is an attempt to account for two striking and unexpected facts of observation which emerge whenever an attempt is made to trace the symptoms of a neurotic back to their sources in past life: the facts of transference and of resistance. Any line of investigation which recognizes these two facts and takes them as the starting point of its work has a right to call itself psycho-analysis, even though it arrives at results other than my own.
—Freud, "On the History of the Psycho-analytic Movement"

Le transfert c'est le concept même de l'analyse, parce que c'est le temps de l'analyse. [Transference is the very concept of analysis, because it is the time of analysis.]
—Jacques Lacan, *Le séminaire I*

The focus of this chapter is on Freud, although my approach is informed by certain aspects of post-Freudian analysis. In the works of Freud, however, history in the ordinary sense often seems lost in the shuffle between ontogeny and phylogeny. When Freud, in the latter part of his life, turned to cultural history, he was primarily concerned with showing how the evolution of civilization on a macrological level might be understood through—or even seen as an enactment of —psychoanalytic principles and processes. And he openly acknowledged the speculative nature of his inquiry into prehistory, "archaic" society, and their putative relation to the civilizing process.

One might nonetheless argue that throughout Freud's work there are theoretical bases and fruitful leads for a more delimited investigation of specific historical processes for which documentation is, to a greater or lesser extent, available. This kind of investigation is, moreover, required to test the pertinence of Freud's speculative and at times quasi-mythological initiatives. At present one can perhaps do little more than tentatively suggest how such an investigation might proceed and the sort of issues it might conceivably illuminate; for its elaboration has been relatively underdeveloped in the research of those who look to Freud for guidance.

In psychoanalysis itself, there has been a widespread concern for the refinement of theory and its application to individual case histories. Distinctive in the recent French initiative is a textual focus, often with only an allegorical sense of the relation of textual to other historical processes. The succinct editorial introduction to an issue of *Diacritics* on "The Tropology of Freud" provides a lucid epitome of the assumptions of those looking to the "French Freud":

> Tropology: 1. "A speaking by tropes" (Blount, 1656); the use of metaphor in speech or writing; figurative discourse. 2. A moral discourse. 3. A treatise on tropes or figures of speech. OED.
>
> In these essays the writing of Freud is considered from the triple perspective of tropology. Freud's topics and descriptions are taken to constitute a new rhetoric or treatise on tropes—versions of the mind which are themselves new figures for classifying and describing the structure and movement of texts, according to what Nicolas Abraham and others here call an 'anasemic' transcription of the very concept of figure under the influence of the 'radical anasemic change that psychoanalysis has introduced into language' (Abraham, "The Shell and the Kernel"). At the same time Freud's scientific project is itself an example of figurative writing, examined here in several of these essays as if it were a literary text, a piece of poetic language, or a narrative fiction. Finally, since psychoanalysis is not merely a rhetorical exercise but an instrument of ethical and therefore eventually political power, these essays in turn raise questions about the ethics and politics of rhetoric.[1]

[1] *Diacritics* 9 (Spring 1979), 1 (special issue conceived by Richard Klein).

This program guides much valuable work in the wake of Freud. One of its incentives is a "Freud-on-Freud" rereading of Freud's own texts, oriented toward the disclosure of how those texts both "act out" and try to account for (or "work through") processes, such as those of dreamwork, that Freud investigated. This program is enhanced and, to some extent, redirected when history and its representation are seen as a crucial mediation (if not the "missing link") between "rhetoric" and ethicopolitical concerns. The difficulty is to take the understanding of history beyond the point of allegorical implication, or at least to inquire more closely into the nature and workings of that implication.

Existing research and reflection among professional historians are, unfortunately, of only limited value in confronting that difficulty. Psychohistory has won its way as a subdiscipline in the historical profession, although it is still able to raise the hackles of some traditionalists.[2] Yet the typical procedure of psychohistorians has been to make more or less selective use of psychoanalytic concepts as they proceed to put individuals or groups from the past "on the couch." Whatever may be their interest, studies of John Stuart Mill's or Max Weber's Oedipus complex, the phantasms of the Nazi youth cohort, the phobias of the other Victorians, or even the discreet sexual charms of the Victorian bourgeoisie tend to remain on the level of the application of psychoanalytic concepts to historical objects. History as applied psychoanalysis does not confront the broader problem of how psychoanalysis can lead to a basic reconceptualization of historical self-understanding and practice or even to a mutual rearticulation of both history and psychoanalysis as implicated in a reciprocally provocative exchange. (It is, after all, this kind of "de-definition" and rearticulation of concepts that motivates the notion of "anasemia.")

A second approach to Freud prevalent among historians is, in certain respects, even further from the perspective I want to explore. It is the straightforward contextual "explanation" of Freud as symptomatic of his own circumscribed society and culture. Here Freud is

---

[2] For a defense of psychohistory, see Peter Loewenberg, "Psychohistory," in *The Past before Us: Contemporary Historical Writing in the United States*, ed. Michael Kammen (Ithaca, N.Y., 1980), pp. 408-32. See also the disparaging comments dispersed throughout John Lukacs, *Historical Consciousness, or, The Remembered Past* (New York, 1985).

seen as more or less blindly effecting a self-deceived "escape" from reality, politics, society, history, and so forth, into the egocentric and phantasmatic labyrinths of the isolated self.[3] Freud's thought does have significant "symptomatic" aspects in its less examined relations to culture and ideology—a point certain recent feminist critics have developed in an especially forceful way. But the danger in the interpretation of Freud as symptom (or as disease posing as cure, in the phrase of Karl Kraus) is the propensity to abstract one reductionist (or "vulgar Freudian") dimension from Freud's own texts and then to apply it to the interpretation of those texts without countering or at least qualifying it with other tendencies also active in Freud. The very understanding of "reality," "politics," "society," and "history" operative in such "critiques" is often precritical. In any event, this approach may not question the extent to which Freud's texts intimate how these concepts may be reworked in ways that at least resist symptomatic replication of some of the most dubious and destructive forces in modern history. To make these points is not to eliminate the complex problem of determining a text's relation to hegemonic or dominant discourses. Nor is it to subscribe to an indiscriminate pluralism or a displaced, talk-show variant of dialogism ("equal time for all 'voices'"). It is rather to insist upon a careful and self-critical investigation of both the possibly divided movements in certain texts and the question of their specific relation to larger discourses and practices. It is also to raise the question of the implications of psychoanalysis for one's own protocols of inquiry and criticism.

One may begin an inquiry into the exchange between psychoanalysis and history with the issue of the relation between history and historiography—or, to change the terms somewhat, between the historical process and its representation in the historian's account of it. This relation is complicated by two factors: one finds repetition on both sides of the equation, and the relation is mediated by various traces of the past (memories, documents, texts, monu-

---

[3] See, for example, the influential interpretation in Carl Schorske, *Fin-de-siècle Vienna: Politics and Culture* (New York, 1980). I shall return to the recent rendition of the "escape from reality" view of Freud in Jeffrey Moussaieff Masson, *The Assault on Truth: Freud's Suppression of the Seduction Theory* (New York, 1984). See also the lucid analysis in Michael S. Roth, *Psycho-Analysis as History: Negation and Freedom in Freud* (Ithaca, N.Y., 1987).

*33*

ments, icons, and so forth) through which the historian reconstructs the historical process in his or her account.

The historian repeats an already repetitive historical process—a process that variably combines repetition with change. I shall later try to indicate how psychoanalysis construes temporality as a process of repetition with change on all levels, from the drives to the attempt of the analyst to control repetition (both through its limited enactment in the analytic situation and through the effort to "work through" repetition in transference). Historians have traditionally accepted the Aristotelian stabilization of repetition/change by confiding in the binary opposition between the universal and the particular, between intemporal "synchrony" and changing "diachrony." In this decisive gesture, repetition is idealized and fixated on an ahistorical level while "history" is identified with a dissociated, equally idealized and fixated concept of change. This binary allows for a neat separation, if not isolation, of philosophy and history (with "poetry" as a rather unstable mediator or supplement between the two).

The reductive stabilization of potentially uncontrollable repetitive processes is necessary and inevitable. But it may be both contested and effected through more problematic distinctions that themselves hold out the possibility of a different articulation of relations allowing for a significant measure of responsible control. In Freud temporality is understood both in stabilizing terms (the quest for a primal origin or scene, the elaboration of stages of development, the construction of linear narratives) and in more disconcerting ways. The mechanisms of dreamwork—particularly displacement, condensation, and staging (or considerations of representability)—indicate the role of nonlinear, repetitive temporality. (Secondary revision is itself a stabilizing form closer to processes prevalent in waking life, notably in the daydream, but dreamwork itself cannot be entirely confined to literal states of sleep.) "Deferred action" (*Nachträglichkeit*) is of course the most patent form of repetitive temporality, and while its significance is heightened in Freud's later work through his insistence upon the repetition compulsion, it plays an important role throughout his career. For Freud a traumatic influx of excitation—an overwhelming rupture that the subject cannot effectively bind—is brought about not through an original event in isolation but through repetition: an event becomes traumatic retrospectively when it is recalled by a later event. In the trauma one thus has a conjunction of repetition and change. As Freud put it as early as the *Project for a Scientific Psychology* (1895): "Here we have the case of a memory arousing an affect which it did not arouse as an experience, because in the meantime the changes [brought about] by puberty had made possible a different understanding of what was remembered. . . . We invariably find that a memory is repressed which has only become a trauma by *deferred action* [*nachträglich*]."[4] The later event, seemingly trivial in itself, may recall the earlier one in only the most indirect manner. (Here the event that triggers a trauma through "deferred action" resembles the insignificant event in the "forward repetition" of displacement,[5] and the often remote linkage between significant and insignificant events signals the difficulties of tracking figurative processes in a "new rhetoric.")

Jacques Lacan has referred displacement to the trope of metonymy (understood as the mechanism of desire), and he has correlated condensation with metaphor. This initial step in the development of a new rhetoric (whose end is not yet in sight) provides valuable insight into temporal processes as well as into the attempt to represent them. Metonymy constitutes a time line of different, serial events which one tries to integrate through a metaphoric concordance of beginning and end. For Lacan this effort can never fully succeed, for desire (unlike need) cannot be satisfied, although the quest for satisfaction (the prototypical *quête de l'absolu*) motivates utopian yearning (including the yearning for full narrative closure and theoretical totalization). The further implication for rhetoric in a different key comes with the elusive dialogic dimension of transference, which for both Freud and Lacan is an axial aspect of the analytic relation.

The tendency of psychoanalysts to emphasize the importance of transference in the relation between analyst and analysand has often

[4] Sigmund Freud, *Project for a Scientific Psychology*, in *The Standard Edition of the Complete Psychological Works of Sigmund Freud*, ed. and trans. James Strachey, 24 vols. (London, 1953-74), 1:356.
[5] I here of course adapt a term from Kierkegaard.

had the unfortunate consequence of diverting attention from its role elsewhere. The restriction of transference to the analytic situation may even be seen as an unwarranted domestication of the notion. As Freud noted: "It must not be supposed . . . that transference is created by analysis and does not occur apart from it. Transference is merely uncovered and isolated by analysis. It is a universal phenomenon of the human mind, it decides the success of all medical influence, and in fact dominates the whole of each person's relations to his human environment."[6] Historiography is no exception to this bold generalization.

It may be argued that the historian is implicated in a twofold dialogic relation that involves transference in somewhat different ways. The closest analogue to the analytic situation (with its displaced repetition of the Oedipal scene) is found in the historian's relation to other students of the past, whose renditions of it must be taken into account in his or her own work. Indeed the very delimitation of inquirers whose views are deemed pertinent for historians—those whose influence is sufficiently proximate to cause anxiety—is a vital constituent of the discipline. The turn toward currently avoided or marginalized interlocutors (such as philosophers, literary critics, or novelists) is part and parcel of an attempt to reorient priorities or alter the horizons of the discipline, which has been drawn toward a certain kind of social science in the recent past. A questionable feature of professionalization is the attempt to establish clear-cut if not unbreachable boundaries separating history from other disciplines, thus giving the historian an unequivocal identity, and even historians more than one generation back may become not vital interlocutors but only objects of innocuous ritual invocation. Hence one has the oft-noted divide that marks the distance between "methodology" and "research" seminars. (To put the point simply: in methodology seminars, one reads past historians and theorists; in research seminars, one proceeds as if one had never read them.)

The most easily located instance of transferential relations in historiography (and in academics more generally) is probably to be

---

[6] Freud, *An Autobiographical Study*, trans. James Strachey (New York, 1963), pp. 79-80; all further references to this work, abbreviated *AS*, are included in the text.

found in the nexus between teachers and students. These relations are most intense in graduate study, particularly in the initial period: the teacher (who may, for the student, initially be an imago projected from written texts) is often intent on establishing a "presence," and the student, in a particularly vulnerable or even "regressive" position, confronts for the first time the problem of a near total (and often phantasmatic) identity between his or her professional and personal self. Peter Loewenberg has discussed this dimension of transference, and, despite certain overstated aspects of his account, his thought-provoking initiative deserves to be followed up and extended in other directions.[7]

Instead of pursuing this route, I would like to stress an equally important but often unnoticed sense in which transference is at play in history, that is, in the very relation of the historian to the "object" of study. Transference in this somewhat more indirect and attenuated sense refers to the manner in which the problems at issue in the object of study reappear (or are repeated with variations) in the work of the historian. "Transference" offers a better way of understanding a complex relation to the past than do standard, round-robin debates about objectivity or subjectivity, truth or relativism. It may even provide perspective on aspects of those debates that cannot be entirely transcended but perhaps can be rethought in a less compulsively predictable fashion.

In one important sense, objectivity refers to criteria of meticulous research in the accurate reconstitution of events through the critical examination of all relevant sources. Formulated another way, objectivity implies an injunction to face facts that may prove embarrassing for the theses one would like to propound or the patterns one is striving to elicit. It is reciprocally related to a "coefficient

---

[7] See Peter Loewenberg, *Decoding the Past: The Psychohistorical Approach* (New York, 1983), pp. 45-80. Bruce Mazlish writes in his review of this book: "As for educating psychohistorians (and historians), I fully applaud Loewenberg's call for a greater diffusion of knowledge of psychoanalysis, but I wonder about his compulsive attention to the infantilizing pressures in history graduate students, exacerbated by unacknowledged sadism, hostility, and so forth on the part of their mentors (surely this was not Loewenberg's experience with his teacher, Carl Schorske)" (*American Historical Review* 89 [1984]: 94). One may, however, note that the actual nature of an authority figure does not determine all aspects of transference.

of resistance" both in the "textual" material one is interpreting and in the modes of empirical reality one is inferring from that material or its cognates. Whatever the problematic nature of reconstituting events, given available documentation, or the necessary interaction between the construal of events and one's theoretical assumptions, the notion of objectivity is valuable even for approaches that stress the mediating and supplementary role of texts (including documents) in all historiography. Freud tried to maintain this notion of objectivity, and it underwent one of its greatest trials (as we shall see) with respect to the so-called seduction theory.

In Freud's work, moreover, objectivity might be correlated with what he called *gleichschwebende Aufmerksamkeit*—"evenly suspended" or "poised" attention. In accordance with this rule—which was the analyst's counterpart to the analysand's "fundamental rule" of reporting everything that came into his or her mind—the analyst should try to be attentive to all material, including any that upset expectations or had no place in preexisting theoretical assumptions, even material that seemed to contradict them. "Poised" attention might enable access to phenomena that themselves would have a meaning only *nachträglich* if at all, and it also allowed for the play of the analyst's unconscious in responding to that of the analysand. The very poise of the analyst might be upset by what he or she was led to notice through an attentiveness that might rub against the grain of method without ever simply eliminating the need for it. As J. Laplanche and J.-B. Pontalis put it, *gleichschwebende Aufmerksamkeit* is the rule "which in Freud's view allows the analyst to discover the unconscious connections in what the patient says. Thanks to it the analyst is able to keep in mind a multitude of apparently insignificant elements whose correlations are only to emerge later on"; "suspended attention is the only true objective attitude in that it is suited to an essentially distorted object."[8]

Objectivity in this sense clearly does not obviate the role of transference. Indeed it challenges the simple idea of recounting the

[8] J. Laplanche and J.-B. Pontalis, *The Language of Psycho-analysis*, trans. Donald Nicholson-Smith (New York, 1973), p. 43.

past purely in its own terms and for its own sake—the historicist dream that (like its complement, presentism, or the dream of total liberation from the "burden" of history) rests on a disavowal of transference. Objectivity as "suspended" or "poised" attention would also jeopardize the overriding desire (prone to give rise to "secondary revision") that leads the historian to "find order in chaos." It would instead imply the need to investigate the interaction between order and challenges to it in the more or less "distorted" objects of the past as well as in one's own discourse about them. Transference in this sense would highlight the issue of the historian's voice in narration and analysis—an issue prematurely foreclosed when one assumes full unity not only of narrative but of narrative and authorial voice. It would attune one to modulations of voice, both in specifically marked hypothetical forms and in more subtle, often unconscious, movements. It would simultaneously raise the question of the extent to which the historian's voice does or should reveal significant parallels with experiments that have been more pronounced in other genres, such as the modern novel.

Freud himself encountered the tension between "objectivity" and the temptation to impose a convincing, coherent interpretation on the experience of the suggestible patient. A recurrent problem for him was whether (or to what extent) his theories informed the patient's experience or actively formed, indeed constrained, it by imposing compulsive schemata that functioned as surrogate myths. (One of course has here the problem of the status of the Oedipus complex.) Freud moved from hypnosis to free association and the "fundamental rule" in order to mitigate the effects of suggestibility and decrease the incidence of short-lived, deceptive solutions to problems brought about by "cathartic" abreaction. But he never fully achieved the "liberation" from hypnosis that he somewhat histrionically announces at the beginning of chapter 3 of *An Autobiographical Study*.[9] Indeed the ensuing textual movement not only qualifies but threatens to retract the force of his statement, for aspects of what Freud earlier recognized to be problematic in

---

[9] "My expectations were fulfilled; I was set free from hypnotism" (*AS*, p. 52).

hypnosis were regenerated in transference.[10] Transference was thus a "substitute" for hypnotism that at most enabled one to "exclude," or "at all events, to isolate" "the mysterious element that was at work behind hypnotism" (*AS*, p. 50). Transference, however, was explicitly recognized by Freud to be inherently ambivalent, for in replacing the original neurosis it might also generate new resistances, and it could both impede the work of analysis and indicate the direction that work had to take to be effective.

> This *transferenca*—to give it its shortened name—soon replaces in the patient's mind the desire to be cured, and, so long as it is affectionate and moderate, becomes the agent of the physician's influence and neither more nor less than the mainspring of the joint work of analysis. Later on, when it has become passionate or has been converted into hostility, it becomes the principal tool of the resistance. It may then happen that it will paralyse the patient's powers of associating and endanger the success of the treatment. Yet it would be senseless to try to evade it; for an analysis without transference is an impossibility. (*AS*, p. 79)

> It is perfectly true that psychoanalysis, like other psychotherapeutic methods, employs the instrument of suggestion (or transference). But the difference is this: that in analysis it is not allowed to play the decisive part in determining the therapeutic results. It is used instead to induce the patient to perform a piece of mental work— the overcoming of his transference-resistances—which involves a permanent alteration in his mental economy. The transference is made conscious to the patient by the analyst, and it is resolved by convincing him that in his transference-attitude, he is *re-experiencing* emotional relations which had their origin in his earliest object-attachments during the repressed period of his childhood. In this way the transference is changed from the strongest weapon of the resistance into the best instrument of the analytic treatment. Nevertheless its handling remains the most difficult as well as the most important part of the technique of analysis. (*AS*, pp. 80-81)

[10] "Even the most brilliant results were liable to be suddenly wiped away if my personal relation with the patient became disturbed. It was true that they would be reestablished if a reconciliation could be effected; but such an occurrence proved that the personal emotional relation between doctor and patient was after all stronger than the whole cathartic process, and it was precisely that factor which escaped every effort at control" (*AS*, p. 49).

The relation of transference to the process of "remembering, repeat-ing, and working through" may well constitute "the most difficult as well as the most important" problem for any attempt to articulate the relation of psychoanalysis to other disciplines or critical theories. The above-quoted passage provides some insight into this problem. "Working through" allows for limited abreaction in the "acting out" or reenactment of earlier experience in ways both continuous and dis-continuous with the former cathartic method. "Acting out" is to some extent "bound" by its restriction to the analytic situation itself, while it is discouraged in other areas of life. It is further restricted in that it is counteracted by the role of memory. Acting out is phantasmatic: it repeats an earlier experience as though it were a fully present reality. In this sense it is, in Jacques Derrida's term, "logocentric." Freud was at times not sufficiently sensitive to the possibility that memory, in its fully speculative form of "Hegelian" interiorization, also involved a quest for full presence (or totality) on a higher, "sublimated" level and thus was prey to its own phantasmatic investments, notably in the guise of complete self-possession.[11] It too might entail a disavowal of transference—indeed might become a theoretical analogue of psycho-sis or "narcissistic neurosis"—instead of creating the possibility of working through a transferential relation. In an other than totalizing sense, however, memory provided critical distance on the past, allowed for the distinction between mnemic trace and phantasm, and posed the question of the role of judgment in relating past and present. In this sense, remembrance was a counterweight to the compulsive repe-tition of acting out, and it opened the prospect of a more reciprocal relation between analyst and analysand (one definition of cure). Through it, acting out was staged on a larger scene that was not entirely dominated by the repetition compulsion, and there arose a greater chance of responding critically to that "mysterious element" that held blind sway in hypnosis.

The recent debate about Freud's "abandonment" of the so-called seduction theory has an obvious interest for anyone trying to relate psychoanalysis and history. What is striking in *The Assault on Truth* is Jeffrey Masson's compulsiveness in asserting both the reality of scenes of seduction in the genesis of severe disorders and Freud's failure of

[11] See esp. Samuel Weber, *The Legend of Freud* (Minneapolis, 1982).

courage in "abandoning" the seduction theory and with it the "reality" of his patients. (A subplot in the book, which threatens to short-circuit its story line, is of course Masson's own sense of abandonment by the founding father and his legitimate heirs in the psychoanalytic profession.) Equally striking is the lack of a psychoanalytic treatment of the relation between mnemic traces of real events and phantasmatic investments, although this relation is "acted out" in Masson's own passionately Oedipal reactions to the avatars of psychoanalysis. At least mildly surprising, moreover, is the fact that, given his insistence on a certain conception of reality, Masson provides no new evidence—in the form of case histories, for instance—for the seduction theory. He bases his reaffirmation, at best, on a rereading of texts (often an extremely reductionist rereading) and, at worst, on inadequately documented and poorly argued assertions (for example, the assertion, on the basis of "some notes by Ruth Mack Brunswick for a paper she never published," that "as a child [the Wolf-Man] had been anally seduced by a member of his family—and that Freud did not know this"[12]). "Reality"—textual, procedural, and empirical— thus suffers a few assaults at Masson's own hands. But the concerns agitating Masson are important ones. And his book does have the merit of insisting that Freud's own reasons for questioning the seduction theory were not always cogent and that they have often been repeated without further testing by later analysts. (He also brings out the extent of Freud's own strongly transferential relation to Wilhelm Fliess, which at times prompted behavior that was inexcusable, notably in the case of Emma Eckstein.)

The seduction theory might perhaps be better termed the child-abuse theory, and evidence of the prevalence of child abuse makes certain hypotheses less implausible than they might have seemed to Freud. (Freud's own case histories do contain evidence of child abuse in one form or another, and Freud does not do enough with this evidence.) The abuse of a more or less helpless child might even be taken as a paradigm of an event whose reality is not purely psychic. And it is a real event of the sort that attests to the element of enduring validity in certain "naive" responses—an event that makes one uncomfortable, indeed impatient, with the notion of Reality as an asymptote of

---

[12] Masson, *Assault on Truth*, p. xxvii.

the detours of the Imaginary and the Symbolic. However difficult it may be to gather evidence in certain cases, one would certainly like to know how prevalent the abuse of children is, what role it plays in the etiology of pathological conditions, and what it means for the nature of a society and a culture. Indeed it is curious that Freud seemed to be staunchly attached to the "reality" of the primal crime, for which no evidence was available, in contrast to his views on the actual seduction or abuse of children, where gathering evidence was at least theoretically possible. The degree of his attachment to the "reality" of the primal crime might even be interpreted as an overcompensation for his residual doubts about the seduction theory.

Yet the formula stating that Freud simply "abandoned" or "suppressed" the seduction theory is itself far from adequate. As Laplanche and Pontalis point out (in a work that predates Masson's book), "right up to the end of his life, Freud continued to assert the existence, prevalence and pathogenic force of scenes of seduction actually experienced by children."[13] In addition, Freud continued to insist on the importance of deferred action, the traumatizing role of memories that are phantasmatically invested, and the need to "ground" fantasy in reality. Indeed Laplanche and Pontalis argue that the seduction theory is not an alternative to the Oedipus complex but an adumbration of it.

It is nonetheless true that Freud's emphasis shifted after 1897 and that he at times formulated the relation between the seduction theory on the one hand and the Oedipus complex, infantile sexuality, screen memories, and psychic reality on the other as pointing different directions, if not incompatible alternatives, in the elaboration of psychoanalytic theory. One need not go to letters to find rather explicit statements of Freud's change in attitude toward his "neurotica." As Freud put it in "On the History of the Psycho-analytic Movement":

Influenced by Charcot's view of the traumatic origin of hysteria, one was readily inclined to accept as true and aetiologically significant the statements made by patients in which they ascribed their symptoms to passive sexual experiences in the first years of childhood—to put it bluntly, to seduction. When this aetiology broke down under the

[13] Laplanche and Pontalis, *Language of Psycho-analysis*, p. 406. Laplanche and Pontalis refer to such works as *Three Essays in the Theory of Sexuality* (1905) and *An Outline of Psycho-Analysis* (1940).

weight of its own improbability and contradiction in definitely ascertainable circumstances, the result at first was helpless bewilderment. Analysis had led back to these infantile sexual traumas by the right path, and yet they were not true.... At last came the reflection that, after all, one had no right to despair because one has been deceived in one's expectations; one must revise those expectations. If hysterical subjects trace back their symptoms to traumas that are fictitious, then the new fact which emerges is precisely that they create such scenes in *phantasy*, and this psychical reality requires to be taken into account alongside practical reality. This reflection was soon followed by the discovery that these phantasies were intended to cover up the auto-erotic activity of the first years of childhood, to embellish it and raise it to a higher plane. And now, from behind the phantasies, the whole range of a child's sexual life came to light.[14]

There is a similar account in *An Autobiographical Study* where Freud refers to his belief that the seduction theory "might well have had fatal consequences for the whole of my work" and states that, after his recognition that scenes of seduction were "only phantasies," he was "for some time completely at a loss" (*AS*, pp. 62, 63). Freud's apparent disorientation when his belief in seduction was shaken—something he describes as putting him in a helpless, traumatizing position analogous to that of the "seduced" child in the seduction theory itself—attests to the strength of his earlier investment in its reality. It also indicates that he may have been overreacting to a sense of loss when he suggested a break in psychoanalytic theory itself or at least put forth conflicting views about the role of seduction in the etiology of pathology. In any event, Freud did try to maintain that whether or not actual seduction took place, the result would be the same for the patient in light of the "psychic reality" of fantasy.

Masson finds the latter view entirely implausible. Whether or to what extent it is accurate is moot but quite important for our self-understanding, and it certainly deserves further investigation. Masson, as I have already noted, does not offer new evidence but rests his case on a restricted rereading of Freud's texts (including

---

[14] Freud, "On the History of the Psycho-analytic Movement," *Standard Edition*, 14:17-18; all further references to this essay, abbreviated "HPM," are included in the text.

his letters). A more far-ranging if controversial rereading, undertaken from a very different theoretical perspective from Masson's but converging in circumscribed ways with certain of his concerns, is Nicolas Abraham and Maria Torok's *Cryptonymie: Le verbier de l'homme aux loups.*

Freud in his study of the Wolf-Man is undecided about the reality of the primal scene as witnessed by the patient as a child of one-and-a-half. He concludes with a *non liquet*, commenting that the child may have seen dogs copulating and projected this scene back onto the earlier one. But the primal scene Freud has in mind is not child abuse but *coitus a tergo* between the parents. In his own account, Freud has evidence that he either leaves uninterpreted or interprets only in a certain direction. The sister of the Wolf-Man, who was a few years older than the boy, showed "precocious" sexual activity, not only in trying to seduce her little brother but in attempting to take a cousin's member. Freud does not ask the seemingly obvious question: Where could a little girl of five or so have learned such specific behavior? Freud knew that the Wolf-Man's father was "manic-depressive" and that he entered a sanitarium when the Wolf-Man was only six. Freud also knew that the sister committed suicide later. But the most Freud admits is the "suspicion that the father of our present patient used himself to indulge in 'affectionate abuse,' and may have played at wolf or dog with the little boy and have threatened as a joke to gobble him up."[15]

For Abraham and Torok, "affectionate abuse" is not the issue, and the relation is other than a joking one. The plausibility of an infant witnessing coitus between parents pales in the face of the scene Freud did not entertain. Abraham and Torok arrive at another scene on the basis of multilingual analysis both close and at times seemingly outlandish—but with an outlandishness that presumably parallels the "new rhetoric" of the unconscious itself. They argue that the Wolf-Man believed his father had abused his sister and that

---

[15] Freud, "From the History of an Infantile Neurosis" (1918), *Three Case Histories*, ed. Philip Rieff (New York, 1963), p. 300; all further references to this work, abbreviated "IN," are included in the text. On Freud's hypothesis, the Wolf-Man would have shown a phobic response to carnivalesque behavior on the part of his father.

he himself had witnessed the scene and reported it to his nurse, only to see it suppressed by his mother in defense of the family's honor. Abraham and Torok leave it undecided whether this belief corresponded to an actual event, and they even indicate the possibly fictional nature of their own analysis. But for the reader the event may seem to acquire the weight of reality or at least of extreme plausibility by the end of their account.[16]

What is less moot than the role of a real event of child abuse (or "seduction") is another point that emerges from the *Cryptonymie*: even an actual event must be the object of phantasmatic investment to become pathogenic. This point returns in a more qualified way to Freud's insistence on the importance of "psychic reality," and it in no sense implies either a disavowal of the significance of actual events of "seduction" or their incompatibility with the theories of infantile sexuality, the Oedipus complex, screen memories, or the role of "psychic reality" itself. Indeed the intervention of "deferred action" implies that in the time between the unassimilated event of early childhood and the later event that somehow recalls it, the "original" event is transformed through the work of fantasy. The phantasmatic position of the father as a grandiose object of love and hate may itself foster denial of, or resistance to, the possibility of certain actions on his part. The Wolf-Man himself, for Abraham and Torok, incorporated his sister as well as his father in his split or divided self. And they stress the general importance of incorporation (contrasted with introjection) as a phantasmatic activity that "encrypts" others in the split self in a manner that creates a symbolic cyst in the psyche. The power of these phantomlike revenants may require a more complex notion of the unconscious and the "rhetorical" workings of language both in the self and in the discourse of psychoanalysis that tracks it.

While the initiatives of figures such as Abraham and Torok go in directions that at times might have seemed as strange to Freud as his own work did to many contemporaries, it is nonetheless significant that Freud's case histories are complex combinations of narrative and analysis in which a quest for unified theory is recur-

---

[16] See Nicolas Abraham and Maria Torok, *Cryptonymie: Le verbier de l'homme aux loups* (Paris, 1976).

rently rendered problematic. His account of the Wolf-Man, for example, is in no sense a simple linear narrative—indeed a straight-forward chronology is supplied, almost as an afterthought, in a foot-note at the very end of the text.[17] In the case history, as in an analytic session, "interrelated material makes its appearance at different times and at different points in the treatment" (*AS*, p. 78). In fact the very interweaving of linear and nonlinear narrative in Freud's accounts, as well as of narrative and theoretical analysis, is emblematic of larger problems concerning the psyche and its relation to society and culture—and of any discursive attempt to come to terms with these problems, including psychoanalysis itself.

A story becomes followable, linear, and satisfactory in its attempt to integrate "metonymic" desire and "metaphorical" recognition through the structuring role of plots.[18] Freud's own preferred plot or schema was of course Oedipal, with the Oedipus complex grounded in an original or primal crime that actually played it out at the dawn of history. And a crucial question one may raise is whether the Oedipus complex is the key to transference or too one-dimensional and compulsive an interpretation of it. In his study of the Wolf-Man, Freud both invoked his idea of the inheritance of acquired characteristics in culture and (without remarking upon the possibly recursive and self-referential nature of his gesture) used it to explain the phantasmatic potential of compulsive schemata. (His point would of course apply more plausibly to social transmission or tradition than to an unmediated movement from psychology to biology.)

> Phylogenetically inherited schemata . . . like the categories of philos-
> ophy, are concerned with the business of "placing" the impressions
> derived from actual experience. I am inclined to take the view that
> they are precipitates from the history of human civilization.

[17] Juliet Mitchell observes, in a more general vein, "Freud's case-histories show that there is little justification for treating the 'stages' either as absolutes or as even separate and sequential" (Mitchell, *Psychoanalysis and Feminism* [New York, 1974], p. 27).

[18] See, for example, Peter Brooks, "Freud's Masterplot: Questions of Narrative," *Yale French Studies* 55/56 (1977): 280-300; idem, "Fictions of the Wolfman: Freud and Narrative Understanding," *Diacritics* 9 (Spring 1979): 72-81.

The Oedipus complex, which comprises a child's relation to its parents, is one of them—is, in fact, the best known member of the class. Whenever experiences fail to fit in with the hereditary schema, they become remodelled in the imagination—a process which might very profitably be followed out in detail. It is precisely such cases that are calculated to convince us of the independent existence of the schema. We are often able to see the schema triumphing over the experience of the individual. ("IN," pp. 314-15).

Much recent criticism has been devoted to showing, in often brilliant detail, how the very plots and structures Freud seemed to take "straight" theoretically and thematically were nonetheless contested or even radically disoriented by the very movements of his own stories and accounts. (Paradigmatic here is the essay on "The 'Uncanny'" in which the repetitive "return of the repressed" is reduced to castration anxiety and used to "explain" E. T. A. Hoffmann's "The Sandman," only to return in less clear-cut and familiarized form in the intricate and at times uncanny tropisms of Freud's own text.) Instead of venturing to offer another "Freud-on-Freud" reading of a Freudian text, I shall—at the risk of courting reduction—confine myself to a few observations that may perhaps indicate how this proliferating series of readings, while not simply reducible to a single thematic, may nonetheless be seen to point in certain directions.

Freud of course looked to Sophocles' *Oedipus Rex* for a rendition of the Oedipus complex, but he explicitly read the play from Oedipus's perspective and reduced it to a vehicle for a compulsive myth without asking how the play critically staged the myth or situated Oedipus. Yet the way the play enacted its compulsive schema may be argued to disclose a telling relation among myth, narrative closure, and the scapegoat mechanism. Myth (at least in one important narrative sense of the term) collapses levels of intelligibility by attempting to account for structural relations or possibilities (the passage from nature to culture, incest, guilt, and so forth) in terms applicable to particular events (an act of incest or of parricide, for example.) Myth tries to "explain" structures through events that enact them. It thus fixates and "totalizes" repetition through a story of events, and it seeks a point of undivided origin in a first event, which begins the story. Narrative closure is achieved when repetitive processes are reduced to peripeteia between beginning and end, and the original event is ultimately redeemed or "lifted to a higher level." Freud was closest to myth in his story of the primal crime as well as in his tendency to present the drives (from below) in terms of a biologistic fantasia or (from above) as titans engaged in combat for the destiny of man. The original event in Sophocles' play would seem to be the pollution of Thebes with the ensuing effort to find the origin of pollution in a guilty act.

Oedipus himself emerges in the play as a master sleuth who, in one gesture, reduces the drama to a detective story (perhaps the most compulsively reductive of narrative forms). He seeks, through a schema that offers blinding closure, to localize guilt and to impute it to a given agent, if need be by assuming the dual role of scapegoat and victim himself. Never explicitly pertinent in Freud's Oedipal reading of *Oedipus Rex*, however, is the way the play stages rather than simply acts out Oedipus's gesture. For it provides evidence that Oedipus may be no more or no less guilty than anyone else—indeed that the kind of guilt Oedipus seeks may be misplaced.

The play never resolves the issue of whether the murderers of Laius were one or many. The witness who is summoned to give testimony on this issue never addresses it. Instead the inquiry shifts to a question of origins: the origins of Oedipus. The displaced witness is of course the very herdsman who had been charged by Laius and Jocasta to expose the child whose ankles they had pierced and so to avert the oracle's Oedipal prophecy.[19] (It is interesting that the protagonists invoke the parents' mistreatment of the child only as evidence in the attempt to establish the guilt of the adult for other putative crimes. Oedipus is driven to take upon himself the particular guilt of the parents as well as the pollution of the city.) Thus the play does indeed present the Oedipal scenario, complete with the symbolic castration of the child, but it does so in conjunction with a scapegoating scenario that is itself linked to a certain kind of narrative and dramatic intelligibility. *Oedipus Rex* also includes unresolved elements through which one may contest these

[19] See Cynthia Chase, "Oedipal Textuality: Reading Freud's Reading of Oedipus," *Diacritcs* 9 (Spring 1979): 54-68.

scenarios and proceed to the possibility of different readings of both their dubious reductivism and the larger sociopolitical situation in which it operates (for example, a reading that stresses the ideologically stabilizing function of reacting to anxiety through a scapegoat mechanism).

Freud never recognized the extent to which Sophocles' play cast doubt upon the Oedipal scenario, perhaps because the way it questioned that scenario was arguably more explicit than anything to be found in Freud's work. It is nonetheless noteworthy that Freud, in recounting the story of his own life and thought, showed resistance to assuming the Oedipal position. Freud was reluctant to avow a symbolic slaying of his actual or intellectual fathers, and he even shied away from acknowledging the problem of succession. In his well-known reference to his own father, Jacob, in *The Interpretation of Dreams*, Freud has his father undergo "castration" at the hands of an anti-Semitic stranger, and the father's passive acceptance of the insult serves to repeat his castration in the eyes of his son. One might perhaps entitle this scene, reminiscent of one in *The Brothers Karamazov*, "A Father Is Being Beaten":

> I may have been ten or twelve years old, when my father began to take me with him on his walks and reveal to me in his talk his views upon things in the world we live in. Thus it was, on one such occasion, that he told me a story to show me how much better things were now than they had been in his days. "When I was a young man," he said, "I went for a walk one Saturday in the streets of your birthplace; I was well dressed, and had a new fur cap on my head. A Christian came up to me and with a single blow knocked off my cap into the mud and shouted: 'Jew! Get off the pavement!'" "And what did you do?" I asked. "I went into the roadway and picked up my cap," was his quiet reply. This struck me as unheroic conduct on the part of the big, strong man who was holding the little boy by the hand. I contrasted this situation with another which fitted my feelings better: the scene in which Hannibal's father, Hamilcar Barca, made the boy swear before the household altar to take vengeance on the Romans. Ever since that time Hannibal had had a place in my phantasies.[20]

[20] Freud, *The Interpretation of Dreams* (New York, 1965), p. 230.

It is unclear from this passage whether the progressivist reason for the story (so blatantly enmeshed in displacement that its little object lesson is rendered abject) was actually given by Freud's father or was imputed to him by Freud himself. One might also see the story as demythologizing the role of the father in a manner Freud refused to acknowledge. Indeed Freud seems to reverse roles by having the father undergo symbolic castration and to localize in his "bad" example an infantile threat of powerlessness that recurs throughout life. In any event, Freud's affirmed identification with figures such as Hannibal and Moses furnished him with more potent role models and symbolic fathers. In the case of Moses, one had, on Freud's own interpretation, a markedly liminal figure—an Egyptian who became a Jew, and therefore someone who deliberately chose the fate Freud inherited as destiny from his parents. In his *Autobiographical Study*, Freud will implicitly differentiate himself from his father by stating that he "refused absolutely" to feel inferior because he was a Jew and that through his acceptance of an alien, oppositional status, "the foundations were . . . laid for a certain degree of independence of judgment" (pp. 14, 15).

Part of the allure of autobiographical writing is the opportunity it offers to become one's own symbolic genitor. Freud never mentions his mother in his *Autobiographical Study*, and his only overt reference to his father is limited to the remarkably "unpsychoanalytic" statement: "Although we lived in very limited circumstances, my father insisted that, in my choice of a profession, I should follow my own inclinations" (p. 13). Yet his autobiography is, after all, intellectual and professional, and in recounting the story of his thought, he confirms the impression of self-genesis rather than of Oedipal anxiety—although the two may of course be interpreted as having a compensatory relation to one another. Freud provides little "ancestry" for his ideas and highlights the image of the lonely discoverer by stressing his isolation for ten years as the first psychoanalyst. (This image is duly replicated in the "filiopious" biography of Ernest Jones.) Freud avoided reading thinkers, such as Nietzsche, who might undercut his sense of creativity, and he even saw his position as founding father as authorizing him to maintain that "no one can know better than I do what psycho-analysis is, how it differs from other ways of investigating the life of the mind, and precisely what should be called psycho-analysis and what would better be described by some other name" ("HPM," p. 7).[21] When he did acknowledge the role of three powerful fathers—Josef Breuer, Jean Martin Charcot, and Rudolf Chrobak (the latter being "perhaps the most eminent of all our Vienna physicians")—it was to indicate how they had blinded themselves by not seeing what was plainly before them (the importance of sexuality in the etiology of neurosis). Freud did not have to rise up against them; he had only to complement their blindness with his insight by noticing or paying attention to what they unknowingly transmitted to him. And he did so in a manner that confirmed his theory of *Nachträglichkeit* (thereby managing to qualify the thesis of absolute originality in a rather original way).

> These three men had all communicated to me a piece of knowledge which, strictly speaking, they themselves did not possess. Two of them later denied having done so when I reminded them of the fact; the third (the great Charcot) would probably have done the same if it had been granted me to see him again. But these three identical opinions, which I had heard without understanding, had lain dormant in my mind for years, until one day they awoke in the form of an apparently original discovery. ("HPM," p. 13)

A final instance of Freud's resistance to assuming the Oedipal position, being faced with the threat of castration and having to work through it to "maturity," is provided by *Civilization and Its Discontents* (1930). I shall later quote the famous passage concerning the possibility of pathological states of society. Here I simply note that the repeated detours in his argument—which Freud himself remarks upon—as well as the suspicious demurrers intimating that he is merely stating the obvious, may be related to his reluctance in taking up the position of social critic. Such a step would cast him in the Oedipal role writ large: that of someone challenging the collective superego of society. As a psychoanalyst, Freud always experienced a perhaps necessary role tension between the status of

---

[21] The claim of course prefaced an attack upon the apostasies of Jung and Adler.

the practitioner dealing with people on a one-to-one basis (a professional status) and that of the social critic addressing structural problems (a nonprofessional status).[22] And there were good reasons for hesitancy and self-doubt in making sweeping judgements about the state of society or the course of civilization. But, on Freud's own "authority," one might argue that his hesitations concerning social criticism were overdetermined and that the Oedipal scenario was at play—notably in a resistance to having it set fully into motion, a resistance that need not be taken in a simply negative sense but in one that may help generate questions about the "imperial" scope of the scenario itself. Especially in his own narrative practice, there may on some level have been—however problematically—a bit of the *Anti-Oedipe*.

In Freud's theoretical rendition of the Oedipus complex and in his thematic application of it in the explicit interpretation of other narratives, however, the Oedipus complex tends to be portrayed as an unproblematic discovery, and castration anxiety tends to function as an ultimate sanction—the penal confirmation of the law of the father and the closure of one crucial stage of the life cycle. The boy in accepting the threat of castration undergoes a *Bildungsreise* cum *Biedermeier* saga in which he learns that a deferral of gratification will in time enable him to assume the role of the father and find a substitute for the mother. He will thus enter into a legitimate heritage wherein he will be like (but not too incestuously like) the father and be rewarded for giving up union with the mother. In its more general function as a structure of closure, castration anxiety seems to provide a definite reduction of the anxiety of ambivalence, divided origins, and repetition (as it seems to do in the essay on the uncanny). It furnishes a clear-cut answer to the possibly uncertain origins of anxiety and converts a potentially intractable problem into a puzzle that detective work may solve. (It thus operates as a

---

[22] This tension is eliminated by the adamantly collectivist and revolutionary position taken by Herbert Marcuse in *Eros and Civilization: A Philosophical Inquiry into Freud* (Boston, 1955). The role tension in Freud had an "economic" dimension: the individual practitioner did not engage basic social problems but had a greater chance of success, if only in returning people from "hysterical misery" to "everyday unhappiness"; the social critic probably had less chance of success but directed attention to structural causes of "discontent."

good, orthodox historian presumably does.) With it, we know what the boy wants in his *Heimweh*; we know why he cannot fulfill his primal wish to return to the womb (the once familiar place later defamiliarized through repression); and we know how the boy may achieve a modified, domesticated happy ending in founding a family of his own (the existential and hermeneutic pot of gold at the end of the psychoanalytic rainbow).

But castration anxiety also opens another story and unfolds other narrative sequences with consequences that may themselves generate anxiety over the status of the entire theory. The girl cannot resolve problems as readily as the boy, and for her, castration anxiety is a point of entry to, rather than exit from, the Oedipus complex: it presumably inhibits the formation of her superego and threatens to underwrite her position of sociocultural inferiority. One also has the genesis of what might be called a castration narrative that may impede the boy's own *Bildung* through its phantasmatic snares.

The bizarre narrative of castration anxiety tells the story of fetishism. It begins with a nonevent, a disavowal of perception, a refusal to see what is there. For "in the beginning" the vagina is foreclosed—a derealized reality. It is replaced by another reality that is "perceived" as absent—something one "knows" should be there: the penis. This "knowledge" is of course based upon an invidious comparison with a privileged object. But the even more decisive step is the conversion of what is absent into what is missing. This is perhaps the true *coup d'Oedipe*, for at this point the narrative becomes blatantly phantasmatic. (There is a crucial relation between the conversion of absence into loss and the genesis of the phantasm.) What is missing is the very phallus that the woman (the phantasmatic phallic mother) had "in the beginning" but lost through some misdeed—an obvious lesson for the boy himself. The fetish, for Freud, is itself the narcissistically invested surrogate for the phantasmatic lost totality—a totality that never existed and whose imaginary constitution requires a conversion of absence into loss on the basis of a nonperception. Yet with the appearance of the imaginary totality, the castration narrative becomes a variant of (or perhaps the prototype for) the greatest story ever told—the classical apocalyptic narrative (as well as the displaced narrative of speculative dialectics) in which a totality fully present at the origin is lost through a sinful fall, only to be a regained in a utopian future.[23]

In the remainder of this essay, I shall speculate on ways in which my discussion bears not only on the history of psychoanalysis but on history and criticism in general. An obvious question is the extent to which the ideal of providing comprehensive accounts or global theories that "bring order to chaos" entails phantasmatic investments—notably when this ideal prompts questionable methodological solutions, for example, in the form of classical narratives and noncommittal analyses of situations in which one is transferentially implicated. The archive itself may become a fetish when it is seen not as a repository of traces in the inferential reconstruction of historical processes but as a surrogate for the missing thing itself—*l'histoire totale*. But a more general approach to the problem of articulating history and psychoanalysis would, I think, have to begin with the contention that it is inadequate to rest content (as Freud sometimes did) with the *analogy* between ontogeny and phylogeny or between the individual and society. Instead one must actively recognize that the analogy itself conceals the more basic interaction of psychoanalytic and sociocultural processes involving social individuals. This interaction calls for an investigation of specific historical processes that cannot be treated as simple derivatives of a totalizing, macrological schema of the civilizing process or the evolution of the species.

Freud's very understanding of temporality as a repetition/change, bringing with it deferred action and transference, itself implied the importance of displacement over (or as) time. Freud's own second

---

[23] For sympathetic portrayals of the apocalyptic narrative, see Frank Kermode, *The Sense of an Ending: Studies in the Theory of Fiction* (New York 1967), and M. H. Abrams, *Natural Supernaturalism: Tradition and Revolution in Romantic Literature* (New York, 1971). Marx's understanding of "commodity fetishism" is itself indentured to the "castration narrative" insofar as it assumes a human essence or social totality from which one is "alienated" under capitalism. To this extent, what certain Marxists oppose to alienation may be part of the same complex as their object of criticism. The further question, however, is whether there are in Marx other dimensions of the critique of commodity fetishism and alienation as well as other possible bases for alternatives to them. On this question, see my "Marxism and Intellectual History," *Rethinking Intellectual History: Texts, Contexts, Language* (Ithaca, N.Y., 1983), pp. 325-46.

topology (ego-id-superego) did not simply supersede but displaced his first topology (conscious—unconscious—preconscious) in a complex network of continuities and discontinuities. It required an attempt to resituate the earlier concepts, with portions of the ego and the superego placed in the unconscious and the earlier notion of the "censor" expanded into a larger understanding of sociocultural norms (prohibitions and prescriptions). It also signaled the mutual articulation of the psyche and society. However one further explicates the notions of the superego and the ego, it is evident that they are constitutively implicated in sociocultural and historical processes. But what is less apparent is that a similar point may be made about the id and the drives. Freud called the drives the myths of psychoanalysis—its sometimes substantialized postulates that could never be directly perceived but could be inferred on the basis of their effects, traces, or "representatives." They may also be called the myths of historicity. When Freud asserted that the unconscious was intemporal and knew no contradiction, he relied for the contrast on a classical notion of history as chronological change and on an equally classical notion of the law of noncontradiction. In terms of his own notion of "contradictory" temporality as repetition with change (at times traumatically disruptive change), the drives themselves became historicized. They were not purely static or intemporal entities, and they could not be defined according to the law of noncontradiction. They mutually marked or supplemented one another, and they shared predicates in a complex exchange of continuity and discontinuity. Freud's own flexible, if not labile, determination of the drives (first, sexuality and self-preservative or ego drives, then "life" and "death" drives) is itself emblematic of their historicity. The drives were internally divided ("life" involving both free-flowing energy and binding into higher unities, with a tendency toward constancy or lowest possible tension; "death" involving both aggression and unbinding, with a tendency toward nirvana or absolute discharge), and their relation to one another was not that of simple binary opposition but rather of "chiasmatic" pairing.[24] In this sense, it is more accurate to speak not of the

---

[24] See J. Laplanche, *Life and Death in Psychoanalysis*, trans. Jeffrey Mehlman (Baltimore, 1976).

dualism of Freud's basic concepts but of their duality—a duality allowing for contradiction as well as for more undecidable modes of exchange. The historicity of the drives was further compounded by their interaction with the ego and superego in a subject that was decentered both "internally" and socioculturally but was also in quest of unity—phantasmatic unity and unity in more viable forms of "binding."

The entire question of psychoanalysis and history might be posed with respect to the notions of "binding" and "unbinding" as they bear upon sociocultural processes. Institutions (in the largest sense) are normative modes of "binding" with variable relations to more ecstatic, sublime, or uncanny modes of "unbinding." They require repetitive performance that may become compulsive but may also facilitate exchanges. Freud often referred to "mental work" in its *Wechselwirkung* with free-flowing, "primary-process" energy, and his thought in this regard opens onto the problem of institutions as loci of work that interacts with more or less "unbound" play. And it directs attention to the modalities of displacement in the history of society and culture.

Freud himself was preoccupied with secularization as a displacement of religious onto secular phenomena, including psychoanalysis itself. Indeed Freud's own "Enlightenment" hostility to religion may have been exacerbated by similarities that were too close for comfort. Not only did psychopathological symptoms seem like religious rituals or beliefs that had lost their collective institutional moorings to reestablish themselves in markedly self-punitive forms in the "private" psyche. (As Freud wrote to Fliess: "By the way, what have you to say to the suggestion that the whole of my brand-new theory of the primary origins of hysteria is already familiar and has been published a hundred times over, though several centuries ago? Do you remember my always saying that the mediaeval theory of possession, that held by the ecclesiastical courts, was identical with our theory of a foreign body and the splitting of consciousness?"[25]) But the psychoanalyst might himself bear an un-

[25] Freud, *The Origins of Psycho-analysis: Letters, Drafts, and Notes to Wilhelm Fliess, 1887-1902*, ed. Marie Bonaparte, Anna Freud, and Ernst Kris (Garden City, N.Y., 1957), p. 90.

57

canny resemblance to the exorcist—a similitude that was anticipated as early as the sixteenth century, when ecclesiastical authori-
ties preemptively attacked, as the ultimate ruse of the devil himself,
attempts to construe demonic possession in terms of madness.[26]

In *The Future of an Illusion*, Freud both disarmingly invokes "our
God *logos*" and tries to distinguish between religious "delusions"
and his own "illusions" on the grounds that the latter are open to
correction and would be given up if experience were to contradict
the expectations they fostered.[27] Weighting continuities and discontinuities in historical displacements in order to arrive at specific
delineations that are neither identities nor simple differences is an
extremely difficult, perhaps intractable, problem.[28] And it is a problem that is not limited to the already vast ramifications of the process of secularization. Indeed it raises the general question of the
extent to which what is repressed or suppressed historically and
socioculturally tends to return as the repressed in psychology.

One issue here is the formation of levels of culture in the modern
period. The distinction among popular, mass, and elite (or high)
culture seems to parallel and in certain respects may shape Freud's
topology of id, ego, superego. Particularly in the late sixteenth and
seventeenth centuries in Europe, elite culture (in the sense of artifacts of creative elites) became, to a significant extent, aligned with
official state culture in a hegemonic formation that (notably in a
country like France) tried to establish a shared superego (or what

---

[26] See Mary R. O'Neill, "*Sacerdote overro strione*: Ecclesiastical and Superstitious
Remedies in 16th-Century Italy," in *Understanding Popular Culture*, ed. Steven L.
Kaplan (Berlin, 1984), pp. 53-83.

[27] See Freud, *The Future of an Illusion* (Garden City, N.Y., 1964), pp. 86 and 89.
This text would repay an extended reading, particularly in view of its explicitly
dialogic format, in which Freud at times gives voice to the *advocatus diaboli* yet
softly affirms the abiding power of reason and experience.

[28] It is too simple to argue, as Hans Blumenberg does, that the displacement in
secularization is functional, not substantive—that is, it constitutes a different
answer to similar questions as were posed in religion. That the similarities and differences, continuities and discontinuities cannot be isolated or so sharply separated
is intimated in Blumenberg's own attempt to ground the so-called legitimacy of
the modern age on self-assertive will—what Heidegger took as the modern displacement par excellence of the traditional metaphysical quest for an ultimate
ground. See Blumenberg, *The Legitimacy of the Modern Age*, trans. Robert M. Wal-
lace (Cambridge, Mass., 1983).

Emile Durkheim would call a *conscience collective*) extending to other sections of society and culture. Language was normalized according to elite standards. And the very definition of what constituted popular religion was the work of ecclesiastical elites concerned with circumscribing and controlling "superstition" and heterodoxy.[29] More generally, religious reform, the development of capitalism, and the rise of state bureaucracies combined to create more disciplined forms of social life in which priority was given to the delay of gratification and the minute surveillance of activity, including the role of "spiritual" exercises. As Michel Foucault has argued with some exaggeration in *Discipline and Punish*, the nineteenth century witnessed an expansion of technologies and mechanisms of surveillance and control, with Jeremy Bentham's Panopticon serving as a normative model for all bureaucratic institutions in which close and constant regulation of personnel was at a premium. Punishment itself was displaced from the physical to the psychical with the decline of torture and the generalization of incarceration as the homogeneous response to a wide variety of crimes.

For Foucault, the psychoanalytic session is the heir of the confessional in its scrutiny of the interior life and sexual desire of the individual. One might add that Freud's all-seeing superego is the internalized counterpart of the techniques of surveillance and control that were being disseminated in public life. The very opposition between public and private opened the public sphere to regulatory agencies while the private sphere was to be kept inviolate from "external" control, only to be subjected to extremely demanding "internal" strictures. (This division of labor is evident in the thought of both Mill and Herbert Spencer.) Civil rights and freedom of speech in public life were thus offset by internal norms and mechanisms that set up "private" parameters to freedom of "inner" life and thought. For such figures as Mill and Spencer, it went without saying that sexual life would be subject to the strictest

[29] My generalizations barely scratch the surface of an inordinately intricate and differentiated series of problems. See, for example, Roger Chartier, "Culture as Appropriation: Popular Cultural Uses in Early Modern France," and Jacques Revel, "Forms of Expertise: Intellectuals and 'Popular' Culture in France (1650-1800)," in *Understanding Popular Culture*. See also my comments in *History and Criticism* (Ithaca, N.Y., 1985).

of inner controls. (One may note in passing the need for a general genealogy of the concepts of the public and the private.)

For a multiplicity of reasons, elites in the modern period tended to withdraw from participation in certain "popular" forms, including carnivalesque activities, which then became severely regulated and even repressed. Especially for the rising middle classes, the carnivalesque became the object of equivocal fascination and phobic investment. The very idea of either a communally festive consumption of an economic surplus or an exchange that did not seem determined by the profit motive might appear as the height of irrationality itself. The carnivalesque was domesticated and made to serve either the state in nationalistic celebrations or the family in both the situation comedies of daily life and the private observances of special occasions ("there's no place like home for the holidays"). Older and now suspect popular forms became something like a collective id, and they were relegated, at times in vestigial form, to the "folkloric" if not opaque world of the peasantry, the dangerous subculture of the urban proletariat, and the shocking antics of *la bohème*. Yet these forms might also threaten to return in distorted, indeed sadomasochistic, variants. (In this sense there may be no contradiction between the interpretations of the Wolf-Man's father offered by Freud and by Abraham and Torok. Indeed a crucial problem in the modern period—ignored in the work of Norbert Elias and only intimated in Foucault's critique of the "repressive hypothesis"—is the conjunction of extremely "civilized," if not "repressive," control and at times "neobarbaric" excess, including sadomasochistic variants of the carnivalesque.)

The rise of mass or commodified culture, particularly in the pervasive forms it has taken in the recent past, added another dimension to this complex of forces. Mass culture was distributed to various levels of society but of course consumed differently by different groups. It nonetheless acted as a "relay" system that might threaten to reprocess older popular forms in more acceptably commodified and marketable packages. It "liberated" artists and intellectuals from aristocratic patronage, but by the nineteenth century it also came to define a culture from which artistic and intellectual elites often felt "alienated." Elite culture itself became inward turning and often inaccessible, not only to popular but to many middle-class groups—for example, when it made use of older popular forms (such as the carnivalesque) in difficult, hermetic guises. It also became internally fragmented in ways the so-called two-cultures thesis vastly oversimplifies. Its artifacts entertained (and continue to entertain) a complex, internally divided relation to society and culture at large, involving both a reinforcement of newer forms of hegemony and contestation of them.

This brief, overly selective, and inadequate sketch of cultural processes in modern history, made with reference to certain psychoanalytic concepts, at least suggests areas for the articulation of psychoanalytic and historical research. The very definition of levels of culture raises the question of processes of boundary formation (with its inclusions, exclusions, isolations, and so forth) that psychoanalysis has explored in terms of the psyche. More pointedly, Freud looked to all signifying practices with specific concern for the role of the body as an organizing trope. (As he puts it with tragicomic, perversely carnivalesque force in his study of the Wolf-Man, "his bowel began, like a hysterically affected organ, to 'join in the conversation'" ["IN," p. 265]). The paradigm of the trauma was the rupture of the skin, and the body provided a reference point for divisions between an "inside" and an "outside." The body might well serve as tropaic matrix in the investigation of sociocultural processes, including the opposition between public and private spheres as well as the formation of disciplines on both discursive and institutional levels. What is good to "ingest" in a given group or discipline, what should be "expelled" as indigestible, and what metabolism is considered "normal" in the rhythm of social life are only some of the most pressing questions in this respect.

On a more directly institutional plane, the network formed by family, educational system, state, organized religion, and commodified economy has complex connections with levels of culture and psychic processes. Freud focused on the family as the "relay" between the child and the larger society and culture. Yet the family itself might of course seek closure as a proverbial haven in a heartless world. Freud himself seemed symptomatically to underwrite this closure in his restricted ability to thematize the problem of the relation of the family to other institutions and discursive practices. But he also introduced considerations of authority and power into the seeming haven of the family itself, intimating one direction for an analysis of the politics of everyday life. His own accounts of the family, moreover, included, however equivocally, the presence of interrupters of family closure and uneasy participants in the family romance. This was notably the case of the maid or nurse as a liminal figure between the family and the larger society—an "other" from a lower social class who partially shared the intimacy and even the secrets of the family without being a full-fledged member of its charmed circle. (It is significant that the embarrassing scene between Freud and a woman patient, which he employs in his *Autobiographical Study* to introduce transference as a displacement of familial relations, is itself interrupted by a maid whose "unexpected entrance" relieved the psychoanalytic couple from a "painful discussion."[30]) In contemporary society, the mediating and supplementary function of the maid in the family is to a large extent taken by the peer group and the media—two "interrupters" of familial closure given scant attention in Louis Althusser's discussion of so-called ideological state apparatuses.[31]

The apparent problem is how to extend further Freud's analysis of the relation of the family to other institutions and to join it with sociocultural criticism. (This is of course a problem that has bedeviled intellectuals, especially on the Left, since Freud's own time, and a prominent form it has taken is the attempt to "build a bridge" between Marx and Freud, often with assistance from such other

[30] See p. 49. On the role of the nurse, see, for example, Jane Gallop, *The Daughter's Seduction: Feminism and Psychoanalysis* (Ithaca, N.Y., 1982), pp. 141-48.
[31] See Louis Althusser, "Ideology and Ideological State Apparatuses," *Lenin and Philosophy and Other Essays*, trans. Ben Brewster (New York, 1971), pp. 127-86. Althusser of course tries to link Marxism and Lacanian psychoanalysis in a theory of institutions and ideology in modern society. His important effort is limited in a number of ways. He attempts to position Lacan in relation to Freud on the analogy of his own relation to Marx, as he conceives it. This results in a rather misleading image of Lacan as providing a "science" of a new "object": the Freudian unconscious. Althusser's definition of ideology as centered on the subject, moreover, both occludes the problem of the subject in the constitution of science and obviates the possibility of an objectivist or scientistic ideology (toward which Althusser himself at times inclines). The notion of ideological state apparatuses itself begs the question of the relation of the state and official culture to other institutions and levels of culture, and the overdrawn conception of hegemony tends to respond to the deficiencies of economic determinism with an equally one-sided and deceptively generalized construction of the political and sociocultural order.

classical social theorists as Durkheim and Weber.) The locus classicus of Freud's own confrontation with the issue is the following passage from *Civilization and Its Discontents*:

> I hasten to come to a close. But there is one question which I can hardly evade. If the development of civilization has such a far-reaching similarity to the development of the individual and if it employs the same methods, may we not be justified in reaching the diagnosis that, under the influence of cultural urges, some civilizations, or some epochs of civilization—possibly the whole of mankind—have become 'neurotic'? An analytic dissection of such neuroses might lead to therapeutic recommendations which could lay claim to great practical interest. I would not say that an attempt of this kind to carry psycho-analysis over to the cultural community was absurd or doomed to be fruitless. But we should have to be very cautious and not forget that, after all, we are only dealing with analogies and that it is dangerous, not only with men but also with concepts, to tear them from the sphere in which they have originated and been evolved. Moreover, the diagnosis of communal neuroses is faced with a special difficulty. In an individual neurosis we take as our starting-point the contrast that distinguishes the patient from his environment, which is assumed to be "normal". For a group all of whose members are affected by one and the same disorder no such background could exist; it would have to be found elsewhere. And as regards the therapeutic application of our knowledge, what would be the use of the most correct analysis of social neuroses, since no one possesses authority to impose such a therapy upon the group? But in spite of all these difficulties, we may expect that one day someone will venture to embark upon a pathology of cultural communities.[32]

Recently Jürgen Habermas has found his own reasons for backing away from the earlier effort of the Frankfurt school to answer Freud's expectation by converting psychoanalysis itself into a paradigm for critical theory, and he has turned to his own version of macrological evolutionary theory and "universal pragmatics." Martin Jay provides this lucid summary of Habermas's position:

[32] New York, 1961, pp.102-3.

Whereas the patient and analyst shared an a priori interest in relieving the patient's neurotic symptoms, in society no such consensus
could be assumed. Indeed, insofar as certain men or classes benefited
from the maintenance of ideological distortion and exploitative
power relations, there was no reason to assume they would willingly
enter the process of dialogic enlightenment suggested by the psychoanalytic model. Nor would their improved understanding of
reality necessarily generate a desire to transform it. Symmetrical relations in a truly democratic public sphere could not be seen as a condition for social change, when in fact they were one of its goals.[33]

Here one may call into question not the insistence on impediments
to discursive enlightenment or dialogic reciprocity in existing societies but the basis of the contrast with the psychoanalytic model.
It is not true that the analyst and the patient simply share the goal
of relieving symptoms or of "entering the process of dialogic
enlightenment." Habermas's own understanding of analysis is
overly predetermined by an "ego-psychological" perspective. The
difficulties in working through transference, countertransference,
and resistances pose severe obstacles to consensus, as does the difference in authority (or relative helplessness) between analyst and
analysand. Freud, moreover, stressed the secondary benefits from
illness that create major blocks to the dissolution of symptoms; he
also recognized the danger that even more severe symptoms might
replace those that were eliminated. There are of course analogues
of these problems in social life. The most obvious is the risk of
radical change, especially when there is little idea of viable alternatives or even the tendency to confide in blank utopianism and apocalyptic euphoria. But one may also mention the way established
regimes institute (as Foucault has argued) systematic and at times
flagrant discrepancies between affirmed norms and actual performance. In this manner, "pathology" is "normalized": normative
expectations are continually frustrated but in a way that evokes
recurrent attempts at reform, sustained by rhetorical appeals to a
founding program, constitution, or charter.

One may also argue that Freud's own "analogy" is both better

---

[33] Martin Jay, *Marxism and Totality: The Adventures of a Concept from Lukács to
Habermas* (Berkeley and Los Angeles, 1984), pp. 480-81.

and worse than he thought. It is better because psychoanalysis and social theory face similar problems. These problems tend to be obscured by the assumptions active in Freud's passage: the enabling idea that someone (presumably the analyst supported by social forces) has the authority to impose therapy on the patient (which Freud elsewhere questioned) and the initial postulate that existing society is normal (which takes psychoanalysis in the direction of uncritically adaptive therapy). Yet Freud's analogy is also worse than he thought. It reverts to the macrological parallel of ontogeny and phylogeny. More important, it takes as an analogy between entities presumed to be discrete and to have autonomous origins and evolutionary paths what is both more and other than an analogy—what in fact involves the interaction of social individuals and the mutual articulation of psychoanalytic and social categories. As we have noted, Freud sometimes emphasized the fact that, in elaborating psychoanalytic concepts and theories, he was already working on and transforming existing sociocultural material.

The very concept of normality is normative and implicated in sociocultural judgments, and for this very reason it calls for critical reflection. Yet it often functions as a residual category in Freud — a category he relies on but defines largely in terms of its implicit contrast with pathology. (It is also noteworthy that there is no entry for "normality" in Laplanche and Pontalis's *Language of Psycho-analysis*.) In this sense, "normality" functions as the absent center of Freud's thought.

It must, however, be added that one of the most forceful incentives in Freud is to question the simple binary opposition between normality and pathology and instead to see these concepts in terms of interacting differences of degree problematically related to judgments of kind. He will refer at most to the "approximately normal person" (his self-designation in *The Interpretation of Dreams*), and he will show how pathogenic forces are not only active to different degrees in all people but ambivalently related to the most "positive" forces in life. Transference itself is a bridge between normality and pathology (both within and between selves)—a sign that movements in both directions are possible, short of irremediable psychosis (if indeed there is such a state beyond transference). But the absence of critical reflection about the category of normality facilitates its identification with conformity or adaptation in the existing soci-ocultural state of affairs.

The concepts of social normality and pathology are both highly problematic and probably necessary. Their status in this respect is no more and no less questionable than their psychoanalytic counter-parts. Indeed the task (as Durkheim saw) was how to articulate the relations between the two sets of concepts. The active recognition that this task is itself normative and ethicopolitical and that it can-not be neatly disjoined from research and analysis is the sine qua non of any attempt to work through it toward that "elsewhere" which, Freud noted, had to be found for social criticism to be possi-ble. In that attempt, transference is at its most intense; yet the chances of acquiring critical perspective may also be greatest.

# 3

## Chartier, Darnton, and the Great Symbol Massacre

This is a privilege coveted by every society, whatever its beliefs, its political system or its level of civilization; a privilege to which it attaches its leisure, its pleasure, its peace of mind and its freedom; the possibility of *unhitching*, which consists—Oh! fond farewell to savages and explorations!—in grasping, during the brief intervals in which our species can bring itself to interrupt its hive-like activity, the essence of what it was and continues to be, below the threshold of thought and over and above society: in the contemplation of a mineral more beautiful than all our creations; in the scent that can be smelt at the heart of a lily and is more imbued with learning than all our books; or in the brief glance, heavy with patience, serenity and mutual forgiveness, that, through some involuntary understanding, one can sometimes exchange with a cat.

—Claude Lévi-Strauss, *Tristes Tropiques*

For all our anthropological and anthropocentric concern with seeing things from the perspective of the "native," we have yet to empathize with the cat—that exemplary victim of cruelty and "fun." Yet we historians do seem to be turning at long last to the problem of "reading" and even indicating an openness to the "jargon of

The works discussed here are Roger Chartier, "Text, Symbols, and Frenchness," *Journal of Modern History* 57 (1985): 682-95; Robert Darnton, "The Symbolic Element in History," ibid. 58 (1986): 218-34; and idem, *The Great Cat Massacre and Other Episodes in French Cultural History* (New York, 1984). Page references in the text are to these works, the latter abbreviated *GCM*.

textuality"—or so it would seem from the exchange between Roger Chartier and Robert Darnton occasioned by Darnton's recent book, *The Great Cat Massacre*. But the aperture through which reading and textuality make their entrance into the historical profession may at times be no larger than the proverbial squint of the cat's eye. While the issue raised by the Chartier-Darnton exchange is that of the nature and import of reading texts in history, their treatment of this issue is rather narrow in focus. Could a different approach to reading make room for the excluded perspective of the cat and thereby attenuate the species imperialism and methodological scapegoating of the "other" that even the most generous and latitudinarian of humanistic or anthropological perspectives seem to entail? Would there even be a point in not trying to get the "joke" of the "great cat massacre" to which Robert Darnton tries to make us privy as he unveils the seemingly opaque secrets of the Old Regime—a "joke" that was not terribly funny for its feline victims? What are "reading" and "texts" all about, anyway—these uncanny code words that often seem to be encased in more opacity than anything the Old Regime might offer to our probing ethnographic curiosity?

The very exchange between Chartier and Darnton may itself provide some ethnographic insight into the present state of the historical profession, for Chartier is a notable affiliate of the *Annales* school who has been questioning some of its long-standing assumptions about the nature of research, while Darnton has often been perceived as a primary mediator of the "message" of the *Annales* on this side of the Atlantic—a message that, in recent years, he has recoded in anthropological terms (particularly those provided by Clifford Geertz). Thus the exchange between these historians—even when it fails to take place—may teach us something about the nature of reading, meaning, and communication in our own tribe as well as about the habits of a distant past. Indeed, it may lead us to conclude that self-reflective and substantive processes of inquiry cannot be dissociated insofar as there is a mutual implication of self and other in any act of historical understanding or interpretation.

As Chartier takes up the "invitation to reflection" that Darnton's book extends to him, he seems initially to be most concerned about the false image of the contemporary *Annales* that Darnton conveys.

While readers outside the orbit of the *Annales* might not see this problem as central to the book or, at most, might read Darnton as proposing a relatively anodyne emendation of prevalent procedures in social history *à la française*, Chartier takes Darnton to be throwing down the gauntlet, and the stakes are apparently high. The injunction not to read but to count cultural objects in order to analyze "massive amounts of homogeneous, reiterated data," which was prompted by the application of serial history to the study of culture, may have been representative of the history of *mentalités* twelve years ago, but, Chartier asks, is it "a fair expression of what French historians are producing today?" (p. 683). While this interrogation conforms to Chartier's recurrent procedure of raising quasi-rhetorical and at times meditatively indeterminate questions, his answer in this case seems relatively clear. It is not a "fair expression," and the primary reason is the putative attention paid by recent affiliates of the *Annales* to the problem of reading texts—a problem given its most extended and forceful expression toward the end of the essay where Chartier discloses what he thinks Darnton has not been doing, notably in the first two essays of his book (those on folktales and the cat massacre). For Chartier, the historian must confront "three ineluctable demands on anyone who sets out to decipher the symbolic system that underlies a text":

> first, to take the text as a text and to try to determine its intentions, its strategies, and the effects produced by its discourse; next, to avoid supposing a stable, full value in its lexical choices, but to take into account the semantic investment or disinvestment of its terms; finally, to define the instances of behavior and the rituals present in the text on the basis of the specific way in which they are assembled or produced by original invention, rather than to categorize them on the basis of remote resemblances to codified forms among the repertory of Western folk culture. (P. 694).

This format is admirable, but one might qualify it in at least three ways. First, what is at issue is precisely the question of what it is "to take the text as a text." Second, the "hermeneutic" attention to lexical and semantic considerations—a text's meaning or message—often excludes or obliterates a "poetic" concern for syntax and form—that is, how the text is put together and the way it

69

"generates" or does not "generate" meaning or message. Third, "original invention" is a notion that is in jeopardy in ideas of textuality as different as those of Hans-Robert Jauss, Michael Riffaterre, Paul de Man, and Jacques Derrida (to restrict oneself to this series of figures). The problem, I would suggest, is not "original invention" but how the text inscribes, reworks, and perhaps transforms its various pertinent contexts, the latter possibly including "codified forms among the repertory of Western folk culture." There would also be the question of what motivates the selection or emphasis of certain contexts rather than others.

In all fairness to Darnton, it must be noticed that while he does state that he especially questions "number crunching" in *Annales* historiography, he also makes a noteworthy *profession de foi*: the school has "contributed enormously to our understanding of the past—more, I should think, than any other trend in history writing since the beginning of the century" (*GCM*, p. 258). He nonetheless puts forth tentative criticisms of two methodological tenets that Chartier mentions only en passant: "that one can distinguish levels in the past" and "that the third level (culture) somehow derives from the first two (economics and demography, and social structure)" (*GCM*, p. 257). Is it fair to say that this methodology—if not metaphysic—for the study of historical reality has been substantially challenged in what is loosely called *Annales* historiography? If not, would it be more subject to contestation if there were greater sensitivity to problems of reading, interpretation, and textuality? Indeed, where is the evidence that *Annales* historians are confronting even the limited set of textual problems Chartier specifies? It is significant that he refers only to two of his own recent essays. I suggest that the older methodology still has much staying power, that twelve years do not a *longue durée* or even a *conjoncture* make, and that the *événement* of "reading" is still very much resisted both in the *Annales* and outside it. Concern for this and for its bearing on more established procedures of research is indeed noteworthy to the limited extent it has occurred, but even in the work of someone like Chartier, who is among the most sophisticated of recent French historians, receptiveness to the problem of "textuality" and the attempt to relate it cogently to historical inquiry in general remain quite restricted. This restriction is, I think, evident in his essay on Darnton.

I maintain that a concern for textuality and reading requires attention to the problem of the contestatory interaction between the desire for a unified framework (at the limit, totalization—including *l'histoire totale*) and the forces that challenge or even disorient that desire. Inadequate attention to this problem, which may come in the form of either an unquestioned assumption of unity or an unqualified assertion of disunity (including so-called splintered history), results in uncontrolled equivocation, while an attempt to work through the problem holds out the possibility of at least some responsible control over processes (notably including linguistic ones) that cannot be absolutely mastered. These processes, I further suggest, pose the problem of rethinking temporality as involving both repetition and change in variable and intricate articulations. Chartier points to a blatant equivocation in Darnton's book between his recurrent stress on the wondrous difference and opacity of the past and his insistence on an essential identity conveying a perdurable "Frenchness" across the ages: "What is still difficult to sustain, however, is the double and contradictory affirmation of a radical discontinuity between old and new ways of thinking about the world and of acting on it and a discernible continuity of a French 'cultural style.' Either this continuity exists, in which case the old ways of thinking are not so strange, or else those old ways were truly different from our own, in which case they could never be found in our present world" (p. 687). According to Chartier, you cannot have it both ways. I contend that you in fact do, but in terms of repetition and change that pose a problem in understanding and interpretation—should one say in "reading"?—that both Darnton and Chartier ignore.

Chartier, moreover, does not notice the equivocations in his own account. He emphasizes the need to read all texts, including documents, with an eye to their rhetoric and polyvalency, and on this basis he sees an "incontestable rupture" in Darnton's book between the first two essays (on folktales and the cat massacre) and the last four. The first two presumably treat texts as mere transparencies, while the last four are more sensitive to problems of reading. Chartier himself questions the feasibility of treating all phenomena as "texts," and he asserts a radical if not total difference between "actual" events, such as an oral telling of a tale or a massacre of

71

cats, and written texts. Indeed, he perceives "two sorts of logic, the logic of written expression and the logic that shapes what 'practical sense' produces" (p. 685). The first two chapters of Darnton's book apparently try to get at actual events and "practical sense" and in the process are insufficiently attentive to the fact that all one has are texts that must first be read. The last four chapters presumably operate on a purely textual and intertextual level and pose no problems. (In any case, Chartier devotes little if any attention to them.) According to Chartier,

> a common question underlies both groups, to be sure: How do men organize and manifest their perception and evaluation of the social world? But whereas the views and judgments of the peasants who told or heard the tales and of the workers who did away with the cats are accessible only through the mediation of texts relating what they are supposed to have heard, said, or done, the views of the burghers, administrators, and Philosophes are available to us in the first person in texts wholly organized according to strategies of writing with their own specific objectives (recasting social order, keeping track of the literary world, substituting the authority of the Philosophes for that of the theologians, remaking individual lives through a reading of Rousseau). This perhaps explains the contrast between Darnton's treatment of Contat's narration, which is obliterated as a narration and held to be a transparent account of the massacre it recounts, and his treatment of other texts, considered, to the contrary, in their full textuality and analyzed for their conceptual categories and the rhetorical formulas that shape their intended effects. (Pp. 686-87)

The terms in which Chartier draws his contrast strike me as questionable. First, the texts treated in the last four chapters are not uniformly first-person accounts. Second, these chapters try to reconstruct "realities" that are not purely intratextual (in the literal sense): an anonymous writer's understanding of the social layout of a city; a police inspector's perception of the world of "intellectuals"; the organization of knowledge in the *Encyclopédie*; and a bourgeois reader's response to the writings of Rousseau. Darnton is always in quest of a "worldview," and there are recurrent difficulties in his conception of the nature of "symbolic" meaning. The attempt to reconstruct a "lived" world through inferences from written texts is, of course, always risky, as is the use of the textual metaphor as the vehicle for this reconstruction. But the problems in Darnton's book are more specific in nature, and they are not restricted to the first two chapters. The "incontestable rupture" is as contestable as Darnton's own idea of the radical if not total alterity of the past. Moreover, the notion of "different logics" between written texts and "lived" events is dubious in the terms Chartier tries to pose it. He himself, after all, refers to something he calls "practical sense." Is "practical sense" prelinguistic or only prewritten? If it is prelinguistic, what is its relation to language? If (as would seem to be the case) it is restricted to the prewritten, what is the significance Chartier attributes to the opposition between the spoken and the written and how justifiable is his reliance on this opposition? Can one really speak (or write—the difference would seem minimal) of "different logics," or does one actually have differences in social conditions in oral and written cultures—differences that remain to be specified? Chartier's own mode of interrogating the textual "metaphor" seems to rely on an unexamined metaphysical opposition between writing and speech (which is also active in the work of a colleague to whom he often refers, Carlo Ginzburg). And it does not address the more "infrastructural" sense given to the notion of "text" in the work of Jacques Derrida—that is, his notion of the text as a network (or interweaving) of relations among instituted "traces." Derrida's "text" is not reducible to the Geertzian idea of a "text analogue" (an idea still indentured to an uncritical dichotomy between action and language), and it renders problematic the opposition between speech and writing as well as between the literal and the metaphorical. In any event, the point is not to posit a difference in "logics" but to inquire into the various and variable articulations between language (whether spoken or written) and the activities with which it is bound up, including the activity of inferring a "lived" past from textual or documentary traces. What is dubious in the extreme is the idea that one can make some general pronouncement about the relation between language (or any signifying practice) and seemingly nonlinguistic (or nonsignifying) activities; for in making any pronouncement one is inevitably situated inside language that is in multiple ways articulated with activities. To think otherwise is to assume a transcendental position outside language from which one can then pronounce on the relation between language and something else (which is, of course, designated in linguistic terms such as "practical sense"). (One could argue, *pace* Saussure, that the same point holds on the level of the sign, which can neither be asserted to be natural nor asserted to be arbitrary in its relation to a signified or referent.)

The further equivocation in Chartier's essay concerns the nontransparent status of any text and the problem of the instability of language itself. In criticizing Darnton's conception of the "symbol," Chartier asserts:

> Even when defined more precisely, the notion is not easy to use. First, we can hardly postulate stability in the relationship connecting the symbolic sign and what it represents and presents to our eyes. Variation springs from many sources: regarding the sign, a plurality of meanings can be carried by any given symbol; regarding circumstances, a sign may or may not be invested with a symbolic function, depending on the conditions of its use; regarding comprehension, it is inevitably highly uneven from one group or one individual to another. It seems risky, then, to claim that symbols are 'shared like the air we breathe.' Quite to the contrary, their significations are unstable, mobile, equivocal. They are not always easily decipherable and not always well deciphered. (P. 689)

One may note that this is the only basic point Darnton takes up in "The Symbolic Element in History," and it is not so much to respond to Chartier's argument as to accept the point in his own behalf and to construe the problem of polysemy in his own manner. Darnton focuses only on one decontextualized element of Chartier's discussion of the symbol as it was presumably understood in the eighteenth century—the notion that the lion is the symbol of valor. To this notion Darnton opposes precisely the polysemy of the symbol, and he uses it to defend his account of the overdetermined nature of the cat massacre in which workers engaged in a sort of bricolage of preexisting items in the cultural repertory (witchcraft, carnival, charivari, dramaturgy, etc.). Chartier, by contrast, invokes the instability and polysemy of the

74

symbol to question Darnton's postulation "that at a given moment and in a given place, a particular culture (for example, that of Parisian printing workers in the beginning of the eighteenth century) is organized in accordance with a symbolic repertory the elements of which are documented at various dates between the sixteenth and the nineteenth centuries and in multiple sites" (pp. 689-90). At the very least, this nonexchange between historians with a marked degree of common culture and even of shared assumptions attests to the difficulties of communication not only across time but also at any given time, even within a relatively homogeneous segment of the population.

Yet Chartier to some extent invites Darnton's (non)response. For just before his passage on the instability of symbols and the riskiness of postulating common cultures, he invokes the 1727 edition of Antoine Furetière's dictionary as evidence of the nature of the "native's" definition of such key terms as *sign* and *symbol*. Not only does he employ this source in a canonical way, but he also glosses over the internal difficulties in its various definitions of symbol and sign, reducing symbol, for example, to only one stratum of Furetière's rather puzzling and sometimes opaque discussion. (Chartier, in a manner reminiscent of Michel Foucault, asserts that "symbol" implies a relation of "representation," a term as problematic as "symbol" and into which he provides little insight. Nor does he puzzle over Furetière's more extensive definition of symbol as "sign, type, sort of emblem, or representation of some thing moral, by the images or the properties of natural things" [p. 688]—a definition latitudinarian if not "Borgesian" enough to encompass the lion as symbol of valor, the ball as that of inconstancy, and the pelican as that of eternal love.) Chartier himself proceeds, moreover, as if Furetière's "definitions" applied to the workers in the cat massacre—or, in any case, he does not raise the question of their range of applicability other than to assert that they "reflected" and "popularized" the theory of the sign as formulated by the logicians and grammarians of Port-Royal. Furthermore, he again resorts to Furetière when he raises doubts about Darnton's interpretation of the cat massacre as involving "ceremonial and symbolic" themes from the witch-hunt, the charivari, and the carnival mock trial, in each case invoking an extremely strict and narrow definition of the phenomenon in question to raise doubts about Darnton's account but without raising any doubts about the applicability of the definition.

A comparable equivocation in the relation between a unified definition and challenges to it arises in Chartier's discussion of genre and its relation to specific texts. Chartier rejects Darnton's idea that Nicolas Contat's *Anecdotes typographiques*[1] (which contains the story of the cat massacre) can be considered as an autobiography. Chartier contends that it belongs to "the time-honored tradition of texts that purport to reveal to the public the secrets and the practices, true or supposed, of particular professional, ethnic, or religious communities"—a generic tradition that had "new life" breathed into it by two further genres: descriptions of crafts and trades and travel accounts (p. 691). It is interesting that in his essay, Darnton will invoke two more genres: the *misère* and the how-to book. One could easily mention others—for example, the hyperbolic account of the feats of a friend in whose reflected glory one bathes. But the very multiplicity of possible generic sources or resonances would seem to indicate that the point is not simply to "name that genre." The prior consideration would be to ask whether the text is a mixed generic performance—indeed, to what extent it conforms to generic expectations—and, insofar as it is mixed, what weight one should attribute to each pertinent genre, how one should construe the interaction of the various genres in the work and play of the text, and how one should evaluate the extent to which the text exceeds or falls short of the expectations genres create. In this respect, a text may be both autobiographical and an account of trade secrets, and one cannot identify autobiography with the explicit use of the first-person narrative. More generally, genres create both constraints and possibilities for specific texts, and a given text may combine various genres in a manner that sets up a problematic interaction between generic unity and forces contesting it. This point applies to texts not only in the past but also in the present, including those written by the historian.

Darnton would probably not disagree with the last point. As Chartier fully recognizes, *The Great Cat Massacre* is itself an extremely ambitious attempt to pose the problem of reading and to relate it to texts and phenomena spanning various levels of cul-

---

[1] [1762], ed. Giles Barber (Oxford, 1980).

ture from the low or popular to the high or learned. One must admire the attempt and the local insights even when one questions the more encompassing assumptions and procedures. One of the great merits of Chartier's own essay is his ability to acknowledge the value of Darnton's undertaking even while he questions it. In my own questioning of Chartier's questions, as well as in the critical discussion of Darnton's book that follows, I too insist on the value of both Chartier's and Darnton's endeavors, particularly in the difficult effort to acquire a greater degree of historiographic self-understanding with implications for the practice of research. Indeed, the rest of this essay may in good part be read as an attempt to follow up Chartier's suggestion that certain borrowings from anthropology "may even create a few problems of their own by destroying the 'textuality' of texts that relate the symbolic practices being analyzed" (p. 690).

What I would especially like to investigate in *The Great Cat Massacre* itself is Darnton's understanding of symbolic meaning and of reading, his conception of the historian's relation to the past, his style in relating popular and elite culture, and the themes he emphasizes or fails to emphasize. Darnton's own (non)response to Chartier is of only limited usefulness in this investigation, except insofar as it repeats certain problems in the book itself. What occurs in the passage from the book to the article is an interesting interplay between stylistic transformation and stylistic continuity. One goes from a book in which the accounts move on the level of flexible if not loose narrative (even more than "thick description") to an essay that is more tightly organized and structural in argumentation. Yet there is a stylistic continuity in which one can read Darnton's "signature" both in the essay and in the book. (I raise some questions later about this resonant, appealing, and highly readable style.) Two further points about the essay do, however, shed light on the book. Darnton invokes a battery of anthropologists to stress the polysemy of the symbol in a manner that might suggest a more theoretical notion of the "overdetermined" nature of an event such as the cat massacre. He also emphasizes the importance of liminality, marginality, and hybridization in culture. The role of polysemy (and overdetermination) is indeed evident in the book, notably in the narrative of the cat massacre, but both there

77

and in the article it is only polysemy that is open at least potentially to full mastery and that raises no difficulty for Darnton's restricted idea of reading and symbolic meaning. The role of liminality or marginality is, moreover, itself at best marginal in the book in contrast to the article; for in the book it is called on only in passing—for example, with reference to the status of apprentices (p. 88) and of certain animals such as pigs and cats (p. 89). It is not systematically investigated. Nor is much sustained attention paid to what typically attends it: scapegoating and victimization.

Indeed, scapegoating and victimization seem to play a role in many of Darnton's accounts, but this either goes unremarked or is underemphasized. One may wonder whether this is the crucial dimension of the "polysemous" cat massacre itself—but a dimension on which one might choose to maintain a critical distance while recognizing the threat and even temptation it poses to oneself and one's own culture. In one sense, there is nothing very opaque about the victimization of helpless creatures when one is unable to get at the perceived sources of difficulty—that is, those more powerful than oneself. It happens all the time, not simply back then in the Old Regime but also here and now. In another sense, there is something about this process, including the hilarity it may provoke, that is not intelligible or "readable" either then or now. It is extremely disorienting in a way that one would prefer to do without and, in any case, in a way that one would want to resist. One might want to "understand" it, insofar as possible, but never with full empathy and always at a distance.

How Darnton himself understands the process of "getting" a joke is not altogether clear, but the tendency to ignore or play down the link among marginality, scapegoating, and victimization is manifest in chapters other than the one on the cat massacre. In the chapter on folktales, Darnton explicitly states, "It would be abusive to take this tale ["Les trois dons"] as evidence that anticlericalism functioned in France as the equivalent of anti-Semitism in Germany" (evident in "Der Jude im Dorn"). His reason is that "the comparison of folktales will not yield such specific conclusions." He nonetheless is willing to make the perhaps even more abusive assertion that such a comparison helps one "to identify the peculiar flavor of the French tales. Unlike their German counterparts, they taste of salt. They smell of the earth" (p. 52). Anticlericalism in general may not even be a significant theme in "Les trois dons," for the more pertinent fact may be that the quasi-feminine, cassock-wearing figure of the priest resembles and becomes a substitute for the hated stepmother with whom he is in any case allied. In any event, whether or not French anticlericalism may be seen as the functional equivalent of German anti-Semitism, Darnton's own argument diverts attention from the role of scapegoating and victimization in both tales (as well as from the problem of French anti-Semitism). Although one should not make too much of them (to do so would itself be dubious and reductive), varied indications of questionable reactions to the marginal appear without comment in later chapters as well. The anonymous writer who describes the social geography of Montpellier evinces his opposition to mixing social categories and insists on the need to patrol boundaries. The police inspector, whose files on the surveillance of intellectuals and other marginal types are the envy of the social historian, has an apparent ambivalence toward the irregular and elusive figures he fits into various pigeonholes. D'Alembert also strains to classify recalcitrant phenomena in establishing his variant of the tree of knowledge, and Jean Ranson—Rousseau's putatively ideal reader—spares no effort in domesticating the writer who insisted on his "otherness."

On a methodological level, an overly reductive process is operative in Darnton's own understanding of reading and symbolic meaning. One no longer seems to have the methodological scapegoating of elite intellectuals (as well as of historians who study their texts) that was at times active in Darnton's earlier work.[2] But the very conception of reading in the book involves an insistent process of domestication, leveling, and reduction of the different to the same. Darnton indeed begins with what is supposedly the most opaque aspect of a text or a phenomenon, and he recurrently insists on the radical alterity of the past. But his initial affirmation of difference is made only to be dissolved in a concordant recognition scene that familiarizes the unfamiliar. Reading, for Darnton, is a rather cozy hermeneutic process in which meaning is fully recover-

[2] On this problem, see my "Is Everyone a *Mentalité* Case? Transference and the 'Culture' Concept," in *History & Criticism* (Ithaca, N.Y., 1985).

able even when it is asserted to be polysemous or multivalent. The focus on message and "worldview" facilitates this unproblematic hermeneutics of reading; for there is little attention paid to the composition, work, and play of texts. Indeed, in the case of Rousseau, meaning is identified with the most simple construal of authorial intention, and the further identification of Ranson as Rousseau's ideal reader itself contradicts the stress on the strangeness of the past, for Darnton shares Ranson's view of how to read Rousseau even if he does not go to the Bovaryesque extreme of seeing *l'Ami* Jean-Jacques as providing a straightforward charter for life. There is an unselfconsciously hilarious moment in the chapter on Ranson that also passes unnoticed in the commentary—a moment that itself questions the idea of a full hermeneutic recovery of meaning (the passage might find its place in Flaubert's *Bouvard and Pécuchet* or in Sartre's *Nausea*).

> Ranson also accompanied the references to Rousseau with remarks on his own life. In June, 1777, when he was about to turn thirty, he wrote [to Frédéric-Samuel Ostervald, the director of the Société Typographique of Neuchâtel]: "I am sure, Monsieur, that you will be happy to hear that I am about to end my bachelorhood. I have chosen and have been accepted by a Miss Raboteau, my cousin, the sister of the young lady whom M. Rother of Nantes married last year. She is also, on her father's side, a relative of Jarnac to the same degree that I am. The happy character of this dear person combined with all considerations of propriety makes me hope in this commitment for the most [here there is a hole in the paper]. (Pp. 235-36)

The more basic point is that the very concept of symbolic meaning tends to be reified or fetishized in Darnton: it is posited as a free-floating "transcendental signified" or an autonomous reality in relation to which language or other signifying practices are mere vehicles or forms of expression. Thus reduced to an instrumental status, language poses no problem for the full recovery of meaning. In addition, the assumption of the alterity and opaqueness of the past, which is to be hermeneutically penetrated and dissipated by the recovery of meaning, is complemented by an assumption of basic agreement in the present. There is little attention devoted to the possibility of significant difference or strangeness in one's own culture, and the entire complex problem of the interaction of proximity and distance between and within past and present is reduced to a rather simple idea of difference back then, which is recuperated and familiarized in the here and now. A passage in the conclusion to *The Great Cat Massacre* is especially instructive in this respect: "Anthropologists have no common method, no all-embracing theory. If merely asked for a definition of culture, they are liable to explode in clan warfare. But despite their disagreements, they share a general orientation. In their different ways among their different tribes, they usually try to see things from the native's point of view, to understand what he means, and to seek out the social dimensions of meaning. They work from the assumption that symbols are shared, like the air we breathe or, to adopt their favorite metaphor, the language we speak" (p. 260).

One might object that the differences among anthropologists, like those among historians, are more significant and less easily resolved than this passage (or Darnton's "The Symbolic Element in History") would lead one to believe. There is a major difference, for example, between so-called material and symbolic anthropologists. Within the symbolic "tribe" itself, there are important distinctions among Geertzians, Turnerians, Lévi-Straussians, and Derridians—to name only a few prominent "clans." Furthermore, the stress on the native's point of view characterizes the "emic" variety of anthropologist, while the "etic" variety emphasizes the "scientific" need to develop a mode of conceptualization that is not the "native's" own. What is most striking about this passage, however, is the adoption of air and language as metaphors for shared symbols—a juxtaposition that attests to the derivative status of language with respect to a fetishized idea of the symbol as well as to a rather "airy" conception of language itself.

One difficulty in Darnton's precipitate turn to anthropology is the implicit assumption that emulating the procedures of the latter discipline (as Darnton via Geertz understands them) may provide a quick fix for the difficulties encountered in historiography. The result would be that the position of the historian in his or her exchange with the past need not be interrogated. This position in Darnton's own writing tends, I think, to be that of the folksy spectator—if not voyeur—of the exotic past. The recuperation of this past is abetted by a writing style that threatens to mediate between elite and popular culture through tacit reliance on a process whose history Darnton rarely sees as posing an explicit problem: commodification. Darnton is an extremely "readable" writer—in a certain sense too accommodatingly readable; for the style of writing in his works at times relies on sure-fire techniques of narration, transitional devices, and catchy phrasemaking that tend to gloss over problems and smooth over knotty points that may call for critical thought. Marx, of course, related fetishization to commodification, and his analysis of the commodity fetish suggested that meaning was stripped from the labor process as the latter became instrumentalized and reduced to an exchange value and that this meaning was then mystified, reified, and projected in a detached, "symbolic" form onto the commodity. Commodified language use extricates the "symbolic" from the work and play of language, where one has a subtle "economy" of losses and gains in "meaning," and makes it into the transcendental object seemingly conveyed in its transparent purity by an unworried, untroubled "style."

What escapes this "style"? Darnton's interpretation of Rousseau is in certain ways an epitome of the promise and the problems of his book. One of his commendable efforts is to append to each chapter a selection from the documents or texts being discussed. Ideally, this practice approximates sociocultural history to intellectual history by making sources public so that the reader is in a better position to evaluate and possibly to contest the reading of the historian. When an archive is used simply as a basis for storytelling or for hypothesis formation and analysis, it remains silent; for it is in practice inaccessible to the public, including most professional historians. Unfortunately, Darnton's selections are so short that they function largely not as critical counterparts to his essays but as extended, illustrative quotations. Even in this role, they occasionally provide enough material to raise questions about the account. In the case of Ranson as reader of Rousseau, however, one has an anticlimactic listing of the books he ordered from the Société typographique de Neuchâtel rather than a substantial selection from his letters. But of course we do have the prefaces to Rousseau's *La nouvelle Héloïse*, which are crucial to Darnton's interpretation, and I would like to say a few concluding words about his treatment of them.

For Darnton, Rousseau's problem in *La nouvelle Héloïse* was to help create, through a new kind of writing, "a new kind of reading, one that would succeed in proportion to the reader's spiritual distance from Parisian high society" (*GCM*, p. 231). This mode of reading would revive that earlier devoted to the sacred text. It would be "reading in order to absorb the unmediated Word of God. Rousseau demanded to be read as if he were a prophet of divine truth, and Ranson understood him in that way" (p. 232). But this project ran into a series of paradoxes that Rousseau had to resolve in order to get his message through to the reader. There was, for example, the paradoxical relation between authentic self-expression or communication and the role of rhetorical artifice—the aporia of reality and fiction.

> Rousseau insisted on the authenticity of the lovers' letters, but he wrote them himself, using all the devices of a rhetoric that he alone could command. He presented his text as the unmediated communication of two souls—"It is thus that the heart speaks to the heart"—yet the actual communication took place between the reader and Rousseau himself. This ambiguity threatened to undercut the new relation between writer and reader that he wanted to establish. On the one hand, it tended to falsify Rousseau's position by making him appear as a mere editor. On the other, it left the reader looking on from the sideline, virtually as a voyeur. . . .
> Many readers of *La Nouvelle Héloïse* believed and wanted to believe in the authenticity of the letters. Rousseau understood their need in advance. So he had his questioner, the sophisticated man of letters "N" in the second preface or *préface dialoguée*, return again and again to the query: "Is this correspondence real, or is it a fiction?" "N" cannot let go of it; it "torments" him, he explains. By letting him give vent to his doubts, Rousseau appeared to square with the reader and to face up to the paradox inherent in the epistolary genre. Although he could not resolve the paradox, he seemed to subsume it in an attempt to reach a higher truth. He asked the reader to suspend his disbelief and to cast aside the old way of reading in order to enter into the letters as if they really were the effusion of innocent hearts at the foot of the Alps. This kind of reading required a leap of faith—of faith in the author, who somehow must have suffered through the passions of his characters and forged them into a truth that transcends literature. (Pp. 232-33)

Darnton reads the prefaces to *La nouvelle Héloïse* as presenting paradoxes—but paradoxes that seem to be resolved through a dialectical process centered on authorial intention. The prefaces are construed as deceptive yet effective resolutions of paradox through an authorial intention that somehow conveys the text's essential meaning or message. The meaning or message is in turn communicated fully to the ideal reader who understands how to transcend the paradoxes and to grasp the author's intention. Thus the hermeneutic circle circumvents the problems posed by the epistolary genre and attains full closure as an unmediated, "heart-to-heart" relation is achieved on a higher level between the isolated writer and the equally isolated reader. One might even extend Darnton's analysis to the point of contending that the writer/reader relation is an unproblematic displacement of that between the Hidden God and the believer in certain Protestant confessions.

One may note in a prefatory way a bizarre dissonance that Darnton's interpretation of Rousseau creates in the book as a whole. The burden of the first chapter on folktales was to establish that "Frenchness exists . . . it is a distinct cultural style; and it conveys a particular view of the world . . . Frenchness makes for ironic detachment" (p. 61). The world in the "worldview" of "Frenchness" is mean and hard, and the message is simple: "The world is made of fools and knaves . . . better to be a knave than a fool." This "message" presumably became "a master theme of French culture in general, at its most sophisticated as well as its most popular level" (p. 64). Rousseau was, of course, from Geneva, but, whether it be classified as emblematic of "Frenchness" or not, his "message" appealed to French readers such as Ranson. For Rousseau the world was corrupt. But, on Darnton's interpretation, the conclusion to be drawn seems radically at odds with the putative "master theme" established by folktales. Without a trace of irony, *l'Ami* Jean-Jacques told people to suspend disbelief in illusion—indeed, to be good or else they would feel bad. One may question Darnton's reading of both folktales and Rousseau. But the "lesson" one may nonetheless draw is that anything as intricate as French culture cannot be approached in terms of stereotypes of national character or "master themes."

The missing link in Darnton's analysis of Rousseau would appear to be situated between the paradox Rousseau seems to transcend (but presumably does not) and the type of reader—presented by Darnton as ideal—who, indeed, does believe that he transcends the paradox in taking literature as an unmediated charter for life. ("Ranson did not read in order to enjoy literature but to cope with life and especially family life, exactly as Rousseau intended" [p. 241].) Are aspects of Rousseau's text elided or obliterated in the now cliché-ridden "willing suspension of disbelief" that Darnton perhaps too readily identifies as the mechanism through which Rousseau seems to transcend paradox and through which the reader, getting the message, apparently does achieve transcendence and unmediated communication with the author? Darnton has located a possible reading of Rousseau that was in fact "actualized" by certain letter-writing readers—a reading with which he agrees. He has also located a stratum or dimension of what may be called, for convenience's sake, Rousseau's text—that in which the author strives for transparency, immediate communication, and authenticity that transcends fiction toward a higher reality or truth. But the work of Jean Starobinski and Jacques Derrida, among others, has alerted contemporary readers to the manner in which Rousseau's repeated quest for transparency, authenticity, and full "presence" of self to self and of self to other is repeatedly displaced and disoriented by "obstacles," detours, doubts, and other paradoxical "remainders" that are at best only seemingly transcended—indeed, at times not transcended but, rather, insistently explored in the text.[3] This point would at least induce one not to take Ranson's reading as canonical but to test it against a critical reading of the text.

It is noteworthy that Rousseau writes two prefaces to *La nouvelle Héloïse*—a fact that alerts one to the general problem of doubling and repetition in the text. Not only are themes and textual strategies repeated from preface to preface but, in addition, the second preface has a dialogic form in which the narrative voice is doubled. The point I want to stress is not that one has a literal dialogue with two separate entities or persons involved in an exchange of views.

---

[3] See, e.g., Jean Starobinski, *Jean-Jacques Rousseau: La transparence et l'obstacle* (Paris, 1957); and Jacques Derrida, *Of Grammatology*, trans. Gayatri Chakravorty Spivak (1967; Baltimore, 1974).

In fact, the full identity of the interlocutors is impeded or even denied in that they are not given proper names but only letters as self-designations: "N" and "R." It would, moreover, be dubious simply to identify "R" as Jean-Jacques Rousseau, biographical author of the text; for the dialogic relation between "N" and "R" is an intense interaction of voices or perspectives that engage, challenge, threaten, tempt, and cajole one another. The interlocutors are hybridized or liminal beings who exist on one another's margins. Indeed, there is some "N" in "R" and some "R" in "N".

Rousseau's own complex relation to the two interlocutors is made textually explicit in the very obsessive question concerning the status of the author and the editor. Indeed, the exchanges concerning this issue might even be read as signs of the "death of the author" in the sense of a full identity or presence whose intentionality masters the work and play of the text. Darnton himself quotes a portion of an exchange relevant to the issue:

> R [Rousseau]: Does a man of integrity hide himself when he speaks to the public? Does he dare to publish something that he will not dare acknowledge? I am the editor of this book, and I will name myself in it as editor.
> N: You will name yourself in it? You?
> R: I, myself.
> N: What! You will put your name in it?
> R: Yes, Monsieur.
> N: Your real name? *Jean-Jacques Rousseau* spelled out in full?
> R: *Jean-Jacques Rousseau* spelled out in full.

Darnton stops his quotation before the next important exchange:

> N: You surely don't think—What will people say?
> R: What they please. I name myself at the head of this collection not to appropriate it but to be answerable for it. If it contains anything bad, let it be imputed to me; if good, I desire no praise. If one finds the book in itself to be bad, there is all the more reason for putting my name to it. I do not want to pass for better than I am.[4]

---

[4] Jean-Jacques Rousseau, *La nouvelle Héloïse*, in *Oeuvres complètes*, ed. Bernard Gagnebin and Marcel Raymond (Paris, 1961), 2:27 (translation is mine); all further references to this work, abbreviated *NH*, are included in the text.

Here "R" in the name of Rousseau disclaims authorship that would allow full appropriation of the text but insists on being answerable for it. But can any writer, who is always involved in tensely negotiating a way among various and often heterogeneous discursive practices, from the particular works of other writers to anonymous currents and clichés—at times to the point of being "ventriloquated" by them—ever claim more? Rousseau would simply seem to be making explicit the role of answerable "editor" that inheres in the practice of writing—a role mystified by any pretension to full authorship. (He would also proleptically cast doubt on any attempt to interpret the text as a mere expression of authorial intention—much less as prophetic utterance—with the prefaces as an unproblematic "how-to" manual for reading.) But with more insistence, passion, and energy than is common, he also inscribes the doubling and internal dialogization that takes place in a critical and self-questioning discourse. His discourse would seem to call for readers who are able to meet or at least to recognize its demands—readers who attempt to come to terms with its complexities but who do not renounce the passion in reading that, for Darnton, "we can barely imagine, that is as alien to us as the lust for plunder among the Norsemen . . . or the fear of demons among the Balinese" (*GCM*, p. 251).

The preface does not "solve" any of the problems explored in the principal text. It "repeats" them in an anticipatory way by reenacting them on another level of discourse. The author/editor relationship is itself doubled by the reality/fiction relation, which is a repeated motif of the two prefaces. In the first preface, Rousseau (who again asserts that he has named himself at the head of the collection "not to appropriate it but to be answerable for it") states: "Although I here have only the title of editor, I myself have worked at this book, and I do not hide the fact from myself. Am I the sole author [ai-je fait le tout], and is the entire correspondence a fiction? People of the world, what does it matter to you! Certainly for you it is all a fiction" (*NH*, p. 5). In this passage, Rousseau is ironic in fending off the question of whether the epistolary novel is real or fictive. For *le monde* it is fictive in the ordinary and somewhat pejorative sense of the term. That is as much as he is willing to concede in a defiant tone. Concerning the truth of the facts in the text, he later states that he has been several times in the country of the two lovers but has not heard of the various characters. Furthermore: "I must also warn the reader that the topography is grossly changed in several places; whether because of a desire to deceive the reader or because of the author's ignorance, I leave undetermined. Let everyone think as he pleases" (*NH*, p. 5). Here again Rousseau does not decide the issue of whether the text is "real" or "fictive" but ironically alerts the reader to problems in reading the text. In the second preface the theme of reality and fiction is treated in a similarly inconclusive way. At the very outset "N" asks: "Is this correspondence real or is it a fiction?" And "R" replies: "I don't see the point of the question. In order to say whether a book is good or bad, what difference does it make how it was made?" (*NH*, p. 11). Later in the dialogue, "R" even raises some extremely disconcerting questions about himself as subject: "Who can say whether I am beset with the same doubts as you are? Whether all this air of mystery is not perhaps a pretence [*une feinte*] to conceal from you my own ignorance concerning what you want to know?" (*NH*, p. 28). Without attempting to trace the further exchanges on the issue, I would simply note that the effect of the continually displaced mooting of the relation between reality and fiction is to question the pertinence to the text of this opposition. The text is neither purely "real" nor purely "fictive" in the ordinary senses of those catchall terms, just as Rousseau is neither simply the "real" author nor the "fictive" editor of the text. The text—and "Rousseau" as writer—are situated in a more problematic zone not entirely defined by clear-cut oppositions.

The shifting relations between "N" and "R" make any determination of their identities and relation to "Rousseau" problematic as well. At times they seem at odds on an issue, but they also converge or even come close to exchanging positions. The very end of the dialogue is particularly instructive in this respect:

> N: I advise you to exchange roles with me. Pretend that I urged you to publish this Collection, and that you resisted. Put the objections in your mouth, and give me the answers. This will be more modest, and will have a better effect.
>
> R: Would that be in keeping with the character for which you praised me a while ago?
>
> N: No, I tried to trap you. Leave things as they are. (*NH*, p. 30)

The seeming agreement achieved by the two interlocutors at the end of the second preface is complex. It cannot be reduced to a full closure of the hermeneutic circle. "N" appears in the role of devil's advocate to tempt "R." He almost seems to express a thought that might have occurred naturally to "R" himself. But the role reversal or substitution that "N" proposes would simply have inverted a hierarchy and recreated an invidious distinction between the interlocutors. "N" would have become a supplicant and "R" a holier-than-thou figure of humility. "R's" loss in rejecting this offer is not total: he intimates that the affirmation of the ways in which one is not praiseworthy is itself quite praiseworthy. But his refusal does reproduce differences between the interlocutors while not going to the extreme of pure opposition or invidious pretense. One may well ask whether this exchange marks the limit of communication itself.

Claude Lévi-Strauss would not be my candidate as Rousseau's "ideal" reader (if such an idealization exists), but he may well be preferable to Jean Ranson. One thing that made Rousseau so appealing for Lévi-Strauss was that, in his quest for a form of agreement respectful of noninvidious differences, *l'Ami* Jean-Jacques made room for nonhuman beings such as the cat. Whether this quest should be classified as "real" or "fictive" may itself be beside the point, although we too seem unable or unwilling to let go of the question. Indeed, the cat might even be said to have a "practical sense" to which we can respond with a glance of involuntary understanding—a glance that neither fully transcends language nor remains totally within its problematic borders. To say this is not to subscribe to the contemplative aesthetic that Lévi-Strauss at times seems to suggest. Nor is it to deny that Rousseau's writing has critical implications for social and political life. But it is to contest the thoroughly domesticated identification of those implications, via putative authorial intention, with the sentimental wedded life of a reasonably wealthy bourgeois of the time and to contest their interpretation, via a so-called ethnographic reading, in terms of an exclusionary, anthropocentric "worldview."

# 4

## The Temporality
## of Rhetoric

> But the question remains how this near obsessive concern with
> mutilation, often in the form of a loss of one of the senses, as
> blindness, deafness, or, as in the key word of the Boy of
> Winander, *muteness*, is to be understood
> —Paul de Man, "Autobiography as De-Facement"

I approach the problem of temporality in history and criticism
through a discussion of two apparently contrasting interpretations
of Romanticism: M. H. Abrams's *Natural Supernaturalism*[1] and Paul
de Man's "Rhetoric of Temporality."[2] De Man's influential essay
appeared two years before Abrams's book, but in many ways it
seems to be a condensed critical response to Abrams's magisterial
and capacious argument.[3] The two works, however, share some features. Both treat Romanticism less as a discrete period in literary
history than as a movement that, although it had deep-seated roots
in the Western tradition, initiated a modern problematic in literature and criticism. Indeed both tend, explicitly or implicitly, to
rethink the concept of temporality itself in terms of interacting

[1] 1971; New York, 1973; all references are to this edition and are included in
the text.

[2] In Charles Singleton, ed., *Interpretation: Theory and Practice* (Baltimore, 1969);
all references are to this edition and are included in the text. The essay also appears
in Paul de Man, *Blindness and Insight*, 2d rev. ed. (Minneapolis, 1983).

[3] De Man does refer several times to Abrams's "Structure and Style in the Greater
Romantic Lyric," in *From Sensibility to Romanticism: Essays Presented to F. A. Pottle*,
ed. F. W. Hillis and H. Bloom (New York, 1965).

processes of displacement and (to some limited extent) condensation. Along the way, a notion of periodicity displaces that of periodization, and uneven developments or modes of repetition with variation or change become evident in the history of literature.

But the two critics differ significantly in their understanding of displacement. Abrams sees it as a nondisruptive modulation or *sanfte Bewegung* in the interest of higher "symbolic" unity; de Man, as radical disjunction or decisive difference. Abrams, moreover, locates "true" Romanticism in the "mature" works of the writers he treats (particularly Wordsworth) and presents "modernism" (beginning with a figure such as Baudelaire) as a "negative" deviation from Romantic "positives." In contrast to Abrams, de Man locates the "authentic" voice of Romanticism in such "pre-Romantics" as Rousseau, Schlegel, and E. T. A. Hoffmann—a voice at times recaptured in late Romantics such as Baudelaire. He views later attempts at "symbolic" resolution or higher unity as falls from insight into mystified blindness. Indeed while, for Abrams, Romanticism is at least a qualified success story on an imaginative level, for de Man it is a tale of repeated defeat and aborted apocalypse. The paradoxical allegory of de Man's own reading is that the "authentic" voice of Romanticism tells of the continual frustration of romantic ideals and dreams, particularly the dream of unity with the desired other. Thus while Abrams seeks to emulate the great Romantic "positives" in his own approach to criticism, for de Man, Romanticism is ever and again a campaign waged disastrously out of season—an internally divided movement misconstrued at times by its proponents and typically by its interpreters.

Yet, in offering their seemingly antithetical appreciations, Abrams and de Man tend to act out, rather than to thematize or work theoretically through, the problem of the relation between continuity and discontinuity, sameness and difference, repetition and change (whether gentle or traumatic). With variations in "blindness" and "insight," their texts tend to transfer into their own dynamics the very problem in the movement of temporality that is their manifest object of investigation. And each in its own way relies on an overly restricted notion of the relation of a text to its pertinent contexts: Abrams, in conventional history-of-ideas fashion, reduces context to mere background for literature; de Man depends upon a displaced formalist version of the binary opposition between "internal" literary intertextuality and "external" empirical history or history of taste. Each thus relies on a prevalent preconceived solution to an intricate problem and fails to pose as an explicit theme for investigation the question of precisely how a text comes to terms with various interacting contexts. The result is a confined and at times dubious notion of historicity and an unargued and equally questionable selection and interpretation of certain contexts rather than others. The (somewhat ironic) point of my own discussion is neither to deny the differences between Abrams and de Man nor to synthesize their perspectives in a higher unity; rather it is to suggest both how they supplement one another and how they require still further supplementation in the interest of a more critically informed and sociopolitically effective inquiry into the historicity of literature, culture, and society.

Abrams's rhetoric may today seem old-fashioned, and his "high argument" has certainly become familiar. Like Northrop Frye and Frank Kermode among others, Abrams maintains that older theological and philosophical patterns of thought, especially biblical ones, were displaced in the nineteenth century. A primary modality of displacement was of course secularization. Yet the problem is obviously the nature of this displacement or transference of the old into the seemingly new. Abrams tends to take the trauma out of displacement in general and secularization in particular; his harmonizing retrospect lacks the atmosphere of crisis so evident at least as a rhetorical topos in the nineteenth century. Instead he tends to stress continuity with the past and unity in the present among those employing traditional patterns. Abrams does note in passing certain differences in the relation of the Romantics to the past. They were "this-worldly," and they put faith in a version of progress toward higher unity instead of a return to a simple, static origin (see p. 183). But his own decided inclination in interpreting Romanticism as "spilt religion" (in the ironic phrase of T. E. Hulme) is to emphasize saving unity and, by the way, to exclude or downplay irony:

> The Romantic enterprise was an attempt to sustain the inherited cultural order against what to many writers seemed the imminence of

chaos; and the resolve to give up what one was convinced one had to give up of the dogmatic understructure of Christianity, yet to save what one could save of its experiential relevance and values, may surely be viewed by the disinterested historian as a display of integrity and of courage. Certainly the greatest Romantic writers, when young and boldly exploratory, earned the right to their views by a hard struggle. (P. 68).

When younger, these writers were often seized by apocalyptic, utopian hope inspired by the French Revolution. When older, they at times became a bit disenchanted and darkly disquieting. But in their virile maturity, they presumably saw the light: the Revolution became a figure of hope betrayed, and they turned from sociopolitical radicalism to the hope for personal secular redemption through an apocalypse of the mind and imagination. Leaving the low road of politics, they took the high road of inwardness in seeking a legitimate marriage between self and nature—a symbolic unity whose desirability it is the task of the humanistic critic to recall in his own "high argument" and to defend against threats of chaos like those posed by an "adversarial" culture beginning toward the end of the nineteenth century.

For Abrams, Wordsworth is a central figure who appears, appropriately enough in the light of Abrams's thesis, at the beginning, the middle, and the end of the book. On one level, the very structure of *Natural Supernaturalism* resonates with the argument about the nature of Romanticism. Why is the Wordsworthian prospect a privileged one? For Abrams, Wordsworth is central because he is an exemplar: both a typical representative of the tendency to displace and secularize traditional patterns and one of the highest and best exponents of this "Romantic" tendency. In Wordsworth the imagination of the individual in direct communication or even communion with nature is the officiant of a legitimate marriage and the means of secular redemption. As Abrams indicates in his discussion of the importance of "inner light" theologians, it is the more Protestant strand of Christianity that is secularized here. (One might even be tempted to speak of the Protestant ethic and the spirit of Romantic poetry.) Poetry brings inner redemption for the individual alone; for the imagination unites the mind and nature in a secular sacrament that transcends or evades intermediaries (including society and politics), depending on one's point of view. Although Abrams intimates that inner redemption compensated for loss of faith in collective salvation when the French Revolution turned ugly and bloody, he insists that the "major" Romantics, including Wordsworth, defended art for the sake of life. Indeed Wordsworth was preoccupied with the common, everyday life of the ordinary person. His democratic, populist ethos itself was a sign of the times that he translated into his own specific idiom. Unlike later "modernists" as Abrams sees them, the Romantics did not espouse an elitist and deadly ideal of art for art's sake.

Yet at times Abrams notices things that may jeopardize his insistence upon inner or personal redemption and upon higher symbolic unity. He notes, for example, the sociopolitical implications of Wordsworth's transformed use of language—a point that does not entirely accord with a purely personal or inwardly imaginative (and rather unworldly) interpretation of his poetry. "In the *Essay* of 1815 [i.e., well after the French Revolution] . . . Wordsworth himself points up the fact that his particular mission as a poet has a social as well as a religio-aesthetic dimension. For if his new poetry of the common man and the commonplace is to create the taste by which it is to be enjoyed, it must utterly reform his readers' characters and sensibilities, which have been permeated with class consciousness and social prejudices" (p. 397). Yet in a contemporary context, the very unfamiliarity of Wordsworth's approach and the lack of ready-made sensibilities to which it might appeal forced the poet, in Wordsworth's words, to "reconcile himself for a season to few and scattered hearers" (quoted p. 398).

Abrams also notes impediments to the quest for higher symbolic unity on a more textual level. On the very first page of chapter I, he indicates how Wordsworth raised difficulties for his endeavor: "In spite of persistent and anguished effort, Wordsworth accomplished, in addition to *The Prelude* only Book I of Part I (*Home at Grasmere*), Part II (*The Excursion*), and none of Part III; so that, as Helen Darbishire has remarked, all we have of *The Recluse* is 'a Prelude to the main theme and an Excursion from it'" (p. 19). We tend, however, in Abrams's focus on Wordsworth's presumed intentions and ideals, to lose sight of the contextual and textual limitations on his overall project and their possible implications for interpretation. (Although he too excludes certain contextual considerations in his own way and brings into play a less harmonistic but still Protestant strand of displaced Christianity, de Man of course places certain textual limitations and considerations in the foreground of his analysis.)

The high Romantic argument that must be preserved centers around what Frank Kermode has called the apocalyptic narrative structure with its relation to speculative dialectics. Narrative provides—in a displaced way—on the level of story and events what speculative dialectics provides on the level of theory and concept. In related but nonidentical fashion (which Abrams does not see as problematic), both traditional narrative and speculative dialectics seek a redemptive, revelatory unity, totalization, or closure—a making whole again. The pattern or paradigm is one wherein a circular but progressive journey or circuitous quest seeks an end that recapitulates its beginning on a higher level of insight and development. (Hence the significance of the image of the upward spiral in Hegel and others.) In a secular sense, one quests after the redemption of meaning and a form of justification—a higher identity. In religion, an original state of innocence (Eden) gives way to a fall (original sin) that is overcome through a redemptive act (the coming of a messiah), and one is born again. In narrative, a beginning gives way to a middle whose ins and outs, ups and downs, are made sense of in a concordant ending. In speculative dialectics, identity gives way to difference that is overcome in a higher identity. Wholeness is broken through alienation and suffering that is transcended in a higher, greater wholeness. For Abrams, these patterns that displace one another in a circle of mutual confirmation may be figures of desire; but they must be maintained, and their approximation, at least in symbolic experience of the sort poetry provides, is a worthy goal.

Abrams steers steadfastly clear of what may be termed lower roads to apocalyptic unity through which religion was displaced and secularized in the course of the nineteenth century. One of the most prominent and powerful was of course nationalism, and it is one legacy of the French Revolution that has continued to affect both social life and thought. The more general point is that for Abrams, such phenomena as the French Revolution and industrialization, while periodically named and invoked, remain mere back-drops. Abrams does not investigate in any sustained fashion the question of the extent to which they were inscribed in texts in symptomatic, critical, or transformative ways. Instead the revulsion certain "Romantics" experienced in life seems to foreclose inquiry into the problem of the Revolution's textual and contextual afterlife and permutations. We get little sense of how the French Revolution, both in fact and in figure, was itself displaced as a traumatic reference point throughout the nineteenth century and even into the twentieth, particularly but not exclusively in France.

We also get little sense of the way in which commodity fetishism provided a form of symbolic unity that itself involved a certain reliance on processes of displacement and condensation; for Abrams does not address this crucial dimension of Marx's thought. In his famous analysis in section 4, chapter I of *Capital*, Marx is quite explicit in asserting that the "social hieroglyphic" represented by the fetishized commodity evokes an "analogy" with "the mist-enveloped regions of the religious world." One may further argue that the commodity fetish is constituted through a displacement of meaning from the work process in capitalism. Work is reduced to technically instrumental labor power and converted into a commodified exchange value that produces other exchange values. The meaning displaced from "living labor" is condensed in the mystified form of detached symbolic value reified in the commodity itself. Thus the commodity not only becomes a substitute for a putative lost totality or essence to be regained on a higher level in a utopian future (the apocalyptic aspect of Marx's thought, to which Abrams gives exclusive attention). It also becomes a surrogate for work that viably engages the problem of meaning. Work in the latter sense suggests a specific alternative to commodity fetishism, an alternative not reducible to the apocalyptic paradigm. Its realization requires basic institutional transformation in the economy, society, and culture. (I note in passing that the critique of commodity fetishism can apply to any form of ideological fetishization or essentialization, including that of pure art or formalism, although it is an open question whether this ideology was affirmed by late nineteenth-century figures such as Baudelaire in the unproblematic form Abrams believes it was.)

An issue more directly germane to the terms of Abrams's argument as he presents them is another low road to higher unity, that of sacrifice involving scapegoating and victimization. In sacrifice, one also begins with an innocent or purified "identity," one dismembers or immolates it (in reality or symbolically), and one returns to "identity" on a putatively higher level. Scapegoating and victimization in general involve processes of displacement and condensation: displacement of pollution or guilt from the community onto a victim and simultaneous condensation of anxiety-producing phenomena on the latter in order to expel or exorcise them. In the wake of the French Revolution, Joseph de Maistre (one of the few significant literary figures of the time not mentioned by Abrams) furnished a version of old-time religious patterns that included a providential and sacrificial interpretation of the Revolution itself—one in which scapegoating and victimization were prominent. Maistre's rendition of apocalyptic paradigms (as well as more secular permutations of them) jars rather disruptively with Abrams's construction of the high Romantic argument. Yet such a rendition cannot be simply ostracized to the exterior, or even to the margins, of the tradition Abrams treats. It is one significant variant of it. And the larger question it raises is whether sacrifice is a ritual analogue (or displacement) of traditional narrative and speculative dialectics—a question Hegel himself seems to anticipate in his reference to history as a "slaughter bench."

A further set of questions Abrams rather self-consciously does not explore, or at least severely underplays, are suggested by the multiple and even heterogeneous ways the often dominant and displaced apocalyptic patterns are also questioned, contested, ironized, satirized, carnivalized, even ragged—and other possibilities suggested. One possibility is that time itself should be seen (and narrative as well as theory articulated) in variably "repetitive" terms instead of simply having its complex displacements and condensations reduced to a "right-angled" apocalyptic model dependent upon a unitary origin, a fall, and a higher-level reunion. An attendant possibility is that difference or otherness is not invariably or uniformly negative and evil (a fall from unity). A difficulty in the apocalyptic paradigm is its fundamentalist identification of all difference or otherness with a fall, so that unity is thereby equated with the good and alterity with alienation. The very tendency to scapegoat the other through exclusion or immolation is of course facilitated by such an equation. Through scapegoating and victimization, we get the other back into the fold in one way or another.

Abrams himself is inclined to present all basic questioning of the dominant patterns as exclusively negative, as affronts to a noble dream or a high argument. And he at times gives way to at least methodological scapegoating of tendencies or figures that depart from his argument. He treats all of "modernism" rather indiscriminately as "other" and as negative:

> Salient in our own time is a kind of literary Manichaeism—secular versions of the radical *contemptus mundi* of heretical Christian dualism—whose manifestations in literature extend back through Mallarmé and other French Symbolists to Rimbaud and Baudelaire. A number of our writers and artists have turned away, in revulsion or despair, not only from the culture of Western humanism but from the biological conditions of life itself, and from the life-affirming values. They devote themselves to a new Byzantinism, which T. E. Hulme explicitly opposed to the Romantic celebration of life and admiringly defined as an art which, in its geometrized abstractness, is 'entirely independent of vital things,' expresses 'disgust with the trivial and accidental characteristics of living shapes,' and so possesses the supreme virtue of being 'anti-vital,' 'anti-humanistic,' and 'world-rejecting.' Alternatively, the new Manichaeans project a vision of the vileness, or else the blank nothingness of life, and if they celebrate Eros, it is often an Eros *à rebours*—perverse, hence sterile and life-negating. (Pp. 445-46)

Similar arguments have been addressed to recent critical tendencies, prominently including deconstruction. We need not reverse the binaries on which Abrams relies (or even deny that dubious features in an argument emerge when one becomes fixated at a phase of simple reversal of an adversary's position) in order to note that Abrams himself tenders an extremely Manichaean argument and proffers a one-dimensional critique of putatively one-dimensional tendencies. The very homogenization of a heterogeneous set of adversarial forces and critical departures from the apocalyptic paradigms itself sets the stage for a scapegoating mechanism.

Even with respect to the early nineteenth century, that is, before the eruption of the "modernist negatives," Abrams is very selective in his treatment of Romanticism, and his procedure intimates that, if "negatives" there be, they cannot be localized in the later nineteenth century. For example, Abrams excludes Byron from his study, and his reason for so doing also affects his treatment of such figures as Carlyle and Nietzsche: "Byron I omit altogether; not because I think him a lesser poet than the others but because in his greatest work he speaks with an ironic countervoice and deliberately opens a satirical perspective on the vatic stance of his Romantic contemporaries" (p. 13). Abrams actually offers an excellent reason for including Byron, insofar as even the "genuinely" highest and best should have their ironic and parodic doubles. Abrams generally excludes consideration of forces grouped by Mikhail Bakhtin under the rubric of the carnivalesque, and his resultant understanding of even figures he chooses to discuss is rather one-sided. He seems unable to entertain the possibility that irony and parody may be both critical and reinvigorating—and in ways that need not necessarily imply disrespect or failure to take seriously, and even value, their objects. (The latter depends on the object and the situation.) Abrams himself refers to Carlyle's *Sartor Resartus* in an excellent formulation that seems to make the same point I am trying to make. He sees the text as "a serious parody of the spiritual autobiography which plays with and undercuts the conventions it nonetheless accepts" (p. 130). (Abrams also notes the humor in Hegel, which is evident, for example, in his use of puns.) But Abrams's own treatment of Carlyle (or Hegel) primarily emphasizes the confirmation of the model of a spiritual quest for higher identity. We get little sense of how *Sartor Resartus* is a tremendously critical, remarkably hybridized, and outrageously funny Menippean satire—a stunning example of carnivalized literature or both high and low comedy of ideas in which the very acceptance of certain conventions is put into "deep" play. Nietzsche himself, in *Natural Supernaturalism*, is tailored into an unproblematic exponent of the dialectical quest for higher synthesis and the pattern of imaginative redemption through art. He becomes a kind of offbeat and dandified Hegelian, treated in the same terms as Marx—terms that suit entirely neither Nietzsche, Hegel, nor Marx (whatever their own differences may be).

If the carnivalesque tends to be mentioned only in passing and to be excluded from sustained investigation, Abrams treats another significant displaced tradition in modern thought in only one of its important guises. He discusses Hermeticism only to the extent to which it, via neoplatonism, conformed to and confirmed Christianity. We see well the importance of Ficino and of those whose perspective was similar to his own. We get little idea of why Hermeticism was opposed by the Catholic church, why Bruno was sent to the stake (a fact not mentioned), or why hermetic tendencies were attacked by Cartesians and often seen as irrational and suspect in later times. More heterodox forms of Hermeticism, for example, in the work of Blake or Nietzsche, go unnoticed.

Abrams, not to put too fine a point on it, is little concerned with the ambivalences, stresses, and strains in the Western tradition—by the internal contestants that can be excluded or confined to its margins and condensed into a homogeneous image of the negative adversary only at the cost of repeating, in however displaced and methodological a form, a scapegoat mechanism. Yet there is a curious if not uncanny way in which *Natural Supernaturalism* threatens to contest or even subvert itself and to indicate however unintentionally a threat to its high argument; for it enacts a kind of textual repetition compulsion. Abrams tends to repeat the apocalyptic paradigms in an almost obsessive way, in wave upon wave of plangent high seriousness, until the hallowed story he tells becomes almost hollow—eroded and made a bit tedious or even senseless. Formulated in less negative terms, the problem posed by this repetition is that of the relations between the quest for unity and the forces, both destructive and possibly enlivening, that challenge it. For the implication of my own critique of Abrams is not that unity in all its forms is mere mystification, inauthenticity, or bad faith but that a crucial problem is the actual and desirable interaction of unity (particularly normative and institutional unity) with its various contestants over time. I further note in passing that, in his later work, as Abrams reiterates the basic arguments of *Natural Supernaturalism*, his articulation of them, despite occasional shrillness, becomes more nuanced and perhaps more persuasive, in part because of his polemical encounter with deconstructive critiques. It is difficult to locate anything that even seems to be a "turn" in Abrams's development, but his later return to his earlier arguments supplements the magisterial sweep of *Natural Supernaturalism* with a pointed confrontation of some of its most forceful contestants.

Paul de Man begins his "Rhetoric of Temporality" with an indication of the temporality of rhetoric—a historical insight that might be taken farther than he intimates: "One has to return, in the history of European literature, to the moment when the rhetorical key-terms undergo significant changes and are at the center of important tensions." One such crucial change occurs in the later eighteenth century when "the word 'symbol' tends to supplant other denominations for figural language, including that of 'allegory'" (p. 173). De Man's argument is that this supplanting marks a fall from insight into blindness, both at the time and in contemporary critics such as Abrams; for the role of allegory, with its complex companion irony, remains active in certain Romantics and reemerges more forcefully in the later nineteenth century in the work of Baudelaire. Indeed de Man seems less concerned with the temporality of rhetoric than with the pseudohistoricization of synchronic or at least recurrent patterns such as the interplay of symbol and allegory themselves. But de Man establishes no simple pattern of rise and fall, progress or regress. In fact he severely criticizes a conventional understanding of history that relies on a simple concept of periodization and that seeks some teleological coding of complex processes and structures. His own procedure at times suggests a more problematic model of temporality in terms of the relative dominance or submission of recurrently displaced forces and tendencies, but the sense of displacement he insistently stresses equates it with disjunction. The question is whether his explicit statements about temporality and history do justice to his own discursive practice and whether that discursive practice in this essay still contains certain blockages (notably in the form of unquestioned binaries) that excessively restrict an understanding of literary displacements.

Adapting arguments made by Jacques Derrida—arguments Paul de Man in his later work would accommodate in his own way—one might maintain that a deconstructive strategy requires a double inscription or a dual procedure involving two interacting "phases": reversal of dominant binary oppositions that inscribe relations of discursive and sociopolitical power, and general displacement and rearticulation of relations in a manner that resists binarism (as well as its attendant scapegoating) and enacts supplementary relations of mutual marking in a transformed field. The phase of reversal is never entirely transcended because binaries tend to be reconstituted and "origins" or "centers" regenerated, but it is important not to remain fixated at the reversal phase, as to do so would bring about an inverted form of ideological fetishization or essentialization. In this sense, deconstruction (like the critique of ideology to which it cannot be reduced but which may be seen as its necessary sociopolitical supplement) does not take place once and for all; it is a recurrent activity that remains marked by its "objects," whose recuperative power it nonetheless resists.

"The Rhetoric of Temporality" was of course written before de Man attempted explicitly to reformulate his approach to criticism in terms of deconstruction. But it already puts into play certain deconstructive strategies: reversal on a thematized or theoretically explicit level and elements of general displacement in its ironic discursive practice. But in this essay there is nonetheless a tendency to remain fixated at the reversal phase, seemingly to generate a new absolute but inverted center or origin, and to allow certain "undeconstructed" binaries (notably that between the "inside" and the "outside" of literature) to remain active even on the level of discursive practice. Hence, at least with reference to this essay, it is difficult to know whether to refer to de Man's rigorous unreliability or to his unregulated equivocation.

With reference to the problem of history, de Man provides cogent and powerful arguments against dubious "traditional" conceptions of temporality, particularly the idea of time as organic continuity or genetic development. But he stops short before arriving at a rearticulation of historical understanding, at times reverting to an insistently negative or "nihilating" notion of temporality. His most decisive gesture is to reverse the binary oppositions operative in the thought of a critic such as Abrams and to oppose the disjunction and difference at work in allegory and irony to the "symbolic" nature of unity and identity. Yet he appears to be involved in the same quest as Abrams; for he ostensibly seeks the true meaning and authentic voice of Romanticism.

Of "allegorizing tendencies" in Western European literature between 1760 and 1800, de Man states: "Far from being a mannerism inherited from the exterior aspects of the baroque and the rococo, they appear at the most original and profound moments in the works, when an authentic voice becomes audible" (p. 188). The use of such terms as "authentic," "inauthentic," and "bad faith" is more than a mannerism in this essay. Insight seems in fact to be identical with authenticity, and blindness with inauthenticity and bad faith. The terms indicate how an existential rhetoric and conceptualization (particularly in its Sartrean variant) double and displace protodeconstructive strategies and motifs. De Man's own rhetoric will of course change in this respect, but the open question is the extent to which his later use of explicitly deconstructive terminology and modes of thematization mark a clear-cut disjunction, a pattern of basic continuity, or a more subtle mode of repetition/change wherein the traumatic breaks or ruptures with respect to the procedures of an essay such as "The Rhetoric of Temporality" are themselves uneven, heterogeneous, and often difficult to trace.[4] The obvious questions agitating this early seminal essay are: What is authentic insight? What is inauthentic blindness or bad faith?

---

[4] De Man's own self-commentary in the foreword to his revised, 1983 edition of *Blindness and Insight* (p. xii) is interesting in this regard: "With deliberate emphasis on rhetorical terminology, ["The Rhetoric of Temporality"] augurs what seemed to me to be a change, not only in terminology and in tone but in substance. This terminology is still uncomfortably intertwined with the thematic vocabulary of consciousness and of temporality that was current at the time, but it signals a turn that, at least for me, has proven productive. . . . When one imagines to have felt the exhilaration of renewal, one is certainly the last to know whether such a change actually took place or whether one is just restating, in a slightly different mode, earlier and unresolved obsessions." One may of course also raise the question of the extent to which de Man, in elaborating a theory of Romanticism in "The Rhetoric of Temporality," rewrites and in certain ways transforms Walter Benjamin's *Ursprung des deutschen Trauerspiels* (Berlin, 1928; rev. Frankfurt, 1963), trans. John Osborne, *The Origin of German Tragic Drama* (London, 1977). The first footnote to "The Rhetoric of Temporality" also indicates a role for Michel Foucault's conception of "epistemological breaks" as elaborated in *Les mots et les choses* (Paris, 1966), trans. *The Order of Things* (New York, 1970). De Man is, however, less concerned with "breaks" between periods than with "breaks" or radical disjunctions within periods that problematize the very conception of periodization.

How do they relate to one another and to the problem of temporality or historicity? And what is one to make of the seemingly "symbolic" relation conveyed in the equations of "insight" and "authenticity," "blindness" and "inauthenticity," as well as in other dimensions of de Man's own argument? For de Man often employs the language of the symbolic to argue for the disjunctive and allegorical.

Issues are further complicated by the manner in which traces of formalism double and displace an existential thematic. De Man often relies on a binary opposition between what is intrinsic and extrinsic to literary texts, most blatantly when he peremptorily dismisses Daniel Mornet's interest in the role of the *jardin anglais* in Rousseau's *La nouvelle Héloïse* as merely superficial history of taste and insists upon the role of literary "intertexts"—as if the significance of the latter simply excluded the pertinence of the former. Moreover, the "undeconstructed" inside/outside binary induces a tendency to conflate the distinction between fiction and nonfiction with the opposition between literature or art and the actual, factual, or sociohistorical world. For example, in discussing Baudelaire and Schlegel, de Man asserts: "Far from being a return to the world, irony, at the second power or 'irony of irony' that all true irony at once has to engender asserts and maintains its fictional character by stating the continued impossibility of reconciling the world of fiction with the actual world" (p. 200). "True" irony is here equated with de Man's own understanding of Romantic irony, especially as infinitely regressive self-reflexivity or linguistic self-referentiality and *mise en abîme*. Yet, in seemingly contradictory fashion, de Man also asserts: "Irony comes closer [than allegory] to the pattern of factual experience and recaptures some of the factitiousness of human existence as a succession of isolated moments lived by a divided self" (p. 207). In this last quotation, de Man may mean "facticity" instead of "factitiousness," but the slip (if it is a slip) in the direction of sham and artifice brings out the problematic nature of any concept of a "world of fiction" inhabited by literary texts or art works cut off from the "actual world."

This two-world theory is a limiting form of binarism (also manifest in the implicit assumption that the only alternative to reconciliation is disjunction). It reifies or ideologically essentializes what is at best a hyperbolic understanding of a "modern" dilemma—one wherein certain possibilities seem excluded from social life, only to be relegated to literature and art construed as a separate realm. Such a theory obscures both the processes by which a "separatist" (albeit for de Man internally riven and unstable) institution of literature is elaborated and the functions it serves; and it simultaneously conceals the role of "fiction" in "actual life." More generally, it provides no critical, nonreductive basis on which to raise the question of the actual and desirable interaction between literature or art and social life. Rather, it leads to an ideological conception of the status of the literary text that may (mystifyingly) see itself as the demystification of ideology—a conception that is a displaced, perhaps abortive form of transcendental metaphysics in the guise of pure figurality or fiction. The result in criticism is to generate a seemingly impenetrable barrier between texts and contexts that, insofar as they are not literary or linguistic in a formal sense, are either ignored or deemed exotopic.

On the level of fixated reversal that generates a new metaphysical center or origin, authentic insight—to the extent one can speak about it at all without immediately lapsing into "inauthenticity" (which is doubtful)—seems to be an unlivably blank apprehension of absence, pure difference, or nothingness—a look into the abyss of radical disjunction. With respect to this blinding "insight," the only language that resists "inauthenticity" or at least asserts the knowledge of "inauthenticity" (without being itself "authentic") is figuration that has an ironic awareness of its own figural or fictional status radically disjoined from phenomenal or empirical reality. This appears to be de Man's ultrasophisticated version of the imagination—the neo-Kantian *Einbildungskraft*. It becomes figurality or fictionality that has an ironic awareness of itself and its uncompromising otherness, indeed its failed transcendence, especially through endless self-referentiality with its negative thrusts and impasses. Inauthentic blindness or bad faith, by contrast, seems to be a "relapse" into modes of "symbolic" unity between language and world, including both putative "marriages" between the mind and nature and realistic representation. This relapse itself presumably engenders a false apprehension of (synchronic) figuration—the (blind) play of tropes—that is identified with (literary) history. The "fall" would thus be a fall not from but into unity. And (pseudo)history would be misconstrued figuration. Authentic temporality, by contrast, would itself seem to be the marking and remarking of pure absence, difference, or disjunction. As a result, history would be the history of error or erring, and an impossible "authentic" historicity would seem to engender nothing except the evacuation of signification in a compulsive reiteration of aporias having "no exit".

> The dialectical relationship between subject and object is no longer the central statement of romantic thought, but this dialectic is now located entirely in the temporal relationships that exist within a system of allegorical signs. It becomes a conflict between a conception of the self seen in its authentically temporal predicament and a defensive strategy that tries to hide from this negative self-knowledge. On the level of language the asserted superiority of the symbol over allegory, so frequent during the nineteenth century, is one of the forms taken by this tenacious self-mystification. (P. 191)

> Irony divides the flow of temporal experience into a past that is pure mystification and a future that remains harassed forever by a relapse within the inauthentic. It can know this inauthenticity but can never overcome it. It can only restate and repeat it on an increasingly conscious level, but it remains endlessly caught in the impossibility of making this knowledge applicable to the empirical world. It dissolves in the narrowing spiral of a linguistic sign that becomes more and more remote from its meaning, and it can find no escape from this spiral. The temporal void that it reveals is the same void we encountered when we found allegory always implying an unreachable anteriority. Allegory and irony are thus linked in their common discovery of a truly temporal predicament. (P. 203)

Earlier in the text, de Man is explicating Baudelaire, but his questionable exegesis seems clearly to merge his own voice with that of his putative object of analysis. The new center is approximated to violence and incipient madness—violence and incipient madness not only as recurrent and variable possibilities (threats and temptations) but as "inherent" and "necessary" components of the seemingly "authentic" human condition. That is, violence and madness are essentialized and foundational features of a fixated synchronicity that itself seems coeval if not identical with the "truly temporal predicament": "Irony is unrelieved *vertige*, dizziness to the point of madness. Sanity can exist only because we are willing to function within the conventions of duplicity and dissimulation, just as social language dissimulates the inherent violence of the actual relationships between human beings. Once this mask is shown to be a mask, the authentic being underneath appears necessarily as on the verge of madness" (p. 198).

Indeed, fixated synchronicity seems tantamount to acting out a repetition compulsion and, as seemingly authentic temporality, it is recurrently contrasted with the mystified phantasm of symbolic unity and totalization. De Man's thought often seems suspended between impossible totalization and a repetition compulsion—a repetition compulsion whose preferred embodiment is a mechanistic play of tropes. One need not agree with M. H. Abrams yet have a critical response to this entire problematic. The obvious question is whether something is repressed or disavowed in the opposition between totality and the repetition compulsion—what Freud referred to as "working through" and Marx as critique. De Man's "protodeconstructive" essay marked by existential and formalist motifs also has its parallels in certain seemingly "post-deconstructive" endeavors. Certain critics, alienated by explicit forms of deconstructive criticism, may well try to amalgamate particular (unnamed) deconstructive features with earlier existential and formalist proclivities. In numerous and overdetermined ways, therefore, "The Rhetoric of Temporality" is far from dead as a factor in contemporary criticism. For many, it may implicitly or explicitly seem a very live option.

I now turn to three important sections of "The Rhetoric of Temporality": its discussions of Rousseau, Wordsworth, and Baudelaire. This sequence of figures may in certain respects reflect de Man's understanding of Romanticism in the late eighteenth and in the nineteenth centuries. After the publication of "The Rhetoric of Temporality," Rousseau became a major reference point for de Man, a fact that gives his treatment of Rousseau a special significance. De Man argues that, given its role in the critical literature, "there is certainly no better reference to be found than *La nouvelle Héloïse* for putting to the test the nearly unanimous conviction that the origins of romanticism coincide with the beginnings of a predominantly symbolical diction" (p. 184). De Man does find such diction in the Meillerie episode in the fourth part of the novel. But he notes that the Meillerie landscape as a wilderness is, in the terms of the novel, emblematic of error. By contrast, the garden functions as "the landscape representative of the 'beautiful soul'" (p. 185). And the garden is treated allegorically not only in its function as an emblem of virtue within the novel but in its literary intertextuality as well:

> From the beginning we are told that the natural aspect of the site is in fact the result of extreme artifice, that in this bower of bliss, contrary to the tradition of the *topos*, we are entirely in the realm of art and not that of nature. "Il est vrai," Rousseau has Julie say, "que la nature a tout fait [dans ce jardin] mais sous ma direction, et il n'y a rien là que je n'aie ordonné." The statement should at least alert us to the literary sources of the passage which Mornet, preoccupied as he was with the outward history of taste, was led to neglect. (P. 186)

Before turning to these literary sources, one may note two features of this passage. First, Rousseau relies on an explicit oxymoron in having Julie say that nature did everything in the garden but under her direction. He thereby marks a disjunction in a nonexclusionary way that seems to intimate the complex role of both nature and human direction or artifice. Affected perhaps by the *vertige de l'hyperbole* that de Man, following Baudelaire, tells us is characteristic of irony, de Man provides an explicit gloss that reductively converts the oxymoron into an either/or choice by maintaining that "the natural aspect of the site is in fact the result of extreme artifice" and that "we are entirely in the realm of art and not that of nature"—hardly what the passage says. Furthermore, his reliance on the opposition between internal literary relations and "the outward history of taste" again implies an either/or decision. What is quite explicit in the exclusion of the seemingly outward in this passage is typical of de Man's treatment of contexts in general. He will refer only to "intraliterary" or "intertextual" relations (in the ordinary sense), and he will not even mention the contexts Abrams at least employs as background. In this limited sense, his reading is formalistic, and he does not attempt to rethink the entire relation between texts and contexts in a manner that would be neither formalistic nor contextually reductionistic and that might therefore question the binary opposition between inner literary history and the "outward history of taste." Indeed de Man here sounds very much like Northrop Frye, and his procedure indicates how even allegory in his sense remains symbolic, that is, separated or cut off ("castrated" in the Freudian sense) from larger, problematic modes of interaction and confined within an internally riven yet specifically literary realm or world.

To make these observations is in no sense to exclude the pertinence of the literary aspects of intertextuality that de Man brilliantly locates, but it is to question the explicit framework within which he sets them and certain of the conclusions he draws from his analysis. Indeed the combination of literary sources he offers for the garden passage does come as quite a shock, as does the nature of his formulations in articulating their relations to *La nouvelle Héloïse*. The two sources are Defoe's *Robinson Crusoe* and Guillaume de Lorris's *Roman de la rose*. We are told "there is hardly a detail of Rousseau's description that does not find its counterpart in the medieval text" (p. 186). Indeed so commanding is the role of this "source" that "Rousseau does not even pretend to be observing. The language is purely figural, not based on perception" (p. 187). Here, as frequently in the essay, the cogent point that language or any system of signs cannot be reduced to perception is converted into a binary opposition between language and perception (or empirical reality in general), thereby generating a "realm" of language as pure figurality or fictionality.

There is, however, a difference between *La nouvelle Héloïse* and the *Roman de la rose*, and it indicates the role of *Robinson Crusoe* as a second source for the novel. In contrast to the erotic aspects of the *Roman de la rose*, "in *La nouvelle Héloïse* the emphasis on an ethic of renunciation conveys a moral climate that differs entirely from the moralizing sections of the medieval romance" (p. 187). Thus the detailed "counterparts" accompany "a moral climate that differs entirely" as one moves from text to text. The rhetoric is one of "all or nothing," encouraging a starkly paradoxical tendency to qualify an absolute assertion made in the diction of the symbolic (i.e., with reference to counterparts or correspondences) with an equally absolute assertion made in the diction of allegorical-ironic disjunction. The possibility that a certain religious heritage or bundle of tendencies within Christianity may be "displaced" in de Man's own rhetoric is suggested by what he responds to in Rousseau's own response to Defoe. This "displacement" would provide a context of sorts for de Man's reliance on a problematic focused on the "temptation" to "fall" into symbolic unity or meaning—a temptation that must be resisted or even renounced even at the cost of inevitably "relapsing" into an inauthentic mode. Indeed the relatively undisplaced reliance on religious or theological terminology in certain passages of "The Rhetoric of Temporality" is striking. For example:

> The temptation at once arises for the ironic subject to construe its function as one of assistance to the original self and to act as if it existed for the sake of this world-bound person. This results in an immediate degradation to an intersubjective level, away from the *"comique absolu"* into what Baudelaire calls *"comique significatif,"* into a betrayal of the ironic mode. Instead, the ironic subject at once has to ironize its own predicament and observe in turn, with the detachment and disinterestedness that Baudelaire demands of this kind of spectator, the temptation to which it is about to succumb. It does so precisely by avoiding the return to the world. . . , by reasserting the purely fictional nature of its own universe and by carefully maintaining the radical difference that separates fiction from the world of empirical reality. (P. 199)

In contrast to de Man's later "technical" language, this allegory of ironic transcendence and worldly temptation gives a vivid sense of how we still may be fighting, in displaced and more or less symbolic ways, the wars of religion. We also get a feeling for the manner in which a critic like Abrams may appear excessively compromising or "Erasmian" when viewed from a more "rigorous" if not intransigent point of view.

To return to de Man's treatment of Rousseau (have we ever left it?), note that de Man insists that recent interpretations "have reversed the trend to see in Defoe one of the inventors of a modern 'realistic' idiom and have rediscovered the importance of the puritanical religious element to which Rousseau responded" (p. 187).

Indeed "the same stress on hardship, toil, and virtue is present in Julie's garden, relating the scene closely to the Protestant allegorical tradition of which the English version, culminating in Bunyan, reached Rousseau through a variety of sources, including Defoe. The stylistic likeness of the sources supersedes all further differences between them" (p. 188). De Man does not of course present Rousseau simply as a secularized puritan, and we cannot see de Man simply as a secularized sectarian Protestant or Jansenist despite the seemingly obvious relations between "Augustinian" tendencies in Christianity and de Man's ascetic "rigor," stark sense of paradox, ironic (yet somehow Bunyonesque) allegory of temptation and renunciation, and iconoclastic notion of the disjunctive relation between sign and meaning. The tendency to assert the priority of allegory in the diction of symbol ("the stylistic likeness of the sources that supersedes all further differences between them") becomes, however, paradoxically pronounced in de Man's ironically "self-deconstructive" conclusion that *La nouvelle Héloïse* achieves ("symbolic") resolution through renunciation as well as closure through the choice of allegory:

> This conflict [between the erotic and the puritanical] is ultimately resolved in the triumph of a controlled and lucid renunciation of the values associated with the cult of the moment, and this renunciation establishes the priority of an allegorical over a symbolic diction. The novel could not exist without the simultaneous presence of both metaphysical modes, nor could it reach its conclusion without the implied choice in favor of allegory over symbol. (P. 188)

Yet, to paraphrase Derrida, does it not appear that we are here in a region—let us call it provisionally a region of historicity—in which the category of choice seems particularly superficial?

De Man notes a variety of differences between allegory and irony themselves, notably in the extended, diachronic, narrativized, or displaced temporal structure of the former and the pointed, synchronic, aphoristic, condensed temporality of the latter. Yet he also insists:

> The knowledge derived from both modes is essentially the same;
> Hölderlin's or Wordsworth's [allegorical] wisdom could be stated

*111*

ironically, and the rapidity of Schlegel or Baudelaire could be preserved in terms of general wisdom. Both modes are fully
de-mystified when they remain within the realm of their respec-
tive languages but are totally vulnerable to renewed blindness as
soon as they leave it for the empirical world. Both are determined
by an authentic experience of temporality which, seen from the
point of view of the self engaged in the world, is a negative one.
The dialectical play between the two modes, as well as their common interplay with mystified forms of language (such as symbolic
or mimetic representation), which it is not in their power to eradi-
cate, make up what is called literary history. (P. 207)

Nonetheless, the very interaction between "symbolic" unity and
"allegorical-ironic" disjunction is played out in the discussion of
allegory and irony itself, and the way it unfolds induces one to question the clear-cut delimitation of realms of language as well as the
identification of symbol as the sign of mystifying inauthenticity,
disjunction as the sign of insightful authenticity.

De Man concludes his essay with a discussion of Baudelaire's
*De l'essence du rire* as a starting point for reflection about irony,
an exegesis of one of Wordsworth's Lucy Gray poems as a dem-
onstration of the role of allegory, and a brief comment about
Stendhal's *La chartreuse de Parme* as the seeming exception to the
rule of aphoristic brevity of irony and narrativized "duration" of
allegory, in that the novel is a self-conscious, extended ironic
narrative. Yet, what seems to be the exception is not only relevant to the rule but may *be* the rule itself, insofar as irony and
allegory, as well as symbol and disjunction, interact in specific
texts or uses of language. This point is itself intimated in de
Man's ironic choice of an eight-line poem as the exemplar of
allegory and of a fairly substantial essay to motivate the discussion of irony. So, too, is the role of a more complex mode of
temporality that cannot be decisively reduced to the binary opposition between the synchronic and the diachronic or its multiple
analogues—a mode of temporality involving complex relations
between repetition and change over time. De Man seems close
to this notion of repetitive temporality both in his discussion of
allegory ("the meaning constituted by the allegorical sign can
then consist only in the *repetition* in the Kierkegaardian sense of

a previous sign with which it can never coincide, since it is of the essence of this previous sign to be pure anteriority," p. 190) and in his discussion of irony ("irony is not temporary—*vorläufig*—but repetitive, the recurrence of a self-escalating act of consciousness," p. 202). But his formulations remain indentured to tendencies such as binarism that I have already touched upon, and he does not explicitly bring them to bear on the interplay of symbol, allegory, and irony in texts. Indeed his passing reference to literary history as constituted by the "dialectical play" of allegory and irony as well as "their common interplay with mystified forms of language (such as symbolic or mimetic representation)," while richly suggestive, remains abstract, mechanical, and tendentious. (To generalize rashly, one might say that in his later work de Man would often see this interplay in terms of his particular variant of deconstruction wherein elements such as allegory and symbol or metonymy and metaphor mutually undercut one another in aporetic fashion, and the literary or rhetorically self-referential, while somehow specific, threatens to become invasive.) More important, he does not here (and I think he never more than very allusively manages to) relate the notion of repetitive temporality as displacement that involves more or less disjunctive or traumatic change to the attempt to rearticulate the manner in which texts inscribe various contexts within a larger network or "general text." This effort, while not free of its own mystifying temptations (particularly when it takes itself as foundational), may nonetheless intimate a notion of historicity that offers some perspective on the interaction of texts with both "literary" and other contexts of writing, reception, and critical reading—including contexts in the so-called empirical world of "engaged" activity.

De Man turns to the poet who served as the exemplar of the symbolic in Abrams in order to approach the question of whether there can be what Baudelaire terms *la poésie pure* in the form of pure allegory that is truly metaironic in that it has "transcended irony without falling into the myth of an organic totality or bypassing the temporality of all language" (p. 204). He quotes this Lucy Gray poem of Wordsworth:

*113*

A slumber did my spirit seal;
I had no human fears:
She seemed a thing that could not feel
The touch of earthly years.

No motion has she now, no force;
She neither hears nor sees;
Rolled round in earth's diurnal course,
With rocks, and stones, and trees.

De Man asserts that "the text is clearly not ironic, either in its tonality or in its meaning" (p. 205). His genial interpretation presents it as narrating a movement from blindness or mystification belonging to the past in the first stanza to insight or demystification situated in the "now" of the poem in the second stanza. The event that separates the two states is the radical discontinuity of a death that remains impersonal: its moment of occurrence—an "actual now"—is hidden in the blank space separating the two stanzas. The poem thus narrates a series of now-points: the first, past and mystified; the second, actual and deadly; the third, an "eternal" or "ideal 'now,' the duration of an acquired wisdom" engendered by the language of the poem but "not possible within the actual temporality of experience." Moreover, de Man claims that "the fundamental structure of allegory reappears here in the tendency of the language toward narrative, the spreading out along the axis of an imaginary time in order to give duration to what is, in fact, simultaneous within the subject" (p. 206).

In a manner reminiscent of Heidegger in "The Origin of the Work of Art," de Man notes an "ambiguity" in lines 3 and 4 concentrated in the word "thing." Within the mystified world of the past, the word "thing" might have been used "innocently" or perhaps even in a "playfully amorous way." But the innocuous statement becomes literally true in the retrospective of the eternal "now" of the second part, for "she now has become a *thing* in the full sense of the word, not unlike Baudelaire's falling man who became a thing in the grip of gravity." Indeed "the light-hearted compliment has turned into a grim awareness of the de-mystifying power of death, which makes all the past appear as a flight into the inauthenticity of a forgetting" (p. 205). When read "within the perspective of the entire poem," lines 3 and 4 are ironic, "though they are not ironic in themselves or within the context of the first stanza" (pp. 205-6). Irony here thus seems to depend entirely on a sequential temporal structure that is nonetheless positioned as an illusory effect of language.

De Man's reading, particularly within the context of his essay, is extremely plausible and even compelling. I would, however, like to suggest the possibility of an alternative reading that brings out how a repetitive temporality is enacted in the poem and how a less contained interaction of irony and allegory may be active in it. First, an ironic or parodic reading of the entire poem is always possible, indeed perhaps impishly prompted by the ostensible role of sustained high seriousness in it. The reading may be effected simply by the recitation of the poem in a singsong intonation its versification almost seems to invite. (A similar ironic or parodic reaction may also be stimulated by certain phrases in de Man's exegesis that border—intentionally or not—on purplish pop existentialism, for example, "an eternal insight into the rocky barrenness of the human predicament prevails" [p. 206]). Moreover, de Man's hypothesis concerning the role of a sweet young thing in the first stanza is of course fanciful. One might argue that the ambiguity of lines 3 and 4 is much more extensive and that death is already marking life in the first stanza, where these lines could be read quite literally to mean that "she" seemed insensitive to aging as it did its inevitable work. The blank space would thus not simply separate the two stanzas in a before-and-after sequence; it would itself be at work in both of them as well—repeated with a significant, indeed a traumatic, variation. Moreover, rather than being simply a sequence of now-points, the stanzas could be seen as related by the chiasmus of an ironic reversal that would crisscross and contest the allegory. The chiasmus would apply most clearly to the interaction of life and death; for if death already marks life in the first stanza, there is a hint of life emerging from death in the second. The last line is especially significant in this respect. Rocks and stones seem redundant as mineral forms of antilife, but with trees one returns—however faintly and with a "shock of mild surprise" —to life and the promise of renewal. Thus the poem as a whole could be read as bearing witness in a muted, memorialized, and relatively decontextualized manner to a repetitive rhythm of life and death—a fully ambivalent temporality—that in other contexts might be institutionalized in a social institution, like carnival, with a clear bearing on the actual temporality of experience. This reading would also be more in keeping with a Freudian interpretation of the nature of *Nachträglichkeit* or deferred action, toward which de Man himself seems at times to gesture in his exegesis.

De Man introduces his extensive discussion of Baudelaire's *De l'essence du rire* with a point that is in one sense well taken and in another specious. He tries to justify or motivate the difference in his treatment of allegory and of irony by arguing that a "historical de-mystification" was necessary in the case of allegory because its "mystification is a fact of history and must therefore be dealt with in a historical manner before actual theorization can start." By contrast,

> in the case of irony one has to start from the structure of the trope itself, taking one's cue from texts that are de-mystified and, to a large extent, themselves ironical. For that matter, the target of their irony is very often the claim to speak about human matters as if they were facts of history. It is a historical fact that irony becomes increasingly conscious of itself in the course of demonstrating the impossibility of our being historical. In speaking of irony we are dealing not with the history of an error but with a problem that exists within the self. (P. 194)

The later de Man would no doubt substitute "language" for "the self." But even with this substitution, his argument would remain problematic. In one sense, he might be read to mean that the very structure of historicity is in some pertinent sense ironic and thus it makes no sense to try to write a standard history of irony that would, for example, seek some oriented development or delimit well-defined periods in the unfolding of irony. But this reading implies that it is impossible not to be historical or engaged by the problem of irony. On another reading, however, de Man himself relies on the standard and dubious binary opposition between history and structure. He seems to occlude the possibility of significant variations in the recurrent role of irony over time—variations whose different figurations and possibilities could be traced and perhaps have implications for social life. This occlusion affects his own discourse and his interpretation of Baudelaire's essay; for de Man himself seems symptomatically to underwrite certain "modern" tendencies by extracting irony from its possible implication in a larger network of carnivalesque forces and construing it in rather narrow, intellectualistic terms. It seems able to evoke a rictus but never a belly laugh. This approach may itself be a hyberbolic and potentially unsettling testimony to modern problems, particularly insofar as de Man stresses the connections among irony, seemingly openended freedom, and lucid madness. But it provides little critical perspective on these problems and no indication of their possible transformation, and I mean transformation not in terms of the actualization of an impossible symbolic totality or the definitive transcendence of radically disorienting threats and temptations but transformation into a significantly different network of relations, including the relation between work and carnivalesque play.

De Man begins his analysis of *De l'essence du rire* by noting the role of the fall in Baudelaire, specifically the simple but pointed spectacle of a man falling in the street. He quotes Baudelaire as writing: "Ce n'est point l'homme qui tombe qui rit de sa propre chute, à moins qu'il ne soit un philosophe, un homme qui ait acquis, par habitude, la force de se dédoubler rapidement et d'assister comme spectateur désintéressé aux phénomènes de son *moi*" (it is not the man who falls who laughs at his own fall, unless he is a philosopher, a man who has acquired by habit the power to double himself rapidly and to witness as a disinterested spectator phenomena involving his own ego). De Man observes that "the accent falls on the notion of *dédoublement* as the characteristic that sets apart a reflective activity, such as that of the philosopher, from the activity of the ordinary self caught in everyday concerns." He goes on to remark further that it is in seeming side remarks like this one that Baudelaire introduces "the notion of self-duplication or self-multiplication" that "emerges at the end of the essay as the key concept of the article, the concept for the sake of which the essay has in fact been written" (p. 194).

De Man is of course to the point in bringing out the importance of the phenomenon of *dédoublement* in Baudelaire's understanding of irony, although one might contend that this phenomenon attests

117

not to the role of disjunction alone but to the intricate and shifting interplay of disjunction and conjunction in language and the self. Two features of de Man's introductory comments are puzzling, however. In presenting *dédoublement* as the "key concept" of the article, he offers a teleological interpretation, which is precisely what irony was said to jeopardize. Moreover, he fails to note that when the concept reemerges at the end of Baudelaire's article, it is with a significant variation: it is linked not to the philosopher but to the artist and to artistic phenomena. All artistic phenomena are said to "denote in the human being the existence of a permanent duality, the power to be at the same time oneself and another." And "the artist is not an artist unless he is a double being and is unaware of no phenomenon in his double nature." This displacement or doubling is significant; for it intimates that the artist may be seen as a displacement of the philosopher (a theme de Man would himself take up in his later work). In addition, the philosopher, while a "rare" case in life, is not entirely separated from "ordinary reality." He is in fact typified as someone who reacts in a certain self-critical way to one of the most ordinary events in life: falling in the street. Nor, as we shall see, is Baudelaire's idea of art for art's sake totally removed from the world.

A second point is that de Man mentions only in passing a second sense of falling that indicates how it is itself doubled in structure—the religious sense. This slight is difficult to see as unintentional since the religious fall is crucial to Baudelaire's entire argument. Laughter for him is postlapsarian, and the satanic mark of the fall touches all laughter in one way or another. Yet falling, while retaining its religious aura, is shifted in the direction of a repetitive process rather than inserted into an apocalyptic paradigm.

It is, moreover, the height of irony that a reader of de Man's essay would never realize that Baudelaire's *De l'essence du rire* is not about irony. In fact the word is never mentioned. This is not to say that the problem of irony is not pertinent to its argument. It may in its silence say more about irony than many full-length treatises devoted to the elusive topic. But it is noteworthy that Baudelaire discusses caricature, the grotesque, the comic, and laughter—that is to say, a larger "family" or congeries of forces to which irony in some sense belongs. It is de Man who isolates irony without giving the reader an idea of the problematic nature of his analysis or the larger context in which problems are treated in Baudelaire.

Here it is interesting to notice the way Baudelaire presents his argument—his own mise-en-scène, so to speak. He begins by stating that he does not want to write a treatise on caricature but to share with the reader certain reflections that have become a sort of obsession with him. He wants to "relieve" himself (*me soulager*) and give himself a better digestion (*en rendre ainsi la digestion plus facile*). He then employs figures of eating and defecation in describing a psychological or even psychopathological state. A symptom is to be treated through writing that is itself figured in manifestly carnivalesque terms. Baudelaire soon makes a further connection between the carnivalesque and the hermetic as he evokes, in terms reminiscent of his procedure in *Les fleurs du mal*, an alchemical extraction of beauty from ugliness and evil, a spectacle that excites "an immortal and incorrigible hilarity" in man. He adds, "Here is therefore the true subject of the article." It is significant that at least in a brief and allusive way, Baudelaire situates his article with respect to two important "underground" traditions in the modern period—the carnivalesque and the hermetic—and he links the two through hilarity. He thus indicates some awareness of the problem of the displaced recurrence of what has been repressed or suppressed in history. At the very outset, the repressed reappears in more or less distorted or masked form both in the psychopathological symptom and in the work of art, and the reappearance poses the problem of the relation of psychopathology and art to one another and to larger historical and sociopolitical processes. Here we can see how a certain set of problems is inscribed in this text not simply symptomatically but also in a manner that has important critical and possibly even transformative possibilities. We shall note other ways in which this is the case.

De Man devotes much attention to the contrast between the ordinary, social, or "significative" comic and the absolute comic. He identifies the latter with irony although Baudelaire correlates it with the grotesque. And he treats the two largely as a pure binary opposition, with E. T. A. Hoffmann serving as the exemplar of the absolute comic: "Baudelaire insists that irony, as '*comique absolu*', is an infinitely higher form of comedy than is the intersubjective kind he finds so frequently among the French; hence his preference for Italian *commedia dell'arte*, English pantomimes, or the tales of E. T. H. [sic] Hoffmann" (p. 195).[5] Moreover, Baudelaire "rightly considers" Hoffmann "to be an instance of absolute irony" (pp. 198-99). De Man also sees Baudelaire, particularly in his understanding of Hoffmann, as converging with Friedrich Schlegel in an apprehension of irony as *"folie lucide,"* "unrelieved *vertige,* dizziness to the point of madness" (p. 198). In discussing Hoffmann's *Princess Brambilla,* he notes that the drawings of Jacques Callot, which the text itself ends by identifying as the "source" of the story, themselves "represent figures from the *commedia dell'arte* floating against a background that is precisely *not* the world, adrift in an empty sky" (p. 200).[6]

Baudelaire's argument concerning the comic has, however, a ternary, not a binary, structure; and his reading of its terms, as well as of the role of E. T. A. Hoffmann as an exemplary figure, is quite different from, not to say contrary to, de Man's. The three forms Baudelaire refers to are the definitive absolute, the absolute comic, and the significative comic. The definitive absolute—the highest mode—is not discussed by de Man. It transcends laughter and constitutes an impossible ideal or limit. "From the point of view of the definitive absolute, there is nothing but joy."[7] Joy, moreover, is earlier discussed in the text in clearly symbolic terms: "Joy is *one.* Laughter is the expression of a double or contradictory sentiment; and it is for that reason that is it convulsive" (p.374). The definitive absolute and joy are discussed in terms that relate them to other figures or issues in the text: the contemplative sage who laughs only when trembling and whose wisdom approaches a higher innocence; the incarnate Word, Christ, who never laughed; and *la poésie*

[5] It is strange that de Man, in the original edition of his essay, refers repeatedly to E. T. H. Hoffmann. This mistake is particularly bizarre in that someone of de Man's erudition must have known that Hoffmann chose the name Amadeus to mark his respect and love for Mozart.

[6] Actually these caricatures are Hoffmann's revisions of Callot's drawings. The latter do have realistic street scenes as settings. In Hoffmann, the stock figures are set on an abstracted piece of cloudlike turf.

[7] *De l'essence du rire,* in Baudelaire, *Oeuvres complètes* (Paris: Editions du Seuil, 1968), p. 375. All references are to this edition and are included in the text; translations are mine.

*pure*, which is in Baudelaire approximated to the symbolic (and not to the allegoric as in de Man). In "pure poetry, limpid and profound like nature, laughter would be lacking as in the soul of the sage" (p. 373). But all of these "corresponding" limiting cases are inaccessible for fallen man. The absolute comic itself "can be absolute only relative to a fallen humanity" (p. 375). It is nonetheless closer to unity than is the significative or social comic: "The element [of the significative comic) is visibly double: art and the moral idea; but the absolute comic, approximating nature much more, presents a unified species (*une espèce* une) and wants to be apprehended by an intuition" (p. 375). The absolute comic is less reflective than the significative, and it erupts suddenly rather than after the fact; in this, as in other ways, it is closer to the unconscious. "One of the very particular signs of the absolute comic is to be unawares of itself" (p. 378).

It is significant that in Baudelaire the absolute comic is not "infinitely higher" than the significative or social comic. It is certainly seen as superior, but the relation between the two is not a pure binary. There is even a curious sense in which it may be lower; for it seems to posit a superiority of man over the rest of nature (in contrast to the significative comic, which rests upon an invidious distinction between man and man). Yet its seeming superiority, which like that of the significative is a derivative of the fall, may be mistaken. In any case, the absolute and significative comic are explicitly treated by Baudelaire in the "impure" terms of supplementary differences and similarities, and they can be active in the same texts, notably those of E. T. A. Hoffmann.

> The [significative] comic is, from the artistic point of view, an imitation; the grotesque, a creation. The [significative] comic is an imitation mixed with a certain creative faculty, that is to say, an artistic ideality. Human pride, which always gets the upper hand, also becomes the natural cause of laughter in the case of the grotesque, which is a creation mixed with a certain imitative degree of elements preexisting in nature. I mean that in the latter case laughter is the expression of an idea of superiority not of man over man but of man over nature. One must not find this idea too subtle; that would not be a sufficient reason to reject it. It is a question of finding another plausible explanation. If this one seems farfetched and a little diffi-

*121*

cult to accept, it is because laughter caused by the grotesque has something more profound, axiomatic, and primitive that is very much closer to innocent life and absolute joy than is the laughter caused by the comedy of manners. There is between these two laughters, abstraction made of the question of utility, the same difference as between the engaged [*intéressée*] literary school and the school of art for art's sake (*l'art pour l'art*). Thus the grotesque dominates the comic with a proportional elevation. (P. 375)

Thus the explanation of the absolute comic or the grotesque through a superiority over nature is doubtful because the grotesque harbors elements that bring humans closer to other animals. De Man seems to touch on this point and even to provide the better explanation evoked by Baudelaire when he states, "In a false feeling of pride the self has substituted, in its relationship to nature, an intersubjective feeling (of superiority) for the knowledge of difference" (p. 196). What would resist the fall and its effects would then be difference that would not entail invidiousness between humans and other animals. (Recall Baudelaire's observation in *Mon coeur mis à nu* that true civilization is to be found in the diminution of the traces of original sin.) But this difference without invidiousness is not for Baudelaire a pure disjunction. Nor is the distinction between the absolute and the significative comic.

The latter point becomes evident when Baudelaire tells why Hoffmann is exemplary for him; for Hoffmann is not the exponent of the pure absolute comic but a hybridized type in whose texts the two forms of the comic interact.

[Hoffmann] unites to the significative mockery of France the mad, sparking, and light gaiety of the countries of the sun at the same time as the profound Germanic comic. . . . What quite particularly distinguishes Hoffmann is his involuntary—and sometimes very voluntary—mixture (*mélange*) of a certain dose of the significative comic with the most absolute comic. His supernatural and most fugitive comic conceptions, which often resemble visions of drunkenness, have a very visible moral sense: one might believe one is dealing with a physiologist or a very profound alienist (*médecin des fous*) who amused himself by clothing this profound science in poetic forms, like a learned man who would speak in allegories and parables. (P. 377)

Here is a linkage of allegory, the absolute comic, and the significative comic which has moral and social effects. Baudelaire also makes a point of noting the setting of Hoffmann's *Princess Brambilla*: "The joyous, noisy and frightful Italy abounds in the innocent comic. It is in Italy, in the heart of southern carnival, in the midst of the turbulent Corso, that Theodore Hoffmann discerningly placed his eccentric drama, *The Princess Brambilla*" (p. 376). One might suggest that, to the extent that the figures in the text, like Callot's "carnivalesque figures" (p. 375), float against a background that is precisely not the world, it is insofar as the text is both symptom and critique of the fate of the carnivalesque once it is separated from a more or less viable interaction with social institutions.

I conclude by stressing that Baudelaire sees the absolute and the significative or social comic as displaying the same difference as the school of art for art's sake and that of "interested" (or socially committed) writers. The terms of the argument indicate that the former is a higher type, but the difference or disjunction between the two is not pure or total. In Baudelaire's terms, it is all a matter of dosage or hybridization. More precisely, the "doubleness" of the human being is related to an undecidable status between two infinites, and laughter itself is "simultaneously the sign of an infinite grandeur and an infinite misery, infinite misery relative to the absolute Being of which he [or it—the referent is unclear: it could be "laughter"] possesses the conception, infinite grandeur relative to animals. It is from the perpetual clash of these two infinites that laughter erupts [or disengages itself—*se dégage*]" (p. 373). The power of Baudelaire's gesture is related to his attempt to conjoin a Pascalian image of the two infinites with a more modulated notion of necessary hybridization or variable dosage, without postulating that the former points toward an impossible "authenticity" (indeed it generates what may be a mystified human sense of superiority) or that the latter designates a "degraded" compromise or relapse. And while the absolute comic—in its drunken hilarity, its *vertige de l'hyperbole*, its proximity to the unconscious, and its "lucid madness"—cannot be reduced to social and political considerations, neither can it be divorced from them. In any event, it is neither a one-sided, deadly ideal nor a vehicle for an unworldly pure fiction. From this complex perspective,

*123*

we can sense the appeal of a self-consciously impossible desire for purity, even—perhaps, in a certain modern context, especially— when it comes in what might seem to be the terminally secular form of technical linguistic analysis that "rigorously" marks and remarks the ultimate "unreliability" of all language, the impasses of "worldly" compromises, and the tempting "seductions" of recon- ciliation and symbolic meaning. Yet one problem Baudelaire seems to leave us with is how to think further his own conception of the intricate relation between "literary" or "artistic" texts and their per- tinent but variable contexts, such as the carnivalesque. I have tried to suggest that a concern for the text/context relation need not be construed as an alternative to rhetorical inquiry or as an indubitable sign of a reductive if not a "foundational" mode of thought. Indeed a certain kind of attentiveness to this relation may enable us better to trace—and to confront our own implication in—the variable fig- urations of temporality (or historicity) conceived as a recurrent but changing formation combining symptomatic, critical, and at times transformative possibilities.

*Postscript.* In the body of this chapter, I compare and contrast two major contemporary critics on a crucial set of issues in interpreta- tion related to the problem of temporality. M. H. Abrams receives briefer treatment than Paul de Man only because the main lines of his argument are clearly delineated and the details are too multifari- ous to be addressed in one chapter. The impression may, however, be inevitable that Abrams has, by the end of the chapter, been left somewhere in the Shandean dust. Although I have often departed from his own protocols of interpretation, I have devoted to Paul de Man's densely intricate and influential essay the type of close, criti- cal reading he demanded in addressing texts but which has rarely been employed in discussing his own writings. Indeed the discrep- ancy in the space I have devoted to Abrams's large book and to de Man's relatively succinct essay is not without its irony, which may be compared to that evident in de Man's treatment of Baudelaire's *De l'essence du rire* and Wordsworth's brief poem. It would be intel- lectually satisfying to turn at this point to a summary statement that would provide at least some sense of closure and of balance in the appraisal of the two critics. Recent developments have made this option seem altogether unavailable. Indeed they heighten one's sense of the role of temporality, and they may well affect one's rhetoric.

The original version of this chapter was written before the discovery of the journalistic articles Paul de Man published in 1941 and 1942. Although these articles fall outside my topic as originally construed, I think it is necessary to address at least certain of the problems they pose.

One piece entitled "Les juifs dans la littérature actuelle," which appeared in the collaborationist Belgian newspaper *Le Soir* on March 4, 1941, argues in particularly tendentious and misleading terms that Western intellectuals should be pleased that the Jews did not have as great a role in Western literature as was often claimed by "vulgar" anti-Semites. The demeaning reference to "vulgar" anti-Semites does not incriminate anti-Semitism in general or indicate that all anti-Semitism is *eo ipso* vulgar. Nor does it lead to the conclusion that one should leave the Jews alone because the claims about their importance are exaggerated. Rather, it prefaces an argument that Western literature has remained healthy despite the limited role of Jews, who are indeed an invasive "foreign force" and are themselves responsible for spreading the myth of their exaggerated role in Western literature. The article puts into play the logic of scapegoating with respect to an alien pollutant. Its primary concern is to guarantee the status of Western literature, which has been vilified by "vulgar" attempts to associate it with Jews.

For de Man, the "deeper cause" of the "error" or "myth" of Jewish influence is the "widespread belief" that the modern novel and poetry are the "monstrous outgrowth" of the world war. He writes, "Since the Jews have, in fact, played an important role in the phony and disordered existence of Europe since 1920, a novel born in this atmosphere would deserve, up to a certain point, the qualification of *enjuivé*." For de Man, "*the reality* is different" because "aesthetic evolution obeys very powerful laws that continue their action even when humanity is shaken by considerable events." Thus the relative autonomy of aesthetic evolution is invoked to defend the relative purity of Western literature from Jewish contamination. It thereby serves a manifestly anti-Semitic function. De Man does mention Kafka among a series of modern novelists, but the context makes it implausible (but not impossible) that he knew Kafka was Jewish. He also puts forth the following counterfactual:

> On any somewhat closer examination, this influence [of Jews on present-day literature] appears even to have extraordinarily little importance since one might have expected that, given the specific characteristics of the Jewish spirit, the latter would have played a more brilliant role in this artistic production. Their cerebralness, their capacity to assimilate doctrines while keeping a certain coldness in the face of them, seemed to be very precious qualities for the work of lucid analysis that the novel demands. But in spite of that, Jewish writers have always remained in the second rank.

Thus appearances are deceiving, and even those appearances depend upon the invocation of an equivocal stereotype of Jews that can easily cut both ways. An analogous argument would present blacks as having "rhythm," which might seem to make them likely candidates for professional dance (even if they are underrepresented in fact in that profession) but would disqualify them for, say, business management.

The conclusion to the article contains perhaps the most incriminating statement:

> In keeping its originality and its character intact, despite the Semitic interference [*ingérence*] in all aspects of European life, it [our civilization] has shown that its nature was at bottom healthy. Moreover, one sees that a solution of the Jewish problem that aimed at the creation of a Jewish colony isolated from Europe, would not entail, for the literary life of the West, any deplorable consequences. It would lose, all in all, only a few personalities of mediocre value and would continue, as in the past, to develop according to its great evolutionary laws.

This "literary" justification for the ghettoization or even deportation of the Jews is itself deplorable, and its disastrous nature is only compounded by the extent to which it fits into the rhetoric of a historical movement that eventuated in concentration camps and genocide. The status of the comment on isolating the Jews as an aleatory supplement or mere "by the way" only increases the offensiveness and insensitivity it signifies in this text.

The fact that de Man as a young man wrote such an article is clearly objectionable but perhaps understandable given his context and family connections. What may be even more open to objection is that in later life he did not make an explicit public acknowledgment and critique of it. De Man apparently did write a recently discovered letter dated January 25, 1955, to Renato Poggioli, who was director of the Harvard Society of Fellows. In it de Man tries to counter an anonymous denunciation of his activity in Belgium: "In 1940 and 1941 I wrote some literary articles in the newspaper 'Le Soir' and, I like most of the other contributors, stopped doing so when nazi thought-control did no longer allow freedom of statement. During the rest of the occupation I did what was the duty of any decent person."[8] I have not seen the rest of this letter, but the above-quoted portion hardly seems to qualify as a public acknowledgment of the problematic aspects of de Man's wartime writings. Indeed it reads like a self-exoneration. Nor does it sufficently mitigate the fact that there were years of omission or even of cover-up—a fact that must be disorienting not only to those with an interest in de Man's work but to anyone. For de Man's students, it must at some level be shattering. De Man was the object of intense transferential relations. He continued to be the one ghostly ideal reader for his students as well as a charismatic source of solidarity if not symbolic unity among them. In one sense, the crucial aspect of the recent discoveries may well be less what they indicate about de Man than what they indicate about others in the very manner in which they attempt to come to terms with them.

Had de Man publicly acknowledged his early writings, especially the questionable portions of them, and said he had made a catastrophic mistake as a young man, one's reaction would be significantly affected. It would in fact have been preferable had de Man, particularly when he achieved prominence, engaged in self-criticism and explicitly explored the problem of the relation or nonrelation of those early writings to his later work. It would, however, be unacceptable to use the early writings to justify a total condemnation of de Man as an individual or to dismiss the later writ-

[8] Quoted in Jacques Derrida, "Like the Sound of the Deep within a Shell: Paul de Man's War," *Critical Inquiry* 14 (1988), 636n. Derrida's analysis may be contrasted with the one I offer here.

ings. The work of de Man should receive the close critical attention he demanded with respect to other difficult texts. Part of this process will now involve a reading of the at times heterogeneous early writings. (For example, de Man at times praises movements or writers out of favor with the Nazis, and he is caught in a tension between, on the one hand, the reading of literature in the light of its political and social implications, often with an insistent stress upon the need for aesthetic and sociocultural unity, and, on the other hand, an assertion of the autonomy of literature that cannot be subordinated to "moralizing" concerns.) Rereading de Man will also require some attempt to relate the early writings to the later ones. Indeed the later texts will almost inevitably be reread in the light of earlier tendencies, and de Man may be seen as avoiding, arguing against, or continuing in displaced and perhaps transformed fashion predilections that were pronounced in his early writings (such as the intense interest in Romanticism or in the quest for "symbolic" unity and totalization). Even more specifically, the extreme stress upon disjunction in the later de Man might be read as a disavowal of the past or an avoidance of the need to come to terms with it, and the almost gravitational pull toward the aporetic impasse or the allegory of unreadability (so pronounced in de Man's writing after "The Rhetoric of Temporality") might be construed as a seemingly apolitical, formalistic overcompensation for the relatively clear and distinct political blunders of the young de Man. Any extended rereadings, however, would have to be more qualified than the preceding statement, and they would have to include a careful examination of the complexity of the later de Man, including his own exploration of the impossibility of simple disavowal of the past, for example, in "Literary History and Literary Modernity" (in *Blindness and Insight*).

It would also be altogether unacceptable to take the writings of the young de Man as a pretext for condemning deconstruction in general. Especially dubious is the idea that de Man's early anti-Semitism conclusively proves—or at least helps to validate the contention—that deconstruction is an ahistorical, apolitical, and amoral if not immoral theory for which anything and everything goes. Indeed here I may quote the rather biased and dubious reporting of the *New York Times* of December 1, 1987: "Deconstruction views language as a slippery and inherently false medium that always reflects the biases of its users" (p. B6). Such a statement not only gathers up all those with a significant relation to deconstruction and places them in one camp. Like the other predictable reactions to the disclosure of de Man's early writing, it repeats in its very reaction to deconstruction what it seems to excoriate in de Man's anti-Semitism itself. More precisely, it displaces a victimizing scapegoat mechanism through which internal purity for the self or the ingroup is sought through the projection of all evil and corruption onto a discrete outgroup that is to be isolated from the essentially "healthy" ingroup. Nothing could be more "anti-deconstructive" than the early de Man article from which I quoted. While it is impossible to deny the sinister pall cast over de Man's later writings by the early ones, the broad issue of the nature and limits of the political implications of variants of deconstruction—or even the more delimited issue of the relation of the later de Man to politics—cannot be resolved in terms of a simple extrapolation from the journalistic articles of the young de Man.

One very important context that may serve as a complex transition in analyzing the relation between de Man's early articles and his later work is the opposition—so prevalent in German intellectual history—between *Kultur* and *Zivilisation*. This opposition was tortuously played out by Thomas Mann, among others, in his *Reflections of a Nonpolitical Man* (1918), and it was analyzed critically by Norbert Elias as well as by Ralf Dahrendorf.[9] In his early wartime articles de Man is divided between two visions of *Kultur*, as the integrating capstone of society as a whole and as an aesthetic world apart. In his postwar work he is a decisive critic of various modes of totalization. But he at times seems to return to a more problematic, disjunctive conception of *Kultur* in the form of a notion of the figural or the literary. He conceives of the literary as the self-referential rhetoricity of a text that prefigures its own misreading and enacts its own *mise en abîme*. This notion may apply to (or blur if not obliterate the distinctions among) philosophy, criti-

---

[9] Elias, *The History of Manners: The Civilizing Process*, vol. 1, trans. Edmund Jephcott (New York, 1982); Dahrendorf, *Society and Democracy in Germany* (Garden City, N.Y., 1967).

cism, and what are ordinarily classified as "literary" texts. While it may also function to destabilize the opposition between *Kultur* and *Zivilisation*, de Man's notion of the literary has political implications that are at best allusive and indirect, hence eminently contestable.

In view of the extremely intricate and often obscure nature of de Man's style, it is particularly hazardous to generalize about his thought or even to elicit the direction and implications of his argument. One recent attempt to provide a general interpretation is Christopher Norris's *Paul de Man*.[10] Norris argues that de Man's work underwent a "decisive change" (p. 17) from political quietism in early postwar essays to an explicit critique of the ideology of aesthetic totalization in later essays. The later essays may also be seen as an often tortured critique of the totalizing aesthetic ideology of the wartime writings. Despite the many insightful local observations he makes, Norris's interpretation is open to objection for a number of reasons. The wartime writings are divided between a totalizing ideology and a conception of the autonomy of literary form and formal evolution; the latter has a more problematic relation to the postwar work. There is, moreover, a critique of totalization in the early postwar essays, and the rejection of "revolutionary" utopianism in the sense of totalizing secular messianism can be found in various forms throughout de Man's work.[11] In addition, the later essays, like the earlier postwar ones, are insufficiently specific about the relation between their modes of criticism and either political options or a revised understanding of historicity.

After World War II, de Man clearly rejects totalizing, redemptive revolution despite the almost compulsive fascination it sometimes holds for him. But what he defends or recommends is unclear. Even

[10] New York, 1988.

[11] For example, "Wordsworth and Hölderlin" (1966; reprinted in *The Rhetoric of Romanticism*, New York, 1984, pp. 47-65) is for Norris a key case illustrating de Man's early political quietism and anti-Marxism. Yet it is also a critique of totalization. In it de Man traces the movement in Wordsworth that ends at the point where Hölderlin presumably begins, that is, with the collapse of symbol, analogy, and correspondence and the disclosure of gaps, radical uncertainty, death, and failure. Of history, moreover, de Man makes an arresting comment that does take on retrospective significance: "The future is present only as the remembering of a failed project that has become a menace" (p. 58-59). One may also note that the leitmotif of the essays in *Blindness and Insight* is that insights arise through often unintentional or "blind" resistances to systematization and totalization.

a stress on de Man's obsessive insistence on the discursive impasse, the lure of the *mise en abîme*, the random contingency and "violence" of the material signifier, the sheer positing power of language, the repeated naming of nothingness, and so forth produces no definite political implications. The latter could fall anywhere in the broad range from mindless activism to the "activeless" mind, including terrorism, cautionary liberalism, democracy as the best among possible alternatives, nonapocalyptic socialism, limited authoritarianism, and political quietism.

One place where de Man does make a clear-cut political inference of at least a general nature is his very late essay "Aesthetic Formalization in Kleist."[12] Here, however, the inference is, if anything, too direct. De Man links the putatively neo-Schillerian ideal of aesthetic totalization to political structures. This linkage is at best superficially plausible and requires further inquiry into the question of how various figures or movements link the aesthetic and the political. Its most obvious application is to Nazi ideologists who elaborated a direct "aestheticization" of politics. But John Stuart Mill, among others, explicitly saw the aesthetic as a realm of detached contemplation and culture of the feelings that compensated for the losses of daily life. Even if this belief was mystified, it still allowed for a conjunction of "aestheticism" and political liberalism. For Georg Lukács, it was arguably the loss of belief in aesthetic totalization that helped turn him toward totalizing revolutionary politics. De Man does not specify in the essay on Kleist where the critique of aesthetic totalization leads politically, and he may well be open to criticism precisely for this lack of specificity. This is of course not to say that he should have provided "duodecimo editions of the New Jerusalem" (in Marx's phrase), but he might well have been more explicit about the institutional and practical implications of his approach, at least as he construed them.

De Man's writing invites quasi-theological exegesis and projective reprocessing, by both his detractors and his admirers, and it is extremely difficult to engage his texts critically through accurate reconstruction and dialogic exchange. I can by no means claim to

[12] In *The Rhetoric of Romanticism*, pp. 263-90.

have avoided all the pitfalls involved in interpreting his work. Nor have I provided the intricate general account of his writing that would attempt to elicit its historicity in terms of a complex interaction of repetition and change over time. I have simply addressed one pivotal text and hazarded a few incomplete remarks about his recently discovered wartime articles and their relation to aspects of his postwar work. My comments have focused on "Les juifs dans la littérature actuelle" because it is the most objectionable of the early writings. A more comprehensive account would have to relate it more thoroughly to the other wartime articles. Such an account should recognize, however, that readers of the time may well have read "Les juifs" in isolation or with only a vague memory of other articles by de Man. In addition, it should not construe the article as more internally complex and self-questioning than it is or bury it in a larger intertextual reading that cushions or even obscures its dubious nature. While it would undoubtedly have been problematic for de Man to have publicly acknowledged and reckoned with this article in his later life, his unwillingness or inability to make the attempt may well prove to have been even more problematic. Finally I would note that the point of my comments is not to demand with moralistic self-certainty that de Man should have been abjectly apologetic or excuse-making. Nor is it to intimate a false sense of superiority from the safe position of someone who is not confronted with the difficult decisions de Man was forced to confront. It is rather to insist that one is indeed answerable for publications in a special sense, especially if one becomes a well-known and influential figure, for then one's writing and teaching constitute a public legacy, with particular significance for one's students. It is in this sense that the obligation to come publicly to terms with the questionable aspects of one's past is itself an issue whose ethical character cannot be reduced to abject apology and self-serving moralism.

# Culture and Ideology:
# From Geertz to Marx

> The culture concept to which I adhere has neither multiple
> referents nor, so far as I can see, any unusual ambiguity; it
> denotes an historically transmitted pattern of meanings
> embodied in symbols, a system of inherited conceptions
> expressed in symbolic forms by means of which men commu-
> nicate, perpetuate, and develop their knowledge about and
> attitudes toward life.
>
> —Clifford Geertz, "Religion as a Cultural System"

The anthropological concept of culture, of which Clifford
Geertz has been both a notable advocate and an influential definer,
has played an important role in contemporary historiography and
social science. It has focused attention fruitfully on the problem of
meaning and symbols. Especially in Geertz's formulation, it has
combated crude sociological reductionism and engendered a concern for close reading of cultural phenomena construed on the analogy of texts. It has also sensitized researchers to the problem of
attempting to understand groups and societies in terms of their
entire way of life as mediated in symbols. In contrast to both narrowly causal models of explanation and modes of "thin" description, Geertz's nonreductive emphasis upon the interpretation of
symbolic practices has marked a clear advance in the understanding
of culture.

In *The Interpretation of Cultures* (particularly in the essay,
"Ideology as Cultural System"), Geertz has applied his general con-

cept of culture to the particular problem of ideology. In line with his more general concept, he criticizes the reductionism of both the Marxist notion of ideology in terms of interest and the functionalist notion in terms of tension management (or the reduction of "strain"). While not entirely denying the partial applicability of these notions (especially the Parsonian version of functionalism), he insists on the "autonomy" of symbolic processes and finds in it the missing link that redirects attention to the precise workings of ideology: "The link between the causes of ideology and its effects seems adventitious because the connecting element—the autonomous process of symbolic formulation—is passed over in virtual silence. Both interest theory and strain theory go directly from source analysis to consequence analysis without ever seriously examining ideologies as systems of interacting symbols, as patterns of interworking meanings."[1] Geertz, moreover, proposes a "genuinely nonevaluative concept of ideology" (p. 196) as the proper way to examine its interworking meanings, and he concludes the essay with an opposition between ideology and science, thereby reinforcing his own program for a social scientific study of ideology as a cultural system. In his expansive idea of ideology as a system of symbolic meaning as well as in his quest for a science that may be both opposed to ideology and posited as the "nonevaluative" way of comprehending it, Geertz formulates views rather typical of recent social scientific perspectives. For example, there are analogues of Geertz's approach in the work of Alvin Gouldner and the early Louis Althusser.

Without denying the many fruitful aspects of Geertz's approach, I suggest it should be supplemented or emended in at least two significant ways. First, certain complex situations may require a more differentiated analysis of culture; for an anthropological model may prove excessively homogenizing in the modern period, when some societies have been sources of both emulation and imperialistic imposition for others. I shall restrict my analysis to significant features of modern Western societies, although certain problems also have relevance for contemporary state socialist societies. I shall not, however, directly address the intricate processes of cosmopolitan

[1] *The Interpretation of Cultures* (New York, 1973), p. 207.

cultural interaction. Second, there may be good reason to return at least in part to a modified Marxist conception of ideology. Geertz's insistence on the autonomy of symbolic forms may avoid reductionism at the price of regressing to precritical idealism. In any event, it dissolves the problem of ideology into that of symbolic meaning and culture in general, and it gives rise both to a dubious binary opposition between ideology and science and to a social science that lacks a link with critical theory.[2] A more specific concept of ideology may be necessary insofar as ideology in a delimited sense does not exhaust all culture and its relation to given symbolic systems or artifacts remains problematic. In other words, symbolisms or signifying practices may be both relatively autonomous and partially ideological in variable ways, and the concrete task of analysis is to specify the relation between ideological and other than ideological aspects of a complex, ambivalent phenomenon. Indeed one crucial way in which a symbolism or a specific text becomes relatively autonomous is by engaging in a critical relation to the ideologies it conveys. The latter point would apply as much to social science or historiography as to other signifying practices.

In the analysis of modern cultural systems, one needs to distinguish—and to pose the problem of the relations—among several levels: official culture, high or elite culture, mass culture, and popular culture. I have discussed this issue in an earlier work,[3] and here I shall expand upon and partially revise that discussion. To begin with, each of these aspects or levels is internally differentiated or even divided in ways I shall at times try to indicate. In addition, the relation among levels poses the problem of a hegemonic formation and its social correlates or bearers. For, while there is never a simple one-to-one equation between culture and society, cultural differentiation is related to social differentiation and actual

[2] For an approach to the problem of ideology that in important respects converges with the one taken in this chapter, see John B. Thompson, *Studies in the Theory of Ideology* (Berkeley and Los Angeles, 1984). I read Thompson's study only after completing this chapter. Although I do not agree with all aspects of its argument, the degree of convergence in perspectives is an encouraging sign of discontent with more firmly established approaches to the problem of ideology in academia.

[3] See *History & Criticism* (Ithaca, N.Y., 1985), pp. 73-79.

or potential conflict. Indeed this relationship is one reason why there is a place for a specific concept of ideology related to the concept of hegemony. It is, I think, initially plausible to argue that in Western countries, mass culture tends to be the dominant force in a hegemonic formation, while in state socialist countries, official culture, under state and party, tends to be dominant but in ways that must nonetheless confront problems attendant upon mass and even commodified culture (for example, a crucial concern for productivity; the technically rational organization of work; a functional division between work and play; a reliance on public relations and public opinion research; the growing importance of the media, especially among the young; the replacement of publics by audiences; and so forth).

Official culture is culture actively shaped or at least influenced by the state. Political culture is a broader concept encompassing traditions and practices in a polity, for example, the practices of state worship and deference to superior authority, on the one hand, and of constitutional rule, civil liberties, and participation or at least consent of the governed, on the other. Political culture may thus either reinforce or limit the scope of official culture—or at times do both insofar as practices and traditions are equivocal or subject to variation over time. It would be simplistic categorically to contrast West and East on this dimension of political culture; for there are important differences between countries within either bloc (for example, between England and West Germany or Poland and East Germany). The more significant difference, however, results from the relative role of constitutional guarantees that are implemented through the courts and effective in the political process. The state in its more official capacity, moreover, may intervene to shape culture in both direct and indirect ways—directly through support for certain programs (endowments on the level of high culture, welfare on more "popular" levels) and indirectly through the priorities it underwrites and the models of success it projects (the importance of national security, military preparedness, and party loyalty or business acumen, for example). State influence may at times be rather subtle, as when a seeming collection agency, such as the Internal Revenue Service, actually comes to affect life styles insofar as its policy on records and documentation confronts citizens with the option of either paying higher taxes or living as if they were book-keepers. Whether its influence be subtle or not, the massive importance of the state in all modern societies raises the question of its differential impact on cultural processes often treated in abstraction from political ones.

High or elite culture is an equivocal term. It may refer to the artifacts and the general culture (or discursive practices) of elites in the arts and sciences. It may also refer to the culture of other elites—political, military, socioeconomic, bureaucratic, academic, and so forth. In the latter sense, it merges in part with official and political culture. It should be obvious that the degree of integration of various elites and elite cultures is not a foregone conclusion, nor is the relation of elite to hegemonic culture. It is misleading simply to conflate hegemonic with elite culture because this conflation occludes the problematic degree to which there may be critical or contestatory tendencies in elite culture itself.

It is often assumed that the stability of a social and political order depends on a workable degree of integration among elites, or at least on modes of noncommunication and functional specificity that do not undermine the legitimation of the state and the social order. The diversity of historical developments among nations and states in the modern period nonetheless makes generalizations hazardous. For example, the French Revolution created barriers among elites themselves, and the instability of France in the nineteenth century was due in part to the absence of consensus among elites on a legitimate form of government and society. In England, by contrast, there was widespread agreement among elites on the legitimacy of a constitutional monarchy as well as on a capitalistic economy, and the degree of democratic participation enabled issues to be open to resolution through a combination of agitation and negotiation. England had an establishment in a sense not in evidence in France. German national unification was achieved only at the end of the nineteenth century through political and military means (Bismarck's "blood and iron"), and it coincided with problems created by large-scale, rapid, and extremely disruptive industrialization. An older agrarian elite of Junkers retained political and administrative power despite the importance of newer socioeconomic groups. And academics maintained a mandarin position that aligned the traditional ideal of *Bildung* with opposition to newer forms of social activity and political participation. I recall these clichés of comparative social history simply to underline the difficulty in generalizing about the nature and role of elites in the modern period.

I would also observe in passing that a crucial problem in the analysis of ideologies in contemporary Western societies is the complex and to some extent differential relation between integration through shared belief or ideology in the older sense and negative integration or dissensus through an absence of widely shared commitments. Negative integration abets the play of divisive or at least functionally specific interests and inhibits the formation of oppositional movements. In the contemporary context at least three ideological tendencies combine: (1) older ideological formations that appeal especially but not exclusively to lower-middle and blue-collar groups, for example, in terms of national security or "our way of life" (including the "born-in-the-USA" syndrome); (2) particular or functionally specific ideologies that appeal largely to middle- and upper-class groups, for example, on the level of professional concerns; and (3) the weakness or absence of ideologies that enable oppositional groups to articulate their differences and form effective political alliances. This threefold complex is ignored in the notion of an "end of ideology," and it is oversimplified even in Jürgen Habermas's more pertinent and sophisticated idea that in modern societies false consciousness, dependent upon older ideological formations, finds its functional equivalent in *"fragmented* consciousness, which precludes enlightenment about the mechanism of reification."[4] It is also oversimplified in the notion that fragmented ideologies and dissensus, enabling a hegemonic strategy of divide and rule and disabling effective protest, simply eliminate ideology in the older sense of a consensual or shared system in society as a whole or even in significant segments of society.[5]

One generalization that has at least limited validity is that, in the modern period, artistic and intellectual elites—at times scientific

---

[4] *Theorie des kommunikativen Handelns*, vol. 2 (Frankfurt, 1981), p. 522.

[5] This perspective is stressed in Thompson, *Studies in the Theory of Ideology.* To some extent, it may be related to the greater degree of disaffection in contemporary Britain than in the United States.

elites—have had significantly adversarial relations to features of the dominant culture and of state policy, however limited the political effect of these adversarial relations may have been. Even noteworthy conservatives like Edmund Burke and Joseph de Maistre have not simply defended a status quo but often inveighed against it in defense of older values they felt were threatened. To some extent, more recent conservatives, such as William Buckley, have been constrained to follow their example. It is, however, true that the role of the critical intellectual, of whatever ideological bent, has been more enshrined in Western European (especially Continental) than in American culture; for the pragmatic tendencies and commonsensical orientation of the latter have affected the potential of even the questioners of the "system." European transplants, such as affiliates of the so-called Frankfurt school, have recognized this point to their chagrin. In addition, the very antipathy to the term "high-culture" in the United States and the preference for the "pop" distinction among high brow, middle brow, and low brow are themselves signs of the different cultural ambience on this side of the Atlantic. Who, for example, could be considered the American analogue of Jean-Paul Sartre, politically committed, accomplished in so many areas that one is tempted to invoke the phrase "Renaissance man," *and* someone whose funeral could bring out a spontaneous cortege of fifty thousand people? Elvis Presley or some grade B movie actor might elicit popular support of that magnitude, but not an intellectual. Still, the differences between the United States and Europe in these respects should not be overdrawn. There have been important critical currents in the United States with more or less marked connections to European thought. Recent forms of socialism and feminism are among the more prominent, the latter having a greater social and political resonance than the former. And the regard with which social elites and the general public have held European artistic and intellectual elites itself involves the role of what Pierre Bourdieu somewhat indiscriminately terms "symbolic capital." The canonization of classics, including some of the most adversarial works of modern culture, reinforces the tendency to set up artists or intellectuals as fetishized sources of prestige and status for privileged social groups.

The socially stabilizing function of canonization has induced recent critical theorists to embark on a program of canon busting in which attention is paid to works excluded from canons, particularly works of oppressed groups such as women, workers, and ethnic minorities. My own view is that the necessary investigation of noncanonical artifacts and their sociopolitical contexts should not replace but supplement a program of noncanonical readings of canonical texts and artifacts. More precisely, we should attempt to reopen the question of the way given texts or artifacts included in canons have complex ideological, critical, and at times possibly transformative implications for their own contexts and perhaps even for our contexts of reading and interpretation. This kind of inquiry hardly exhausts all significant problems or excludes other modes of investigation, and it may—indeed should—be undertaken in conjunction with broader sociocultural and historical research. But it has its role to play, especially now. It may still be plausible to view certain departments of literature or art history as subsisting on a neo-Arnoldian ideology that upholds a canon as a feature of both intellectual and sociopolitical standing. But to generalize this into a vision of modern, and particularly American, culture is at present extremely shortsighted and narrowly academic. Our culture is not Arnoldian, and attempts to move it in that direction are misconceived. High culture of a traditional sort (particularly print culture) is an endangered species. But any qualified defense of it should be premised on the argument that the abilities developed in a close study of high culture may be one crucial source of critical judgment in coming constructively to terms with the forms of mass and commodified culture that have assumed an important if not clearly dominant role in modern life. It is not, I think, accidental that the most cogent critics of a canon, such as Walter Benjamin or, in a different register, Jacques Derrida, have had an intimate acquaintance with their objects of criticism.

Mass culture evokes the image of large numbers of people who do not form face-to-face publics but, rather, audiences of spectators or more or less organized crowds of participants in such events as rallies and parades. Sociologically, mass culture is related to urbanization, the rise of the middle classes, and the spread of *embourgeoisement* through widening circles of the population. It is also related to the fear of being lost in the crowd and no longer being recognized, as well as to the ambivalent exhilaration that anonymity in an urban environment brings. In these respects, it is a term difficult to extricate from ideological considerations. In a more limited sense, it denotes culture in good part dependent upon mass media for dissemination—what is currently termed "mediated" culture in a specifically modern sense. Particularly in the West, it also denotes commodified culture, that is, culture further mediated by the market and converted into a commodity bought and sold in accordance with market criteria. But even in countries where the media are owned and controlled by the state, procedures perfected under commodified conditions, such as public relations and public opinion research, are employed to curry the favor of large audiences. Advertising may itself either be emulated by other mass-appeal programming or be literally replaced by appeals to patriotic sentiment. (In Western noncommercial, educational television, advertising of course finds its functional equivalent in marathon fund-raising drives that may be so tedious and inept as to make one crave commercials employing professional talent.)

The effect of mass and mediated culture is difficult to calculate. This is particularly true to the extent that it becomes a primary culture, as television assumes the role of a baby-sitter, if not a surrogate parent, and people have fewer alternative sources of culture to serve as countervailing forces. Certainly, mass culture today affects all other aspects or levels of culture, and a crucial question is the extent to which it has passed beyond the status of a technology and now assimilates or modifies various forms of elite and popular culture to become a culture in its own right. In any case, it should be evident that media such as television and film are not simply neutral technologies but forces active in shaping and transforming culture; the product they create is distinctive. I simply note one recent feature of religion on TV that bears on the extent to which the medium affects the message. There is a remarkable similarity in rhetoric, personality type, and pitch between preachers on televised religious programs (so-called electronic evangelists) and proliferating real estate hucksters who have managed to convert advertising into full-time programming. This epiphanic convergence may, moreover, be related to the more general resurgence of evangelical capitalism that has marked the Reagan years—a resurgence abetted by the sort of media hype that has itself helped to create the image of the "great communicator."

Even when the media tend to replicate older distinctions such as that between elite and popular culture, for example, in the case of art films and "popular" films, they do so within a context they help to generate—a context that has more than a mimetic relation to other levels of culture. A crucial question here is whether or to what extent the media reduce other cultural forms to the level of raw material for readily consumable and instantly intelligible, off-the-rack products that in turn become the models for "spontaneous" emulation in "popular" culture. The Madonna look in fashion and even in attitude is one recent serioparodic example of the media's ability to transform older models or schemata.

Advertising itself has in certain ways become the most "advanced" sector of the media and particularly of television. Given its importance in a commodity system, it is heavily funded, and the care with which commercials are made often makes ordinary programming seem amateurish. Ad men were able to assimilate the so-called modernist "tradition of the New" and the cult of formal experimentation by adapting the techniques of the avant-garde to the celebration of the dominant culture. Their success in this venture should give the quietus to any general idea that formal experimentation is invariably contestatory or "subversive" in a sociopolitical sense. The formally aesthetic quality of certain ads is in fact quite remarkable, and it includes the use of self-referential and smugly ironic techniques. Given the nature of recent programming, especially with the movement of soap operas into later time slots and the blending of soaps and comedies into sudsy sitcoms, certain viewers may actually look forward to well-crafted, vaguely adult commercials and experience a reversal of the standard pattern of expectation punctuating television viewing.

Before leaving the topic of mass culture, I would like to point out one of its important features. This is the relation between work and play (a problem I think is radically underemphasized in Habermas's reformulation of critical theory). In modern culture, work tends on one level to be effectively split off or alienated from play in that it is defined in terms of instrumental or technical efficiency, while play is confined to a separate sphere of leisure-time activity. The very idea of work as "serious play" or of a different rhythm between labor and enjoyment may seem farfetched or patently utopian. "Leisure time" is itself organized on a mass-cultural basis, with the individual either in the role of spectator or in that of an amateur performer who tries to do what professionals do better. (The jogging craze is perhaps paradigmatic here; for it presumably has the utilitarian value of improving one's health, and it is an activity that may be performed either alone or while trying to have a conversation with a few huffing-and-puffing friends. The element of invidious comparison with professionals is also reduced to a minimum because distance seems to be the most differential criterion among joggers, which thus makes jogging a rather democratic sport, if not a ritual.) With commodification, moreover, the opposition between work and play—so important on the level of production—collapses on the level of consumption; for leisure time is recycled into a market system and serviced by "culture industries" specializing in the satisfaction of leisure-time needs. It is in this sense that leisure time may be defined as commodified play. I simply propose without further argumentation that a massive problem in modern society and culture is how to give all jobs a craft component and to articulate them with more "playful" or carnivalesque activities in a different rhythm of social life. It is a problem that is denied or occluded both in the rarefied Habermassian ideal-speech situation based on a restricted notion of serious, rational communication and in the prevalent idea that we need to increase leisure time in conjunction with an increase in functionally specific and at times automatic work.

"Popular culture" is an equivocal and ideologically invested term that hovers between a critical fiction, if not a myth ("the world we have lost"), and a residual category (everything that is not elite or mass culture). Its clearest reference is to culture generated or at least enacted in face-to-face groups of people who at least know one another. Its privileged bearers for historians have tended to be peasants and workers, but the disappearance of a distinct peasantry and the decline of a recognizable working-class culture have made its social bases more indeterminate. Today, "popular culture" is often used interchangeably with "mass" and "mediated culture," but this misleading usage begs the question of the historical and sociological relations between levels of culture. In a more delimited sense, "popular culture" is employed to refer to more or less residual traditional forms of various sorts ("superstition," witchcraft, magic, folklore, fairy tales, carnival, and so forth). In a somewhat more general sense, its usage sanctions the investigation of a laundry list of activities and beliefs: family history, peer group relations, the culture of oppressed and minority groups, grass-roots sports, relations to nature and to animals, and so on. It may guide inquiry into less savory topics such as the role of invidious stereotypes, prejudices, and forms of scapegoating or intolerance for outsiders. In a professional sense, it may also have the viciously paradoxical function of underwriting claims to disciplinary hegemony by those who study it, on the grounds that it constitutes the most basic or most significant of social realities.

It seems essential to give the study of popular culture a better theoretical and methodological grounding. It also seems Pollyannaish to believe that this grounding may be fully provided when the phenomenon itself is in such a problematic state in contemporary society. For the uncertainties and hyperboles of the study of popular culture are not unrelated to the condition of popular culture itself in the modern world. One of the telltale uses of the term is with reference to the study of the consumption of mass culture produced by elites. Here the point is that on the level of consumption (or "reader response"), there may be tendencies contradictory to or at least different from those manifest in the artifact taken in isolation or interpreted on its seemingly manifest level. Of course one question is whether the critical or transformative treatment of the artifact by the viewer or reader takes place on the level of the isolated individual and the small circle of family and friends or whether it has a broader resonance that may help convert an audience into a public. Another question is the extent to which there are emergent forms of popular culture that are not entirely consumed by the commodity system. These questions raise the larger issue of the interaction among levels of culture and the role of phenomena or artifacts that represent amalgams of levels. Nationalism, for example, is obviously a phenomenon of modern history that exists on all levels of culture, and an adequate analysis of it would have to investigate the interplay of official, elite, mass, and popular cultures.

I have already referred to the assimilative and assimilating capacity of mass culture and the question of the extent to which it tends to be a dominant force in a hegemonic structure. Mass culture has shown an ability both to recycle popular and elite forms and to affect newer products of popular and elite culture in more or less decisive ways. It is, for example, the rare novel that does not get converted into a soap opera when it becomes a TV drama or even a film, and much talent is currently employed in writing scripts directly for the media. The soap opera form has a tremendous homogenizing effect, as it takes incidents more banal than those of daily life and charges them with a level of emotional intensity rarely achieved in daily life. (A crucial device is eye contact used to generate more or less unearned and evanescent recognition scenes.) To the extent that the soap opera form provides a space for women (its primary audience) to take stock of problems, it is a relatively small space, and the desire to emphasize its importance as a force of resistance may in good measure be a symptom of wishful thinking. The principal point is that at best a mild and readily contained level of social and cultural criticism is the price of access to the mass media, and the exception (say, Monty Python) is relatively rare. There is a sense in which viewing habits may reinforce this point; for one's mind may go into neutral upon switching on the TV, and one may well want a program that does not add critical reflection to the ordinary troubles of the day or the stereotyped disasters of the news. Customized and private modes of viewing, such as cable channels and VCRs, may well have the effect of lessening even the level of awareness of national and local problems necessarily conveyed through regular programming; they enable the viewer to concentrate exclusively on the genre or genres he or she prefers—that is, to consume more and more of them. In addition, the growth of seemingly sophisticated media criticism can accompany a collapse of critical discrimination insofar as the analyst—at times with no sense of critical irony or parody—engages in projective reprocessing of artifacts by providing an intricate semiotic, deconstructive, or dialogic account of *Dynasty* or *Magnum* as if it were *The Brothers Karamazov* or *Moby Dick*.

"Elite culture" at present may to a significant extent mean works that make the kinds of demands on readers that ensure relatively small readerships and dependence on assignment in college courses for dissemination. One technique of the older artifact of elite culture was to take endangered popular forms and translate them into its own medium, in part as a protest against the nature of the dominant culture in which these very forms were undergoing eclipse or repression. For Mikhail Bakhtin, the process of carnivalization in literature began in an interaction with social carnival but became relatively autonomous as a literary genre with the decline of carnival in society. Bakhtin indicated, in his study of Dostoevsky for example, that literary carnivalization might retain an insistence and potency even in the modern period, but he was clear that carnivalization in art or literature remained most vital when it could indeed interact with social and popular currents such as carnival in society. I might add that a tendency in elite culture has been what might be called the hermetic appropriation of the carnivalesque, that is, the insertion of an older popular form into a framework that cuts it off from popular communication and understanding. This phenomenon poses a problem often ignored by those who argue for the political or pedagogic effect of critical tendencies in elite culture (including modes of deconstructive or disseminatory writing). Much art and literature today relies for its knowledge of older popular forms on aesthetic and scholarly traditions; for there is little role for the older forms in many contemporary societies, and what role there is may be highly commercialized (as in carnival in New Orleans). (Here of course certain writers, such as those in South America, may have an advantage to the extent their cultures retain older popular forms.)

Elite culture has increasingly had to come to terms with mass and commodified forms, from advertising to television and beyond. Responses have ranged from assimilation to resistance, with black humor, parody, and satire as prevalent modes of integration. Yet fascination with technology, even when combined with aversion to its excesses or its mindless use, can engender an acrostic ingenuity that threatens to give rise to a baroque technologism in the construction of intricate plots or mechanical wonders. Whether such a procedure is symptomatic or critical of larger cultural trends may at times seem undecidable. Still, one may point to modern works in which the relation to both older popular forms and newer mass or commodified currents is often handled with critical and aesthetic power (for example, William Gaddis's *The Recognitions*).

The very complexity of culture in the modern period and its relation to social stratification and conflict indicate the need for a concept of ideology that is not simply conflated with a homogenized idea of a cultural system. Tendencies in recent history might even lead to a partial rehabilitation of the crudest version of interest theory; for example, David Stockman's revelation that even for some of its promulgators, Ronald Reagan's policy of supply-side economics was little more than media hype devoid of credibility. Indeed there are times when the level of public discourse falls so low that anthropological talk of the wonderful world of meaning and symbols seems like idealistic humbug, and the historical interest in past popular cultures amounts to one more nostalgia trip. Public life then approximates a grade B movie, and the kind of rhetoric and response typical of that genre may have surefire efficacy and significant popular appeal in politics.

A relatively specific sense of ideology refers to modes of legitimation and justification in public life. In this sense, ideology spans what Karl Mannheim distinguished as ideology and utopia, in other words, situationally congruent and situationally transcendent modes of legitimation. One may certainly use the term "ideology" in a sense that equates it with ethicopolitical and publicly normative discourse in general. In the Marxist tradition, however—particularly in Marx and Gramsci—ideology is further specified in certain ways, and this specification has at least limited validity for critical analysis.

I suggest five features of ideology when it is not simply identified as a general "cultural system" or even as a mode of legitimation:

(1) Ideology involves mystification, illusionism, or illegitimate masking in the interest of legitimation or justification. It is in this sense the public and sociopolitical analogue of Freud's concept of rationalization (whether through secondary revision or more deep-seated unconscious processes). I do, however, leave open the question of whether there may be legitimate modalities of masking (for example, in carnival) that have variable interrelations with illegiti-

mate or invidiously deceptive forms. The obvious but extremely difficult task, which is both analytic and critical, is to distinguish legitimate from illegitimate modes of masking and to prevent the latter from dominating the former.

(2) Ideology is illegitimate insofar as it serves the interest of a part of society by generalizing that interest to appear as the good of the whole society. Ideology is in this sense falsely or misleadingly synecdochic in a given social order. I also leave open the question of whether there can be egalitarian ideologies that serve a particular interest or whether egalitarianism may be equated with "truth"—as it commonly if implicitly is, especially by students of popular culture. My own view is that the relation of equality, reciprocity, and difference represents an extremely knotty problem that is avoided by the simple equation of egalitarianism with "truth" and the correlation of ideology with the domination or hegemony of a superordinate class. I have already indicated at least two dubious features of populist egalitarianism: the tendency in populism to scapegoat outsiders and exceptions, and the inclination of at least some students of popular culture to appeal vicariously to the experience of the oppressed to justify their own pretensions to disciplinary hegemony. I might also note that Marx related the "identitarian" logic of commensuration to exchange value and commodity production, but I would add that we must be very careful in critiques of egalitarian populism because they can easily be misconstrued and abused. Although I want to raise questions about certain conceptions and uses of egalitarianism, I do—particularly in specific contexts—defend other appeals to it, for example, in the notions of equality before the law and equal pay for equal work, or even in the general idea that people are equal in a sense more basic than all the senses in which they are unequal.

(3) Ideology presents what is historically variable—although perhaps recurrent (not unique)—as if it were universal or eternal. In Marx's typical example of the naturalizing or essentializing nature of ideology, the economic bases of a commodity market may be construed as if they were conditions of economy and society in general. Gift exchange, from this market-oriented ideological perspective, may be interpreted as an aberrant or incomprehensible form of commodity exchange, and all exchange may be equated with

exchange value (in the specific sense of equalization or commensuration with respect to a universal equivalent). I should note in passing that there is a danger in Althusser's contention, on the basis of his understanding of psychoanalysis via the work of Lacan, that ideology, like the unconscious, is both transhistorical and centered on the subject. This view threatens to repeat essentialism in the very definition of ideology, and it both ignores the historical nature of displacement (or repetition with variation) in unconscious processes and obviates the possibility of an objectivist or scientistic ideology (to which Althusser himself at times falls prey).

(4) Ideology is related to the hegemony of one formation, bloc, or group over others, and hegemony in this sense cannot be reduced to power; for it requires a nexus of power and consent—in other words, a form of authority—that is at least partially accepted and internalized by all relevant groups, including the oppressed. The notion of hegemony casts doubt upon the attempt to analyze social and cultural processes in terms of a concept of power (or even of power-knowledge) alone. It also raises the possibility of self-deception in groups who may believe, to a greater or lesser extent, that something is in their interest when it may not be—or at least when it involves losses that outweigh gains (economic or other). As I intimated earlier, the alternative to the hegemony of an elite is not total egalitarianism or populism, which is typically attended by intolerance for outsiders and exceptions. The alternative should be an articulation of differences, including the differences between the exception and the rule—an alternative that poses the problems of justice and generosity. Here Marx's formula—from each according to his ability, to each according to his needs—remains a fruitful beginning point (yet only a beginning point) for reflection. In any case, the value of this formula, which of course was not confined to Marx, is that it does not restrict us to the binary opposition between hierarchy and equality. It complicates the picture by introducing at least two differential orders of magnitude: abilities and needs.

(5) A particularly prevalent if not typical form ideology assumes is the attempt to see "meaningful" order in chaos. Here ideology most approximates Freud's notion of secondary revision through which the distorted procedures of dreamwork are straightened out

and made compatible with the demands of an ego in quest of coherent meaning and identity. In culture and society, the often incoherent modes of collective life—including the uncontrolled oscillation between excessively restrictive control (for example, in narrow forms of technical or formal rationality) and chaotic excess or transgression—are covered and assuaged by attempts to interpret existence as somehow imbued with satisfying meaning. The very quest for meaning and order that misconstrues its object by infusing it with the overall coherence it lacks may of course be transferred into social science methodology itself. Such methodology deceptively provides methodological or "symbolic" solutions for substantive problems—problems it does more to conceal than to disclose for critical analysis. And it may be seen as the complement to "positivism" rather than its alternative. The two seemingly opposed methodologies—positivism and a harmonizing, often commonsense hermeneutics—feed on one another and collaborate in diverting attention from the possibility of a more critical apprehension of the actual and desirable interaction between "meaningful" order and challenges to it in society and culture. In this sense, one may ask whether Geertz's entire "hermeneutic" orientation is itself ideological; for he has done much to focus if not fixate attention on the problem of social "meaning," including the way ideology presumably furnishes satisfying "meaning" for the collectivity. He has also tended to replicate the providential task of ideology in his own methodology and style—a fast-paced, eminently readable style that threatens to gloss over certain problems in both culture and its own stylized approach to cultural studies.

Here I must raise a difficulty in my analysis of ideology thus far. I seem to have correlated mystification or dissimulation with deceptive, essentializing, hegemonic modes of "meaningful" order, thereby creating at least by implication the impression that we may correlate "truth" or correctness with division, difference, and heterogeneity. I do, however, resist this implication (which is often associated with poststructuralism) or attribute to it at best a provisional significance as a limited strategy of reversal. But it is, for example, possible to introduce divisions, differences, and complexities into an object of analysis in a distorting and deceptive manner, particularly when one believes that in so doing one is invariably furthering a critical if not subversive movement of theory and praxis. An endlessly "differing" procedure may take thought on increasingly involuted and conceit-laden paths that have at best the most problematic of relations with political and social criticism and may even instill more or less compulsive habits of discourse—what might be called discursive tics douloureux—that can be incapacitating in the attempt to confront sociopolitical and institutional issues. In addition, the one-sided stress on difference or disjunction joins the exclusive emphasis on "meaningful" order in diverting attention from the more general problem of the actual and desirable interaction between unity or order and various challenges to it.

This entire line of inquiry suggests a further point. Ideology may be contrasted with critical and possibly transformative (for Marx, revolutionary but not necessarily redemptive) thought and practice. It need not be construed one-dimensionally as "false consciousness" and placed (as it sometimes was by Marx himself) in a binary opposition with absolute truth (itself often equated with positive science). Anything like social or human science arises, both historically and theoretically, in the recurrent yet variable interaction between ideology and critique, and it cannot be given a purely positivistic or value-neutral status (despite Marx's own inclination at times in this direction). Critique discloses what ideology mystifies, and it does so with implications for praxis. But just as ideology itself cannot be fixated or reified in one essential form, be it in the form of essentializing wholeness or "meaningful" order, so critique is recurrently subject to self-mystification and never entirely transcends this possibility in a realm of absolute truth or pure, value-neutral theory and method.

This kind of argument is not without its internal difficulties. It places science and critique within the same larger model of critical theory. And it makes at best a limited and guarded appeal to universal norms that themselves may be seen as ideological naturalizations or fixations of the recurrent process of argument. (In any case, such norms have at best had an abstractly formal rather than a concretely substantive role in thought.) The approach I am suggesting refers critique to a discursive and argumentative context that itself has no absolute or ultimate grounds—a variable context that cannot even be labeled "pragmatic." This approach perhaps has the minimal

*151*

value of making explicit what processes of inquiry and argument have always been, and it does not pretend to any transcendental or fully systematic (or "totalized") perspective. Rather, it insists on, indeed affirms, the problematic connection of scientific inquiry and ethicopolitical judgment. This approach further implies that the notion of unity or order is limited, contextually variable, and internally contested; but it does not simply eliminate that notion. Nor does it invalidate the idea of accuracy in propositions or the role of hypothesis testing. Rather it attempts to connect empirical-analytic procedures with argumentative strategies in a critical and self-critical conception of discourse and practice that does not rest on ultimate foundations and that explicitly emphasizes the difficult problems of "translating" from context to context and making "transcontextual" normative judgments. This idea of critical theory is, I think, necessary to situate both ideology and science within a more comprehensive yet self-questioning model of research.

This is precisely the type of model that is difficult to locate in Geertz's account; for Geertz runs the risks of voiding social science of a critical dimension and of providing deceptive if not ideological definitions of science itself. The terms in which Geertz, in quest of a "genuinely nonevaluative conception of ideology," opposes science and ideology are particularly instructive:

> The differentiae of science and ideology as cultural systems are to be sought in the sorts of symbolic strategy for encompassing situations that they respectively represent. Science names the structure of situations in such a way that the attitude contained toward them is one of disinterestedness. Its style is restrained, spare, resolutely analytic: by shunning the semantic devices that most effectively formulate moral sentiment, it seeks to maximize intellectual clarity. But ideology names the structure of situations in such a way that the attitude toward them is one of commitment. Its style is ornate, vivid, deliberately suggestive: by objectifying moral sentiment through the same devices that science shuns, it seeks to motivate action. . . . The existence of a vital tradition of scientific analysis of social issues is one of the most effective guarantees against ideological extremism, for it provides an incomparably reliable source of positive knowledge for the political imagination to work with and to honor. It is not

the only such check. The existence . . . of competing ideologies car-
ried by other powerful groups in the society is at least as important;
as is a liberal political system in which the dreams of total power are
obvious fantasies; as are stable social conditions in which conventional expectations are not continually frustrated and conventional
ideas not radically incompetent. But, committed with a quiet intran-
sigence to a vision of its own, it is perhaps the most indomitable.
(Pp. 231-33)

One may well agree with some of the sentiments Geertz expresses
in this passage, notably concerning the importance of relative social
stability, groups with roughly equal power, and traditions of liberal
politics and scientific investigation. But his account threatens to
import a metascientific (or "ideological") conception of science into a
seeming definition of science itself, and in so doing it relies on an
"ornate, vivid, deliberately suggestive" opposition between science and
ideology. Science presumably requires a "disinterested" attitude; a
"restrained, spare, resolutely analytic" style; and a disavowal of extremism. One might object that science itself is not defined by questions
of attitude, rhetoric, and political stance but by certain procedures of
inquiry. What attitude, rhetoric, and politics go with these procedures
cannot be derived from a definition of science itself; they at best constitute either empirical generalizations about scientists or normative
prescriptions about the way scientists ought to behave. The fact that
they are masked and naturalized in a seemingly neutral, universal definition of science may make Geertz's approach "ideological" in the
narrower Marxist sense of the term.

In a footnote, Geertz acknowledges that science and ideology,
while "two sorts of activity," may be combined, although "most
such attempts to mix genres are . . . distinctly less happy" [than the
putative success of Edward Shils in *The Torment of Secrecy*] (p. 231).
But what tends to drop out of Geertz's account is the possibility of
an articulation of science and ethicopolitical judgment in a broader
conception of critical theory. This possibility is not adequately covered by a passing footnote about the role of so-called mixed genres
(later thematized in Geertz as "blurred genres"), a notion parasitic
upon an unargued prior analytic definition of pure genres. Also
obscured are the problems engendered when the concerns active in
the object of study are regenerated in one's account of it—what

*153*

might be called a transferential relation to the object that cannot be transcended through seemingly anodyne definitions of culture, ideology, and science but must be worked through in a careful, critical, and self-critical way.

Indeed the belief that one can avoid or transcend a transferential relation to the object of study tends to foster definitions that are covertly ideological and less subject to critical control than they might otherwise be. What is striking is that Geertz implicitly excludes options between extremism and moderation or neutrality, especially the possibility that certain situations may call for basic criticism that cannot be identified in patently ideological fashion with extremism and irresponsibility. One such situation involves a state of affairs in which just conditions for relative social stability are absent, power is distributed among groups in markedly unequal ways, and traditions of liberal politics and scientific investigation are jeopardized. The only gate Geertz leaves open for criticism is that presumably embodied in science itself, in its ability to "force [ideologies] to come to terms with (but not necessarily surrender to) reality" (p. 232). Yet this notion of criticism receives no further discussion in "Ideology as a Cultural System." Nor is there any recognition that it requires an approach to problems that is not defined by the simple binary opposition between science and ideology. It is, I suggest, in developing this approach that both a critical conception of ideology and a viable relation between science and critique may be most cogently elaborated.

# 6

## Up against the Ear of the Other: Marx after Derrida

> We cannot consider Marx's, Engels's or Lenin's texts as completely finished elaborations that are simply to be "applied" to the current situation. In saying this, I am not advocating anything contrary to "Marxism," I am convinced of it. These texts are not to be read according to a hermeneutical or exegetical method which would seek out a finished signified beneath a textual surface. Reading is transformational. . . . But this transformation cannot be executed however one wishes. It requires protocols of reading. Why not say it bluntly: I have not yet found any that satisfy me.
>
> —Jacques Derrida, *Positions*

Derrida's attitude toward a reading of Marx and "Marxism," particularly one sensitive to the issue of contemporary "relevance," often seems to resemble that of certain Marxists toward revolution in certain contexts: the time is not yet ripe. If one does not see this attitude as merely evasive, it alerts one to difficulties affecting any attempt to address the question of "Marx after Derrida." It would not, I think, be fruitful to take the tack of a traditional *Auseinandersetzung*, especially in light of the fact that Derrida strains not to develop a *Setzung* or position that may be compared and contrasted with Marx's "thought," only to be *aufgehoben* in some putatively larger synthesis. Equally fruitless would be an attempt to emulate one of Derrida's other readings and "apply" it to Marx's texts—in other words, to read Marx *d'après* (or à la) Derrida, who would be more than competent to do this himself if he saw fit.

*155*

Indeed the time may be ripe to retire emulations of Derrida, or at least to take a certain critical distance on them, insofar as they tend either toward unintended parody or toward the generation of a routinized "deconstructive" discourse that is perforce self-defeating. The question of reading and estimating the relevance of Marx after Derrida may in this sense be a heightened version of the general question of reading anything after Derrida. The option I take is that of offering a schema for reading Marx that is alert to the issue of his contemporary relevance or pertinence but not written in Derrida's "voice," although I try to contend with a few of its echoes. But I do not pretend to be in possession of the protocols of reading that Derrida finds lacking. Thus the schema or sketch is preliminary and shall remain so.

The direction Derrida would point any reader of Marx is toward the heterogeneity of his writings and the dubiousness—indeed the ontotheological or logocentric nature—of any claim to have discovered the one true or essential Marx. One may still argue that certain tendencies in Marx are more fruitful than others, but the basis of the argument cannot be the belief that one has returned to the one true or original Marx, whether an early Marx or one situated after an epistemological break. A second direction, however, would be the attempt to relate Marx's written texts to what Derrida terms "*le texte général.*" Derrida's notorious assertion in *Of Grammatology*, il n'y a pas de hors-texte, is often translated as "there is nothing outside the text." The translation is misleading insofar as it induces the idea of a pantextualism, either in the literal and bookish sense (only written texts count; all else is insignificant or derivative) or in the sense of seeing "textuality" as an omnivorous metaphor heavy-handedly, perhaps insensitively, applied to everything under the sun. Derrida is of course not presenting the text (or *écriture* in its revised, paleonymic sense) as a simple metaphor, in relation to which everything else may be seen as a "text analogue." He attempts to elaborate a "notion" of the text on a simulated "foundational" level that, through the deconstructive strategies of reversal and generalized displacement, unsettles any attempt to postulate a foundation or a "transcendental signified" purely and simply beyond the work and play of "textuality." In this sense, a somewhat better translation of his assertion might be: "there is no outside-the-text." But, as I have intimated, this translation is better only insofar as one understands it to imply that there is no "inside-the-text" either—no pure and virginal form or meaning amenable to an uncontaminated formalistic or hermeneutic reading and referable to an unconstrained play of liberated or transcendental signifiers. The assertion thus "refers" one to *le texte général*.

To a limited extent, the latter notion may be specified in terms of the relation between written texts and larger discourses and institutions of production and reception. Derrida has increasingly insisted upon the role of discursive and institutional practices, and he has stressed the point that, given its institutional bearing, deconstruction is not simply a hermeneutic but a political practice.[1] Here, however, the "Marx after Derrida" relation may become subject to the figure of chiasmus (fittingly enough, an almost obsessive favorite of both Marx and Derrida), and one may pose the question of Derrida after Marx. This kind of reversal, which is not to be fixated or fetishized, may nonetheless help take deconstruction further into the area in which Marx laid the groundwork and wherein his thought, at least in modified form, retains its "relevance": the critical theory of commodification and of its relation to other discursive and institutional contexts in society.

In Marx's case, I think it is fruitful to begin the elaboration of a schema for reading by relating the question of heterogeneous tendencies or tensions in his writing to that of variations in its reception. For I suggest that different readings of Marx tend, to a greater or lesser extent, to emphasize one or another, or perhaps some combination, of the tensely related tendencies in his writing. With respect to reception, I shall, however, be merely indicative and restrict myself to mentioning some of the more classic, widely disseminated, and influential "interpretations" of Marx among intellectuals and academics. On the more difficult question of the use and abuse of Marx by political regimes, I simply note that the inter-

[1] See, for example, "Entre crochets," *Digraphe* 8 (1976); "Philosophie des Etats Généraux," in *Etats Généraux de la philosophie* (Paris, 1979); *La carte postale: De Socrate à Freud et au-delà* (Paris, 1980); "No Apocalypse, Not Now," *Diacritics* 14 (1984); and *The Ear of the Other*, ed. Christie McDonald, trans. Peggy Kamuf (1982; New York, 1985). The variable cogency and effectiveness of the political analyses or interventions in these works is an issue into which I shall not enter here. My primary purpose with respect to deconstruction in this chapter is heuristic.

pretation of Marx in nonheterogeneous, indeed monolithic, terms serves the interests of both his opponents and his proponents, particularly (but not exclusively) in the Cold War context. If there is one true Marx (say, the Marxist-Leninist Marx, often equated with the later or postepistemological-break Marx), one state or party may plausibly stand forth as the bearer of the Marxist message and justify its actual or desired position of dominance in relation to other Marxist states or parties. Conversely, the idea of one true Marx may be used to reinforce the image of a monolithic world-communist movement, directed from a political center. In both cases, the issue is not simply interpretive but political; for the idea of one true Marx obscures or occults actual differences and divisions within Marxist states, parties, and movements. Even when the homogenizing interpretation of Marx is ostensibly made to oppose pretensions of political dominance (say, by identifying the early, humanistic, Hegelian Marx as the one true Marx), the results are dubious not only as readings of Marx but as bases for democratic politics, because they typically avoid or gloss over less desirable aspects of the putatively homogeneous Marx.

As may be partially anticipated from the foregoing, my schema or sketch entails focusing upon three interacting and tensely related tendencies in Marx's texts, a choice I cannot absolutely justify. Indeed, aside from its inevitable reductionism, this choice courts the danger of adapting my own reading to the model of speculative dialectics (thus paradoxically returning, on a seemingly higher level, what will be the third of my tendencies to the first). This danger too I cannot entirely avoid, although I attempt to resist it through vigilance in articulating both the relations among the tendencies and the limited pertinence of speculative dialectics in a field it does not entirely dominate. Furthermore, while the first two tendencies are to some extent opposed to one another, the third is not their speculative synthesis or *Aufhebung*; at most, it situates certain of their aspects in a displaced and limited manner.

The three tendencies are (1) a Hegelian and utopian tendency related to the widespread idea of a messianic Marx; (2) a positivistic tendency whereby Marxism becomes a deterministic theory of the laws of motion of capitalist society and world history; and (3) a tendency toward what may be termed a complex, supplemented

dialectic. These three tendencies (to which I shall return) are over-
laid by two strains in Marx's thought. The first, related especially
to the Hegelian-utopian and positivistic tendencies, involves Marx's
seeming acceptance of the assumptions of an approach he criticizes
on other levels. With reference to speculative dialectics, which
often appears as the dominant force in Hegel's texts, Marx often
seems to accept a productivist, totalizing idea of historical process
but to replace *Geist* and its modern bearer, the bureaucracy, with
the proletariat as the driving force and the truly universal class.
With reference to classical economics, Marx seems to combine the
idea that it accurately formulated certain "laws" of an alienated
commodity system with the acceptance in his own voice of certain
of its postulates, such as a labor theory of value. (Thus Foucault
was induced, in *The Order of Things*, to situate Marx within the
same *episteme* as Ricardo—indeed to present the two simply as rip-
ples in the same pool.) I see this first strain as inducing a fallback
position. Marx falls back upon, or remains fixated at the "phase"
of reversing the terms of, a form of thought he questions.

A second strain is most closely related to a complex, supplemented dialectic. It involves Marx in a more thorough-going critique of existing theories and practices, a critique both immanent
and situationally transcendent. Marx attempts to dismantle basic
assumptions, render them radically problematic, and indicate the
possibility of a transformed way of thought and life. As Marx put
it as early as his 1844 article "For a Ruthless Criticism of Everything Existing," "We do not attempt dogmatically to prefigure the
future, but want to find the new world only through criticism of
the old."[2] Or as Marx indicated even earlier in a dense and far from
homogeneous passage in his doctoral dissertation, the worldly
transformation of philosophy might be seen as its carnivalization,
and in the process of becoming the world or weaving intrigues with
it, philosophy did not provide total transparency but underwent the
need to wear masks:

[2] *The Marx-Engels Reader*, (2d ed.), ed. Robert C. Tucker (New York, 1978), p.
13. Since the quotations from Marx that I employ are contained in this readily
accessible volume, all further references are to it and are included in the text. This
text (as well as most others cited in my notes) serves my purposes particularly well

As in the history of philosophy there are nodal points which raise philosophy in itself to concretion, apprehend abstract principles in a totality, and thus break off the rectilinear process, so also there are moments when philosophy turns its eyes to the external world, and no longer apprehends it, but, as a practical person, weaves, as it were, intrigues with the world, emerges from the transparent kingdom of Amenthes and throws itself on the breast of the worldly Siren. That is the carnival of philosophy, whether it disguises itself as a dog like the Cynic, in priestly vestments like the Alexandrian, or in fragrant spring array like the Epicurean. It is essential that philosophy should then wear character masks. As Deucalion, according to the legend, cast stones behind him in creating human beings, so philosophy casts its regard behind it (the bones of its mother are luminous eyes) when its heart is set on creating a world; but as Prometheus, having stolen fire from heaven, begins to build houses and to settle upon the earth, so philosophy, expanded to be the whole world, turns against the world of appearance. The same now with the philosophy of Hegel. (Pp. 10-11)

Let us return to the three tendencies without losing sight of the more dynamic relations indicated in the notion of two contestatory strains. Marx always criticized Hegel's contemplative bias or "owl-of-Minerva" conception of philosophy, but he did not consistently attempt a carnivalesque uncrowning of it that would distance a materialist from a speculative dialectic. In one tendency of his thought, Marx adapted the seemingly dominant structure of Hegelian dialectics and simply reversed it or "turned it on its feet" by substituting "material" ("men," the proletariat) for "ideal" agents. This has been termed (for example, by Shlomo Avineri) Marx's

---

in that it is not restricted in its readership to a small group with a particular ideological or theoretical perspective. It has been important in presenting Marx to a rather large audience, especially of students and academics, and its introductory material and notes—often colored by Tucker's own interpretations—should be read critically. Harold Mah's useful critical review of recent literature on Marx, "Marxism's 'Truth': Recent Interpretations of Marxist Theory" (*The Journal of Modern History* 61 [1989], 110-27) appeared when this book was in press. In limited ways, its argument converges with that of this chapter.

Feuerbachian, transformative criticism of Hegel.[3] Relying on Feuerbach's example, Marx inverts the relation between the subject and the predicate in the Hegelian sentence so that humans attain the status of active subjects of history and *Geist* becomes a predicate. But, as Althusser has indicated, a reversal of this sort, while perhaps necessary, is not sufficient as radical critique; for the dialectic on its feet remains "Hegelian."[4] The grammar and syntax of speculative dialectics remain the same even if the lexicon changes. In Derrida's terms, the "phase" of reversal, which is necessary in that binary oppositions like matter and spirit are ordered in a hierarchy, must be supplemented by a general displacement and rearticulation of relations if a "critique" is to be effective.

In my own initial delineation of what I am terming the first tendency in Marx's thought, I linked the Hegelian and the utopian. The two are not identical and from other perspectives (particularly one defining the utopian in terms of situational transcendence) can be distinguished. The sense of "utopian" I am using is, moreover, not Marx's. In *The Communist Manifesto*, Marx characterizes utopianism in terms of a blueprint of the future, local solutions to general problems, and inadequate theory inadequately related to practice. "Utopian" in the sense I am using it may overlap at points with Marx's conception but does not coincide with it. What I am designating as utopian is the hope for a total, definitive solution to problems, in a new society, through total synthesis and reconciliation of opposites. I am, in brief, approximating utopianism to secular messianism. In Hegel, utopianism in this sense takes the form of a philosophy of identity: at (and as) the end of history, total reconciliation, healing the wounds of the past without leaving scars, would terminate and fulfill history as we know it, making total retrospective sense of experience.

Especially in his early work, Marx at times seems close to a "materialist" and activist rendition of this end-game fiction or Chris-

---

[3] See the discussion in Shlomo Avineri, *The Social and Political Thought of Karl Marx* (Cambridge, 1970).

[4] Louis Althusser, *For Marx*, trans. Ben Brewster (1965; London, 1977); idem, *Reading Capital*, trans. Ben Brewster (1968; London, 1970).

tian heresy. One may, for example, refer to the following famous passage from *The Economic and Philosophic Manuscripts of 1844*:

> *Communism* as the *positive* transcendence of *private property*, or *human self-estrangement*, and therefore as the real *appropriation of the human essence* by and for man; communism therefore as the complete return of man to himself as a *social* (i.e., human) being—a return become conscious, and accomplished within the entire wealth of previous development. This communism, as fully-developed naturalism, equals humanism, and as fully-developed humanism equals naturalism; it is the *genuine* resolution of the conflict between man and nature and between man and man—the true resolution of the strife between existence and essence, between objectification and self-confirmation, between freedom and necessity, between the individual and the species. Communism is the riddle of history solved, and it knows itself to be this solution. (P. 84)

This and like passages seem fully to confirm Althusser's understanding of the young Marx as entirely within the problematic of German idealism and as presenting an essentializing humanism as the ultimate solution to the problems of society and history. But, aside from the idyllic portrait of society without the division of labor in *The German Ideology*, such later mainstays as the classless society, the withering away of the state, and the reign of freedom (discussed in the third volume of *Capital*) seem to resonate with an earlier utopianism either in terms of a full reconciliation of opposites or (as with the "reign of freedom") at least in terms of an unproblematic reliance upon simple binary oppositions (such as work and leisure).

Two notoriously dubious aspects of Marx's thought may be correlated with his Hegelian tendency, the first quite clearly and the other more hesitantly: his attitude toward colonialism and his de-emphasis of feminism. His willingness, despite his acute perception of their ravages, to justify colonialism and imperialism as "functional" forces in bringing "underdeveloped" areas, such as India, into the mainstream of world-historical development is itself a function of his acceptance of a totalizing and teleological conception of historical movement. (In the more recent past, a domesticated and more aseptically functionalist derivative of speculative dialectics has of course been prominent, for example, in the understanding of bombing raids in Vietnam as a factor in forced urbanization.) The following quotation from a newspaper article published by Marx in 1853 could quite literally have been written by Hegel as an illustration of the "cunning of reason": "England, it is true, in causing a social revolution in Hindustan, was actuated only by the vilest interests, and was stupid in her manner of enforcing them. But that is not the question. The question is, can mankind fulfill its destiny without a fundamental revolution in the social state of Asia? If not, whatever may have been the crimes of England she was the unconscious tool of history in bringing about that revolution" (p. 658).

The small role played by the question of women's rights in Marx—and in Marxism more generally until recently—can perhaps be understood in part through the inclination to see social and political issues in the light of a dominant contradiction and a dominant historical process of development. The idea that the relation between labor and capital constitutes the dominant issue easily shades off into the idea that other issues can take a back seat and will largely solve themselves, once the primary contradiction is resolved. Barbara Taylor has plausibly argued, in her *Eve and the New Jerusalem*, that the dominance of Marxism in the labor movement by the end of the nineteenth century was itself a principal force in occluding women's issues that earlier had a prominent, albeit problematic, place in Owenite socialism.[5]

I simply note, in extremely abbreviated fashion, that the Hegelian and utopian reading of Marx has, in one form or another, been important to both his defenders and his opponents. His defenders have resorted to it to combat narrowly positivistic readings and at times to oppose developments in existing communist regimes. Hegelian Marxism received its most influential and probably its most powerful formulation in Lukács's *History and Class Consciousness* (1923), but it has also received varied renditions in the work

---

[5] *Eve and the New Jerusalem: Socialism and Feminism in the Nineteenth Century* (New York, 1983). Marx's anti-Semitism derives in part from the anti-particularistic, speculatively dialectical quest for higher unity, but it also draws from "enlightened" cosmopolitan universalism and the civic tradition's suspicion of commerce.

of figures as diverse as Marcuse, Sartre, Fromm, and Jameson.[6] Among critics of Marx and Marxism, it has been instrumental in Popper's indictment of the ideological origins of totalitarianism, Camus's critique of the combination of nihilism and utopianism in revolutionary movements, and Aron's quest for antidotes to the "opium of the intellectuals."[7] It has of course also recently resurfaced in the antigulag liberalism of the so-called *nouveaux philosophes* (whose novelty seems largely restricted to recycling the views of such figures as Camus, Aron, and Orwell). Much academic scholarship has also stressed the Hegelian and utopian roots of Marxism. Robert Tucker's massively repetitive rendition of this theme may perhaps be taken as emblematic of an entire school of liberal scholarship.[8] More subtle renditions may be found in Avineri's argument that Marx's later thought is but a corollory to his early Hegelianism and in István Meszáros's view that *The Economic and Philosophic Manuscripts* is the key that cracks the entire code of Marx's thought through a theory of alienation and its dialectical *Aufhebung*.[9] At times, however, certain of the figures I have mentioned (notably Marcuse, Sartre, and Lukács's disciple, Meszáros) put forth views that sit uneasily with a homogeneous "Hegelian" Marxism (or with an excessively one-dimensional reading of Hegel himself)—views that are closer to what I shall discuss as an open, supplemented dialectic.

The second major tendency in interpreting Marx's thought is to see it as a positivistic "science" giving us facts, laws, and mechanisms of causal determinism or historical inevitability. Positivism in

---

[6] See, for example, Herbert Marcuse, *Reason and Revolution: Hegel and the Rise of Social Theory* (1941; New York, 1954); Jean-Paul Sartre, *La critique de la raison dialectique* (Paris, 1960); Erich Fromm, Foreword to *Karl Marx: Selected Writings in Sociology & Social Philosophy*, trans. T. B. Bottomore (New York, 1956); Fredric Jameson, *The Political Unconscious* (Ithaca, N.Y., 1981).

[7] Karl Popper, *The Open Society and Its Enemies* (London, 1945); idem, *The Poverty of Historicism* (New York, 1944); Albert Camus, *The Rebel* (1951; New York, 1956); Raymond Aron, *The Opium of the Intellectuals*, trans. Terence Kilmartin (1957; Garden City, N.Y., 1957).

[8] See, for example, Robert C. Tucker, *Philosophy and Myth in Karl Marx* (New York, 1961).

[9] See Avineri, *Social and Political Thought of Karl Marx*, and István Meszáros, *Marx's Theory of Alienation* (1970; New York, 1972).

one sense represents the extreme deflation of utopianism. But it may also be combined with utopianism when the laws of economic development are construed as leading automatically to revolution and the realization of the new society. On a more cognitive level, the powerful belief that the economy is determinative "in the last analysis" can itself become a dogmatic center of reliance providing utopian knowledge of history—a center of reliance that becomes utopian in the etymological sense when the "lonely hour of the last analysis," like Godot, never comes. It should, however, go without saying that positivism (or scientism) ought not be identified with science. Indeed, by autonomizing or essentializing the constative dimension of language, positivism obscures both the historical and the theoretical grounds for scientific activity.

Those affiliated with the Frankfurt school often saw Marx as a positivist in order to criticize him for this tendency. For Marx as a positivist was part of the problem for critical theorists of society and culture. In their critique of humanism, productivism, and the "dialectics of Enlightenment," Adorno and Horkheimer were suspicious of Marx to the extent that he saw society as a great workhouse; placed man on top of everything, including mother nature; and one-sidedly stressed the Promethean urge to master the other.[10] Marcuse took his distance from the same Marx and tried to counter him through an appeal to more romantic, receptive, and aesthetic overtures he found in the young Marx himself (among others).[11] More recently, Habermas, from a significantly different perspective, has argued that Marx became involved in a positivistic self-misunderstanding and conflated work and symbolic interaction in a manner destructive to any critical and emancipatory theory of society.[12] For Habermas's disciple Albrecht Wellmer, Marx was not above being a vulgar Marxist, and even a work such as *The German Ideology* is suffused with uncritical positivistic motifs.[13]

Positivist interpretations of Marx are one area in which critical

---

[10] Max Horkheimer and Theodor W. Adorno, *The Dialectics of Enlightenment* (1944; New York, 1972).

[11] See especially *Eros and Civilization* (1955; New York, 1962).

[12] *Knowledge and Human Interests*, trans. Jeremy J. Shapiro (1968; Boston, 1971).

[13] *Critical Theory of Society* (1969; New York, 1971).

theorists are in agreement with social scientists, whom they typically criticize. But these social scientists counter Marx not with an insistence upon the need to integrate empirical and analytic research into a paradigm of critical theory but with even more positivistic research procedures. Max Weber provided the formula for the partial co-optation of Marx into positivistic social science when he interpreted him as furnishing a consistent but one-sided ideal type or model of the relation of the economy to society, a model that had to be complemented with other models. Marx is thus effectively reduced to the theorist of the economic variable.[14]

Yet there is an important sense in which Weber, whatever the unearned benefits accruing to later social scientists from his work, was simply taking Marxists of his own day at their word. For the positivistic interpretation of Marx was canonized by the later Engels and theorists of the Second International. Although his work certainly cannot be reduced to this side of it, Engels did provide a convenient image of Marx as the Darwin of society, who discovered its laws of motion.[15] With a similar caveat, Althusser may be seen in part as elaborating the most subtle positivistic rendition of Marxism in the context of contemporary structural and poststructural thought. With agents as the *Träger* of structural relations and with ideology interpreted, via Lacanian psychoanalysis, as centered on the subject, Althusser could occult the possibility of objectivist ideologies, like the one toward which he at times veered.[16] It is significant that he initially construed *The German Ideology* as the scene of the famous (and increasingly elusive) epistemological break in Marx's thought; it is the very work that Wellmer, from the perspective of critical theory, interpreted as a prime locus of positivistic inclinations.

The complexity of Marx's texts is evident from the fact that one cannot dismiss any of the interpretations I have briefly mentioned as simply wrong. Yet they tend not to pose explicitly the problem of tensions in Marx's thought, and they also tend to take one

[14] See, for example, the selections included under the heading "Class, Status, Party," in H. H. Gerth and C. Wright Mills, *From Max Weber* (New York, 1946), pp. 180-95, as well as the discussion in the introduction, pp. 46-50.

[15] See Engels's "Speech at the Graveside of Karl Marx," in *The Marx-Engels Reader*, pp. 681-82.

[16] See Althusser, *Reading Capital* and *Lenin and Philosophy*, trans. Ben Brewster (New York, 1971).

tendency in Marx as representing the true Marx. I maintain that there indeed are Hegelian-utopian and positivistic tendencies in Marx. And it is plausible to argue that the former are pronounced in the early Marx, while the latter are more insistent in the later Marx. (Who, for example, can read *The Economic and Philosophic Manuscripts* without being aware of the Hegelian subtext even when Hegel is the direct object of criticism?) But there is no total split or break on this basis. The Hegelian-utopian aspects of the later Marx and the positivistic aspects of the early Marx are not insignificant. The problem in the reading of Marx in this respect is that of reading historical processes more generally: to wit, deciphering the interaction between continuity and discontinuity, repetition and change. Change can indeed be traumatically disruptive. The changes wrought by capitalism and secularism were precisely of this sort for Marx, even when he did not construe them in terms of simple discontinuity. How the changes in his own thought over time are to be understood and evaluated is a more difficult problem. And it is exacerbated by the role of an often ignored third tendency (or bundle of tendencies) in his texts, which is difficult to locate in terms of the contrast between the early and the late Marx. It is what I am calling a complex or supplemented dialectic. For convenience sake, I furnish the following diagram of it:

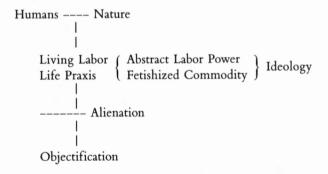

I call this dialectic "supplemented" because its basic terms are not simple binary opposites, and this point helps account for the very complexity of the processes it designates. Humans are part of nature, and there is a natural dimension to human beings. (This is one sense of Marx's materialism.) Neither humans nor nature may be taken as the simple origin of the other. Humans and nature have a "supplementary" relation to one another. In addition, the human being is dual, both active and receptive in relation to others. (Many statements in *The Economic and Philosophic Manuscripts* as well as in the *Grundrisse*, for example, may be read in the light of these contentions.)

The interaction between humans and nature takes place as life praxis or living labor in some unfamiliar, displaced, paleonymic sense; it always produces objectification but not necessarily alienation and ideology, which, under capitalism, assume the form of abstract labor power, exchange value, and commodity fetishism. In *The Economic and Philosophic Manuscripts*, Marx criticizes Hegel for conflating alienation and objectification in that, given Hegel's speculatively idealist assumptions, all objectifications of *Geist* are *eo ipso* alienations that must be overcome. Whether this is an altogether acceptable critique of Hegel or whether Marx's own "supplemented" dialectic is best seen as a more extended enactment and partial thematization of relatively submerged aspects of Hegel's thought, it is quite important for Marx's own argument. But how are we to understand "labor" and "alienation"?

Notably in his later texts, Marx, seemingly in his own voice, will employ labor in the sense of purely economic, narrowly instrumental work—a usage related to his positivistic tendency more generally. But throughout his texts, he also situates this kind of labor—as well as classical economics, which theorized labor's role—as "alienated" aspects of capitalism itself. Under capitalism there is a reduction of living labor to abstract labor power that is construed in technical, instrumental ways as a means toward the end of producing commodities. Labor as life praxis in some fuller, more ambivalent, but less easily definable sense (as it appears in *The Economic and Philosophic Manuscripts* or the *Grundrisse*, for example) involves not one-sided, analytic reductions but modes of interaction between humans and nature, work and play, productivity and receptivity, senses and intellect, men and women. This living labor mediates and supplements relations. It does not entail a unilateral appropriation or domination of nature for restricted and typically self-defeating human interests.

The speculatively dialectical side of Marx readily situates living labor in a lost golden age of primitive communism that, after the trial and turmoil of recorded class history, will be recovered on a higher level in the revolutionary future. It also presents a notion of human essence, often interpreted in terms of infinite potential and Promethean productive power that will be, paradoxically enough, fully realized when humans come into their own. Overcoming ideology itself will bring full truth and transparency, as all relations will become simple and totally intelligible. I could go on, but this side of Marx is well known and has been invoked by commentators time and again.

In a supplemented dialectic, things are significantly different. Overcoming ideology is a recurrent practice that never fully succeeds nor can promise (actually or counterfactually) an "ideal speech situation." It involves recurrent criticism and self-criticism without absolute foundations (however formal), but it certainly requires a measure of distance on the self and a willingness to argue for commitments or courses of action. The very distinction between alienation and objectification requires a nonidentification of alienation and alterity, that is, an active recognition of differences that cannot be fully transcended or reconciled but that can be lived and thought differently. In this sense, there would be otherness and the tension engendered by otherness in any consensus, but not all otherness need give rise to alienation. Nor need any form of otherness, however open to criticism and sanction, be subject to a scapegoating mechanism that provides an unearned sense of purity and innocence for the ingroup. Indeed the question opened (but not definitively decided) by a supplemented dialectic is the relation between modes of difference or otherness that are to be actively tolerated, perhaps even affirmed, and those that call for criticism and transformation. The system of wage labor and capital certainly involved differences for Marx, but they were kinds of differences calling for major change. Indeed Marx's move, which was not simply rhetorical, was to see wage labor as having been equated with prostitution; there was from his perspective little difference between a modern system of sex for money and one requiring the sale of living labor. For when the differences are too "clear and distinct" and too incisively hierarchical, they will involve identities that are too homogeneous (as well as a desire for a grand identity that will bring it all together in the end). Alienation, in a sense distinct from alterity in general, itself involved pure binary oppositions between seemingly homogeneous identities (for example, between capital and labor or, in another register, between instrumental work and meaning or symbolic interaction); it also required ideology to naturalize or essentialize it and conceal its problematic, historically variable nature.

I have of course been interpreting Marx rather freely in my attempt to give some notion of at least general directions indicated by a supplemented dialectic. I have employed the term "supplemented dialectic" rather than simply using "supplementarity" because I think that in Marx there is always a fruitful tension between unification and contestation in the attempt to address issues and to relate theory and practice. However challenged—in enabling or disabling ways—unification may be, there is nonetheless a strong drive toward synthesis and a forceful desire to overcome a historical situation judged to be intolerable. Yet this drive and this desire do not necessarily take dogmatic or speculatively dialectical form *sans plus*. The notion of a supplemented dialectic may help in stimulating our efforts to see how this may be so in Marx's texts and in his hopes for society.

I now turn briefly to two texts to elucidate more specifically what is at stake in this notion and in the way it is intertwined, at times inextricably, with Marx's other tendencies in his textual practice: *The German Ideology* and *Capital*. In the former, I address the problem of the understanding of history and temporality. In the latter, I inquire into the reading of the very difficult initial sections (the portion of the text that Althusser recommends we defer or avoid reading until we have read virtually everything else in Marx).

Early in *The German Ideology*, Marx writes:

> The premises from which we begin are not arbitrary ones, not dogmas, but real premises from which abstraction can only be made in imagination. They are the real individuals, their activity and the material conditions under which they live, both those which they find already existing and those produced by their activity. These premises can thus be verified in a purely empirical way.
>
> The first premise of all human history is, of course, the existence of living human individuals. (P. 149)

Marx here opposes "Hegelianism" by posing an affront to the concept and to logocentrism. A living human individual is not a premise or a point of origin in any conceptual or logical sense. But the opposition to "German ideology" seems to take the form of a regression to empiricism that falls behind the level of critical insight Hegel attained, and it accords both with the repeated, uncritical invocations to the real and the empirical in the text and with its positivistic conception of stages of historical development culminating in a putatively demystified science. The critique of German ideology becomes fixated at the phase of reversal, and Marx's ascension from earth to heaven (in contrast to the idealist descent from heaven to earth) leads him to envision "morality, religion, metaphysics, all the rest of ideology" as derivative phenomena devoid of history—"reflexes and echoes," "phantoms formed in the human brain," "sublimates of . . . material life process, which is empirically verifiable and bound to material premises" (p. 154). There is even a phantomlike echo of the thought of Auguste Comte, wherein philosophy is replaced by scientific abstracts—"a summing-up of the most general results, abstractions which arise from the observation of the historical development of men" (p. 155).

But there are other themes and movements in the text whereby positivism, including a positivist dialectic of stages of historical development, is problematized by a more intricate notion of historical and social processes. When he comes to his section on history, Marx repeats in more extended form the arguments he has already elaborated, and he does so with significant variations that involve curious repetitions in the very replays of the arguments he has already made. He again invokes "a first premise of human existence and, therefore, of all history, the premise namely, that men must be in a position to live in order to be able to 'make history'" (pp. 155-56), and he supplements it with a cryptic marginal note: "*Hegel.* Geological, hydrographical, etc., conditions. Human bodies. Needs, labour" (thus leaving us in doubt whether he is criticizing Hegel or appealing to his authority in contradistinction to the "Hegelian" antics of his successors). He also asserts, "The first historical act is thus the production of the means to satisfy these needs, the production of material life itself" (p. 156). Production to satisfy needs, a rather utilitarian and instrumental activity, thus seems to have priority as the "first historical act." But Marx begins the next paragraph with the words "The second point is that the satisfaction of the first need (the action of satisfying, and the instrument of satisfaction which has been acquired) leads to new ones; and this production of new needs is the first historical act" (p. 156). Thus we have two "first" historical acts—production to satisfy needs and the production of new needs—indicating either that Marx is hopelessly confused or that there is no original act in the historical process. After mentioning the "third circumstance which, from the very outset, enters into historical development"—the family (itself repeated in more extended form in the fourth "moment" of general social relations)—he asserts, "These three aspects of social activity are not of course to be taken as three different stages, but just as three aspects or, to make it clear to the Germans, three 'moments,' which have existed simultaneously since the dawn of history and the first men, and which still assert themselves in history today" (p. 157). And he immediately adds, "The production of life, both of one's own labour and of fresh life in procreation, now appears as a double relationship: on the one hand as a natural, on the other as a social relationship" (p. 157).

Thus, at least at this level of analysis, there is (except for expository constraints, which should not be underestimated) no question of discrete, serialized stages of development or of absolute origins. A process exists of relational interaction among elements that cannot be construed as simple binary opposites. The temporality at issue is repetitive, and it is reproduced with variations in specific historical conditions. Marx, later in the text, even rejects, in no uncertain terms, a teleological understanding of stages of development in particular historical sequences, and he employs the trope of chiasmus to mark its limits:

> History is nothing but the succession of the separate generations, each of which exploits the materials, the capital funds, the productive forces handed down to it by all preceding generations, and thus, on the one hand, continues the traditional activity in completely changed circumstances and, on the other, modifies the old circumstances with a completely changed activity. This can be speculatively distorted so that later history is made the goal of earlier history, e.g.,

the goal ascribed to the discovery of America is to further the eruption of the French Revolution. Thereby history receives its own special aims and becomes 'a person ranking with other persons' (to wit:
'Self-Consciousness, Criticism, the Unique' etc.), while what is designated with the words 'destiny,' 'goal,' 'germ,' or 'ideal' of earlier
history is nothing more than an abstraction formed from later history, from the active influence which earlier history exercises on
later history. (P. 172)

Yet in his own account of historical development after his discussion of the four "primary" aspects, Marx himself serializes stages
leading up to the division of labor, and it is unclear whether he is
proposing an actual historical sequence. In his brief comment on
language, he subordinates the problem of consciousness to it (in
terms both "materialistic" and phonocentric; for "'spirit' is afflicted
with the curse of being 'burdened' with matter, which here makes
its appearance in the form of agitated layers of air, sounds, in short,
language"), and he subordinates both consciousness and language
to "need, the necessity of intercourse with other men" (pp.
157-58). Again, the conception seems positivistic and utilitarian,
but again it is unclear whether an actual sequence is being proposed. A break or disruptive variation does, nonetheless, seem to
supervene, with the division between material and mental labor as
the most essential form of the division of labor in general. Before
this (real or fictive?) point, language is presumably "directly inter-
woven with the material activity and material intercourse of real
men, the language of real life" (p. 154). After it, language becomes
ideological mystification as "'pure' theory, theology, philosophy,
ethics, etc." (p. 159). The conception of language reinforces both
a golden age mythology and the promise of its *Aufhebung* in the
pastoral idyll ("hunt in the morning, fish in the afternoon, rear cat-
tle in the evening, criticize after dinner, just as I have a mind to,
without ever becoming hunter, fisherman, shepherd or critic," p.
160) that Marx proposes as the positive transcendence of the division of labor. (I must confess that this idyll has, for some time, sent
chills down my spine, for it actually seems to correspond to the
lives of people I know in Ithaca, New York.) This pastoral utopia
is of course rather atypical in Marx, and it jars with his frequent
argument that a transformed society must integrate the achieve-

*173*

ments of science and technology. (Naturally, it is more difficult to imagine being a brain surgeon in the morning, a roofer in the afternoon, a nuclear physicist in the evening, and a more or less informed literary critic after dinner.) Marx's naive utopia has the merit, however, of forcing the issue of simplification and the economy of losses and gains it entails. It also is a hyperbolic version of the demand for significant work that is viably related to play in a rhythm of social life beyond the institutional possibilities of instrumentalized labor and leisure time. Thus reaction to its naiveté should not be made to obliterate the critique of extreme division of labor, prominently including the divorce (or binary opposition) between manual and mental labor.

The heterogeneous currents—indeed the divisions—in the textual movement of the initial sections of *Capital* are no less marked than those in *The German Ideology*. In the afterword to the second German edition, Marx provides his retrospective self-interpretation. In it he is both positivistic and dialectical in a reversed "Hegelian" manner, and he even seems to identify the two tendencies. With apparent agreement, he quotes from a Russian reviewer's analysis of *Capital*, which concludes with the words "The scientific value of such an inquiry lies in the disclosing of the special laws that regulate the origin, existence, development, death of a given social organism and its replacement by another and higher one. And it is this value that, in point of fact, Marx's book has" (p. 301). Marx immediately adds, "Whilst the writer pictures what he takes to be actually my method, in this striking and [as far as concerns my own application of it] generous way, what else is he picturing but the dialectic method?" (p. 301). Thus Marx's method appears to be identical with the positivistic method, indeed with a variant of social Darwinism, which discloses in purely objective fashion the laws of motion of the modern economy that lead to the collapse of capitalism and its transcendence by a higher social organism. And "Hegelianism" is reversed: "With him [Hegel] it [the dialectic] is standing on its head. It must be turned right side up again, if you would discover the rational kernel within the mystical shell" (p. 302). The rational kernel in this proleptic reading seems to be a positivistic dialectic conflating what I earlier distinguished as two tendencies in Marx and leaving little room for the third.

174

Yet the text of *Capital* can itself be read, against the grain of the afterword, in at least two ways. It can indeed be (and of course quite often has been) read as an exposition of the positivistic dialectic of the laws of capitalistic development that automatically lead to the collapse of the system (either in fact or as a tendential regularity of the system analyzed in model-like, laboratory conditions). Here Marx seems to elaborate concepts, make distinctions, and develop arguments in his own right (or in his own unified voice) to show how capitalism will lead to collapse. In so doing, he seems to be the most lucid of the classical economists (vide Foucault). Read in another way, however, *Capital* is a critical theory of classical economics and the market-based commodity system it was supposed to ground (and legitimate) theoretically. Here Marx is inquiring critically, systematically, and historically into the assumptions of a system and its theoretical foundations in a fashion that renders them radically problematic. And the role of agents is crucial in the attempt to change that system. The nodal point in this second reading is not the automatic working out of laws of motion but the assumptions involved in reducing living labor to abstract labor power and exchange value, bringing into being a quasi-deterministic but alienated world.

These two readings, and the two levels or movements of Marx's text that they portend to disclose, coexist, but their relations are agonistic if not contradictory. On the first reading, Marx seems altogether committed to the validity of concepts like abstract labor power, the binary opposition between use and exchange value, and "naturalistic" historical inevitability. He calls the "recent discovery that the products of labour, so far as they are values, are but the material expressions of the human labour power spent on their products" something that marks "an epoch in the history of the development of the human race" (p. 322). On the second reading, he is taking a critical distance on these concepts and indicating that they apply only to an alienated state of society. The status of [exchange] value, as the expression of abstract labor power, is itself that of an expression or articulation of alienation. Often in the opening theoretical sections of *Capital*, Marx seems closest to a positivistic dialectic, at least before the section on commodity fetishism. But there are important signs of a supplemented dialectical model and of critical theory.

The principal text of *Capital* begins with a discussion of the com-modity form, but it does so in a confusing way, at least for the reader. Marx starts by making abstract distinctions to investigate the commodity form in a seemingly value-neutral fashion, and he appears to be speaking entirely in his own voice. He distinguishes between use-value and exchange-value as if this binary opposition were altogether clear and unproblematic. In discussing these con-cepts, Marx is heavily indebted to the metaphysical tradition. Use-value, we are told, relates to the utility, intrinsic nature, substance, quality, and materiality of the commodity. As use-values, commodi-ties are purely different from one another. Exchange value, by con-trast, relates to the form, extrinsic character, magnitude, exchangea-bility, and substitutability of the commodity in relation to other commodities. Exchange-value is on the side of identity. Indeed, use-value seems to be the rational kernel and exchange-value the mystical shell of the commodity. Use-value is presumably immedi-ately transparent and poses no problems. One wears a coat, for example, to keep warm. Yet there is a sense in which use-value is difficult to understand. As the binary opposite of exchange-value, it would seem implicated in the same general system, and the very dichotomy between utility and exchange should pose a problem as a mode of alienation. At most, the stress on use-value would be stra-tegically significant as a reversal of a dominant hierarchy, but once again Marx seems fixated at this "phase" of a critical operation, and the tendency to take use-value as entirely unproblematic is ques-tionable. (Whether use-value itself intimates a generalized displace-ment of assumptions as a "deconstructive lever" tending toward some less restricted notion of use is a question whose answer would be more available if we had a critical genealogy of the concept.)

Exchange-value, for Marx, is mysterious. As exchange-values, commodities are exchangeable in that they may be replaced by or equated with one another. For this equalization to be possible, Marx asserts, exchange-values must share something common. They must have what in traditional philosophy was called a quiddity or essence that secures their identity as values. In Marx's words, "first, the valid exchange-values of a given commodity express something equal; secondly, exchange-value, generally, is only the mode of expression, the phenomenal form, of something contained in it, yet distinguishable from it" (p. 304). This shared something in exchange-values, in virtue of which they may be exchanged as equal, is identified by Marx as abstract labor power: "Along with the useful character of labour embodied in them, and the concrete forms of that labour, there is nothing left but what is common to them all; all are reduced to one and the same sort of labour, human labour in the abstract" (p. 305). And Marx characterizes the common essence of commodities as "the same unsubstantial reality in each, a mere congelation of homogeneous human labour, of labour-power expended without regard to the mode of its expenditure" (p. 305). From this point, one proceeds to the equation of exchange-value, abstract human labor power, and the universal equivalent ultimately in the money form.

I have rehearsed this familiar argument as a prelude to the question of how we are to take it. If there are metaphysical moves or contradictions in the argument, are they Marx's or do they inhere in the theoretical foundations of classical economics Marx is excavating critically? Is the primary problem for him the existence of unpaid labor and the extraction of surplus value within the system, or is it the reduction of living labor to abstract labor power as the precondition for commensurable exchange-values? Is he in his own voice simply making better use of the language of commodities, or is he indicating that there is something profoundly wrong with the entire language?

Despite the positivistic tenor of the initial sections, at least before the section on commodity fetishism, there are signs that Marx presents the "discovery" that exchange-value is based upon abstract labor power as the scientific structure of an alienated system. One indication of double voicing in the text is the appearance of jarringly ironic comments that disrupt the neutral facade of the analysis: "As a use-value, the linen is something palpably different from the coat; as [exchange] value, it is the same as the coat, and now has the appearance of a coat. Thus the linen acquires a value-form different from its physical form. The fact that it is value, is made manifest by its equality with a coat, just as the sheep's nature of a Christian is shown in his resemblance to the Lamb of God" (p. 317). By the time one gets to the section on commodity fetishism, the criticism of the phenomena discussed is blatant and extensive.

When I state that coats or boots stand in a relation to linen, because it [linen as equivalent value] is the universal incarnation of abstract human labour, the absurdity of this statement is self-evident. Nevertheless, when the producers of coats and boots compare those articles with linen, or, what is the same thing, with gold or silver, as the universal equivalent, they express the relation between their own private labour and the collective labour of society in the same absurd form.

The categories of bourgeois economy consist of such like forms. They are forms of thought expressing with social validity the conditions of a definite, historically determined mode of production, viz., the production of commodities. (P. 324)

Here the restricted validity of concepts such as abstract labor power which formulate the conditions of an absurd system is explicit. The prior absurdity is the very reduction of living labor to abstract labor power and the binary opposition between instrumentalized work and abstracted, mystified meaning in the fetishized commodity. And a crucial problem is posed by the very idea that living labor can be bought and sold.

It is, moreover, significant that the commodity fetish can itself be read in at least two ways. First, it may be taken as a surrogate for a missing or lost essential totality such as species-being (*Gattungswesen*) that lies at the origin of a speculative dialectic. Yet this is an ideological understanding still within the logic of essentialism and fetishism. One may recall that for Freud the fetish was the narcissistically invested substitute for the phallic mother— another avatar of the lost totality at the putative origin. Yet for Freud the lost totality was itself imaginary or phantasmatic.

A second way of understanding the commodity fetish is as a fixated product of a disrupted work process wherein there is a binary split between instrumentalized abstract labor power, on the one hand, and detached, mystified symbolic meaning, on the other. From the perspective of a complex, supplemented dialectic, the mechanism of commodity fetishism involves the reduction of living labor to abstract, instrumental labor power. One might extend Marx's train of thought and argue that meaning divorced from an intricate relation to the work process is projected and fixated in a detached symbolic form into the mystified commodity as fetish. In this sense, the problematic interaction of meaning and work is reduced, and meaning receives a deceptive totalization in the fetishized commodity (the alternative to which is at times misleadingly seen in binary terms as *fully* and unproblematically meaningful—typically dedifferentiated or "holistic"—work). Instead of an interactive rhythm of work and play involving the problem of meaning, one has meaningless abstract labor power as instrumentalized work and the commodity fetish as the locus of mystified meaning (as well as leisure time as alienated symbolic interaction or commodified play). One also has the divorce between the work-a-day language of needs and the tendency of language to gravitate toward pure play—often commodified play—as cliché or as autonomized, self-referential literature.

One may also note that Marx's critique of commodity fetishism in Section 4 of *Capital* remains too narrowly humanistic or anthropocentric in orientation. Marx asserts that in commodity fetishism the social relations among men are distortedly seen as relations among things. One seems to have a simple reversal in the reification of social relations and human labor that a further simple reversal will set right through the return to genuinely human relations. Yet the more basic question one may raise is whether the pure opposition between humans and things as well as between use and exchange-value is problematic. The critical question is not simply whether one treats people as things, as Marx seems to suggest and as existential thought made into a cliché. It is also whether one treats things as things in the sense of mere raw material for production or use-values subordinated to separate and distinct human values. One might argue that it is misleading to see the world only in terms of restricted human interests or use-values—to see only potential coats or lamb chops in sheep, iron in mountains, or experimental objects in animals. Such a view fosters the belief that one can base the emancipation of society on the exploitation of nature. In contrast to *The Economic and Philosophic Manuscripts* where there was some idea (however problematic) of a different kind of exchange with nature, *Capital* often seems more narrowly humanistic in assumptions. Yet it does furnish elements for a different understanding of labor and of relations more generally, particularly in terms of what I have sketched—only sketched—as a complex, supplemented dialectic.

*179*

Jürgen Habermas among others has successfully specified ways in which aspects of, and extrapolations from, the arguments in *Capital* no longer apply to contemporary capitalistic societies. Yet the role of a critical theory of commodity production in its relations to other dimensions of society and culture remains, in modified and even intensified form (given the expansion of mass or commodified culture and its assimilation of other levels of culture and, indeed, of portions of social life in a "consumer" society), a Marxian legacy that retains contemporary significance. So, I suggest, does what I have sketched as a model of a supplemented dialectic, and it is in elaborating and specifying its features that the exchange between Marxism and deconstruction may take some of its more fruitful turns. I have tried to indicate that, in terms of this model, the antidote to ideology is not simply science but critique. Science emerges in the struggle between ideology and critique. When "science" is autonomized, the result is a positivistic ideology in which the subject does not disappear but is effectively occluded. To this extent, it is misleading to define ideology as centered on the subject; the "imaginary" can assume the form of a denial of the subject or of the answerable, responsible agent, including the role of the subject or agent in science. Nor should the critical and self-critical contention that ideology and the possibility of alienation reappear with significant differences in different social formations be transformed into the idea that ideology is a transhistorical requirement of all societies (at least "for the people"), for the latter idea is itself much too close to a legitimating secondary revision or readily manipulable mystification. It also tends to obviate undertaking a project whose importance Derrida has at least signaled: the rethinking of institutions.

An institution interweaves discourse and practice and it may be seen as a displacement of a text (or, more precisely, as a crucial aspect of the *texte général*). In the modern context, the almost inescapable temptation is simply to identify institutionalization with routinization and institutional norm with normalization. This temptation, however, should itself be situated as a symptomatic response to modern (particularly bureaucratic) institutions; it should also be taken as a caveat concerning a possibility of institutions in general. An essentialistic or universal identification should nonetheless be resisted in that it both inhibits inquiry into more or less marginal areas of modern institutional life that counteract routinization and eliminates the very project of rethinking and recasting institutions in significantly different terms. Here it is, I think, also deceptive to rely on the simple binary opposition between dominant, normalized forms and marginal parasites, with the implication that the margin, if it is not to remain a harmless safety valve, must become the center, either by mutating into a new form of oppressive dominance or by assuming the impossibly utopian guise of total liberation, carnivalization, free play, permanent revolution, and so forth. The very difficulty in the project of rethinking institutions lies in the attempt to elucidate how thought and practice may further the emergence of a situation in which social life has a rhythm that may, to varying degrees in different areas of society and culture, be open to the interaction of norm and transgression, rule and exception, centrality and liminality, commitment and criticism, significant work and carnivalization. Posed in these terms, however, the project may be situated after Marx after Derrida.

# 7

## *Intellectual History*
## *and Critical Theory*

> Each of the distinguishable significative elements of an utter-
> ance and the entire utterance as a whole entity are translated
> in our minds into another, active and responsive, context. *Any*
> *true understanding is dialogic in nature.*
> —V. N. Volosinov, *Marxism and the Philosophy of Language*

In this chapter I am somewhat polemical and at times even
assume the role of devil's advocate in my attempt to put forth provocative arguments. Specifically, my purpose is to explicate and
explore aspects of a project to which I have been committed in my
teaching and publications: the attempt to forge a link between
intellectual history and critical theory. As will become evident, I
contrast a critical-theoretical approach with both historicism and
formalism. Max Horkheimer of course contrasted critical with contemplative theory, but I maintain that this contrast should not be
taken as a simple binary opposition leading to an either/or choice.
The critique of contemplative theory still has limited relevance.
But it should not be made to deny all value to contemplativeness
and particularly to a certain mode of receptivity. The difficulty is
to see how certain features, which serve to counteract dogmatism
and the cult of productivity, may connect with more critical and
practical orientations. I think that receptivity is necessary for a certain openness to nature and to language of the sort Heidegger tried
to evoke in perhaps too abandoned and incantatory a manner. It is
also a component of a mode of objectivity to which psychoanalysis

has been particularly alert—what Freud termed *gleichschwebende Aufmerksamkeit.*

In my own approach to intellectual history, I have tended to focus on so-called canonical texts of elite culture. But I in no sense attribute to this approach a higher value than to the study of peasant or worker culture, for example. Indeed one of the crucial problems in historiography at present is to work out better mediations between intellectual and social history, in part by elaborating an analysis and critique of the formation of levels of culture in the modern period and their relation to social groups or categories. I do, however, think that the study of so-called canonical texts has been excessively underemphasized in recent historiography and that this underemphasis has had some negative consequences, particularly in the education of historians who can supplement their scholarly and professional expertise with a certain interpretive and critical sensibility. I also think that a major problem, which is often denied or repressed, is that there is not at present a viable congruence between significant problems and disciplinary frames or boundaries in the humanities and social sciences. To the extent that certain problems, such as the relation between research and critical theory or between texts and contexts, are not coterminous with—and may even be poorly housed within—existing disciplines, there may be something to be said for more exploratory, hybridized, or even "transgressive" discourses in academics. One such transgressive discourse is deconstruction. Yet deconstructive criticism has often seemed to parallel if not replicate New Criticism and formalism in general in its proclivities: apparently remaining within the text, referring directly only to "the metaphysical tradition" (which itself at times appears to be a massive abstraction), leaving other contexts a matter of allusion or extremely indirect inference, elaborating an ahistorical reading technology, and at times confining itself to what might be called trope plumbing (in both senses of the word).

While this conception of deconstruction may have limited applicability, it is nonetheless too general and imprecise, both because tendencies labeled deconstructive show appreciable differences between and among one another and because there are prominent efforts to question the assumptions on which this conception is based. Derrida, for example, has stressed the point that metaphysics is not an isolated area of thought; it has displaced resonances in contemporary "human sciences" that are the more unexamined to the extent one believes one has transcended metaphysics and traditional philosophy. And Derrida has of course also tried to undercut the opposition between the inside and the outside of texts, proposing instead the notion of a general text in a special infrastructural sense. But much remains to be done in tracing the mutual implications of metaphysics and secularized discourses and practices, for example, on the level of theoretical grounding and basic assumptions. One cannot rest content with the partially valid idea that the deconstruction of philosophical and literary texts is in and of itself a form of political intervention. (I would interject here that this idea is partially valid because of the relation of deconstruction to the undoing of binaries, which are crucial for the scapegoat mechanism. This undoing is necessary but not sufficient with respect to social and political criticism.) Nor can one construe deconstruction as a universal solvent to be applied in the same terms to Plato's dialogues and Reagan's speeches. Deconstruction is most powerful and least unselfconsciously self-parodic when undertaken with respect to texts with strong internal forms of self-contestation, and its undoing of binary oppositions eventuates in an undecidability that is itself operative on very elementary levels, such as the relation between world and inscription, self and other, or seriousness and laughter in the response to the world.

To put the point another way, deconstruction is an acritical "critique" of foundational philosophy, and it undoes elementary binary splits. But it need not induce the obliteration of all distinctions, and a crucial problem is how it may be distinguished from ordinary equivocation and conjoined with criticism of institutions and practices on other sociocultural and political levels. The more general problem posed by deconstruction is how to articulate differences that may neither be equalized and reduced to identities nor dissociated and placed in hierarchically ordered binary oppositions. (In this sense, deconstruction does not eventuate either in simple egalitarianism or in elitism. It poses the problem of how to articulate differences—in ethical and political terms, the problem of justice and liberality.) One also needs a fuller elaboration of a notion of history as a process of repetition with (at times traumatic) change—a process not equated with "dialectical" development in the clichéd Hegelian sense; with empty homogeneous, chronological time; or with the historicist idea of unique periods (an idea rehabilitated in Foucault's early notion of epistemologically defined period "breaks"). Especially in the absence of this revised notion of historicity, there is a danger that the focus on metaphysics may engender a bizarrely meta-metaphysical discourse obsessively fixated, in ahistorically essentializing and ideological fashion, on the relation between origin and displacement, absolute and aporia, seeming stability and sublimely abysmal emptiness. At best such a focus may result in the reduction of history to one rhetorical topos among others or make of it the elusive object of a diaphanous outreach program.

A tortuous and at times contradictory conception of history typifies the writings of Paul de Man wherein "history" itself may be in the position of the unconscious. One may quote, for example, the famous or infamous opening lines to the preface of de Man's *Allegories of Reading*:

> *Allegories of Reading* started out as a historical study and ended up as a theory of reading. I began to read Rousseau seriously in preparation for a historical reflection on Romanticism and found myself unable to progress beyond local difficulties of interpretation. In trying to cope with this, I had to shift from historical definition to the problematics of reading. This shift, which is typical of my generation, is of more interest in its results than in its causes.[1]

One might try to argue that a close reading of de Man would modify the apparent meaning of this quotation by indicating how a rejection of a "classical" or conventional concept of history in terms of linear development or the unfolding of teleologically coded meaning leads de Man both to act out and to indicate the importance of processes of repression and displacement. Working through such processes may enable the elaboration of a more complex, "deconstructed" concept that at least prepares the ground for a different understanding of historicity itself, including the intricate

[1] New Haven, Conn., 1979.

role of the return of the repressed. But the surface meaning of de
Man's statement clearly seems to posit an opposition between historical study and a theory of reading as well as between historical
definition and the problematics of reading. On an explicit level, de
Man's thought at times seems to rehabilitate and refurbish certain
binary oppositions, notably that between phenomenal reality and
language or form, and then to question or even collapse binaries in
a way that obliterates distinctions. The serious preparation for historical reflection seems to eventuate in aporetic impasses and "local
difficulties in interpretation" that postpone sine diem the elaboration of what de Man elsewhere terms "any expectation of ever
arriving at a somewhat reliable history." In this respect Derrida's
own explicit references to history have a very different tenor and
import. As he puts it, for example, in *Positions* (as supplemented by
a self-quotation from the essay "*Différance*"):

> Although I have formulated many reservations about the "meta-
> physical" concept of history, I very often use the word "history" in
> order to reinscribe its force and in order to produce another concept
> or conceptual chain of "history": in effect a "monumental, stratified,
> contradictory" history; a history that also implies a new logic of rep-
> etition and the trace, for it is difficult to see how there could be
> history without it. . . .
> If the word "history" did not bear within itself the motif of a final
> repression of difference, one could say that only differences can be,
> from the outset and in all aspects, "historical."[2]

It must be noted, however, that Derrida himself, in his *Mémoires
for Paul de Man*,[3] has placed in question the pattern I seem to have
posited in discussing the relation between his references to history
and de Man's. In an extended reflection on memory, Derrida takes
note of the contrast in de Man between *Gedächtnis* (in the sense of
material inscription including even mechanical or rote memorization) and *Erinnerung* (in the traditional "Hegelian" sense of total
mastery and anamnesic interiorization). He also contrasts de Man's

[2] *Positions*, trans. and annotated by Alan Bass (Chicago, 1981), pp. 57, 104.
[3] New York, 1986; all further references to this work, abbreviated *Mémoires*, are
included in the text.

stress on disjunction with Heidegger's seemingly dominant quest for *Versammlung* or gathering in Being. But toward the end of his discussion, Derrida implies that both *Gedächtnis* (at least in the sense of purely mechanical or rote memorization) and *Erinnerung* are ideal limits and that a "deconstructed" sense of *Gedächtnis* as "thinking memory" would undercut the opposition between de Man's stress on discontinuity and what seems dominant in Heidegger. "No doubt, thinking memory (*Gedächtnis*) is itself the gathering of this difference, and it could be the same for all disjunction as such. But this gathering does not gather in an *'état présent'*" (p. 146). *Gedächtnis* in this displaced sense would seem to move somewhere in the space—perhaps one might call it historical in a different sense—between rote memorization (which is never entirely transcended) and *Erinnerung* (which is never fully achieved). Writing of de Man's discussion of Rousseau's *Social Contract* in *Allegories of Reading*, moreover, Derrida quotes this passage:

> Just as any other reader, [Rousseau] is bound to misread his text as a promise of political change. The error is not within the reader; language itself dissociates the cognition from the act. *Die Sprache versprict* (*sich*) [language promises (itself)]: to the extent that it is necessarily misleading, language just as necessarily conveys the promise of its own truth. This is why textual allegories on this level of rhetorical complexity generate history. (*Mémoires*, pp. 94-95)

Unlike Derrida in his exegesis of this passage, I question de Man's attempt to relate the political promise of a text exclusively to misreading and not to treat the manner in which texts may validly have a prescriptive dimension that may be read as well as misread. Performativity may be seen as unqualifiedly "perverse" only with respect to a "constative" model of language. In terms of a more complex and problematic understanding of language, performative and prescriptive dimensions are as "normal" and "readable" as any other, and they may arguably become "perverse" only in more specific circumstances. In addition, the one-sided emphasis upon dissociation between cognition and act tends to polarize (or construe in terms of a binary opposition) a more complex network of possibilities. More generally, de Man in this pas-

187

sage tends to reduce the rhetorical mediation of theory and practice to perversion or misprision rather than to pose in a more intricate manner the relation between cognition and act, reading and mis-reading. To some limited extent, however, this passage helps to elucidate de Man's elliptical reference to the "materiality of actual history" in contradistinction to teleological and "dialectical" pseudo-history, which Derrida mentions earlier in *Mémoires* (p. 52). Concerning the notion of the genesis of history through rhetorically complex textuality, in which language, in excess of the constative function, has performative and generative force, Derrida observes, "It [de Man's sentence] assigns to textuality, as *versprechen* (the performative and generating perversion of the promise but also, if we can say this, the *Ur-sprechen*), the condition of the possibility and generation of history, and of historicity itself. No history without textual *versprechen*" (p. 98). With respect to the closely related issue of de Man's usage of "aporia," Derrida states:

> The word "aporia" recurs often in Paul de Man's last texts. I believe that we would misunderstand it if we tried to hold to its most literal meaning: an absence of path, a paralysis before road-blocks, the immobilization of thinking, the impossibility of advancing, a barrier blocking the future. On the contrary, it seems to me that the experience of the aporia, such as de Man deciphers it, gives or promises the thinking of the path, provokes the thinking of the very possibility of what still remains unthinkable or unthought, indeed, impossible. The figures of rationality are profiled in the madness of the aporetic. (*Mémoires*, p. 132)

Without entering further into its labyrinthine complexity, I simply note that I find it difficult to decide whether Derrida's genial gloss of de Man brings out a convergence (without identity) between their readings of "history" or whether it represents an amicable and generous "allegorical" rewriting of this dimension of de Man's thought in terms that make it approximate Derrida's own initiatives. To the extent one disagrees with it, one may suspect it of a troubling tendency to suspend critical rationality or at least to put it in provisional abeyance (perhaps in the overriding interest of offering a memorial to a friend). Indeed Derrida, for understandable reasons given the context of the lectures on which *Mémoires for*

*Paul de Man* were based, would seem to be underwriting and authorizing the questionable tendency simply to amalgamate his thought with de Man's to furnish the more or less unified basis for deconstructive criticism.

To the extent that one agrees with Derrida's gloss (or at least finds it acceptable), one may see in it the best possible way to make selective use of de Man both in the wake of his death and as a promise for the future; this interpretation of de Man intimates what "deconstruction in America" should be. The danger is that this kind of gloss induces projective reprocessing of the texts being read and interpreted. The "dialogue" in question in *Mémoires for Paul de Man* is, however, of such a level of difficulty and involves such a subtle interplay of proximity and distance between self and other that one must in this case be hesitant in locating clear-cut projective elements in the interpretation.

However one may respond to certain of its features, Derrida's reading pointedly directs one's attention to the "history-making" role of rhetoric as mediation and supplement between theory and practice—a role it performs through the very performative dimension of language itself. The ensuing questions (which Derrida himself has broached) would seem to be how to relate the textual "condition of the possibility and generation of history" to actual historical processes (including historical accounts), how to situate the role of an active exchange with the past, and how to articulate the relation between the "acritical" deconstruction of foundational binary opposites and the role of critical theory, notably including the decisive (or at least effective) criticism of aspects of sociopolitical and economic institutions.

On the side of more insistently political criticism (including much Foucauldian and Marxist criticism), where one might expect to find ways of answering these questions and thus compensating for certain perceived defects of deconstruction, there has been a marked—perhaps even an exasperated—tendency to turn away from patient, subtle, and painstaking analysis of texts or particular artifacts and to stress the role of collective discourses, ideologies, codes, and institutions. There is even a tendency to dismiss textual analysis as an anachronistic residue of bourgeois liberalism. And when texts or other specific artifacts are treated, it may be only to subsume them under larger interpretive categories and historical processes. The very code words in handling—at times manhandling—texts have been "symptom" and "emblem." A text is often seen as a symptomatic or emblematic precipitate or expression of some more encompassing discursive and institutional phenomenon or stage of development. Hence "realism" may be taken as emblematic of early market capitalism, "high modernism" of imperialism, and " postmodernism" or "poststructuralism" of contemporary consumer, multinational capitalism. A text or artifact in this light may become a mere token or illustration of a type or a collective entity. And the priority of collective political demands is readily linked to "canon busting" in the insistence that the "great tradition" has served the status quo and that the need is to turn to the excluded, more popular manifestations of collective activity and expression.

While explicitly political and more circumscribed Foucauldian or Marxist modes of criticism are sufficiently heterogeneous to warrant a caveat similar to the one I put forth with reference to deconstructive criticism, the tendencies I have listed, however briefly and tendentiously, are, I think, sufficiently prevalent to cause concern, and they threaten to replicate (at least with reference to the treatment of specific artifacts) the domesticating and reductive, at times even the imperialistic, features of ideologies they attack. They may even be conjoined with a disinterest in (or divestment of) art and literature or, more poignantly, with a conviction that art and literature (as well as art and literary criticism) are diversionary activities that may be redeemed only to the extent that they are strictly subordinated to clear and manifest political concerns—with politics itself understood in a very conventional manner as centered on the state.

The New Historicism is of course a term made current by the *Representations* group at Berkeley and particularly by Stephen Greenblatt. (Its partial analogue in American Studies, which I shall simply mention, is usually linked to the name of Sacvan Bercovitch.[4] Despite its notable accomplishments, the "American Studies" variant of historicism often tends in the direction of the

---

[4] See esp. *The American Jeremiad* (Madison, Wis., 1978).

kind of symptomatic readings I have already discussed.) While the *Representations* group in its individual publications is quite diverse, they have to some extent tended to generate a collective methodology if not an ideology—something that manifests itself in the editorial policy of their journal and at times in the more manifestolike aspects of their writings. (Here I must, however, be extremely cautious in generalizing, lest I regenerate in my own account the associationist if not scapegoating kind of thinking I criticize elsewhere, a possibility particularly difficult to avoid altogether when stylizing arguments for polemical effect. Thus I cannot pretend to have entirely avoided this questionable possibility in my own account, although I think that my objects of criticism are at present in the ascendent and not in the helpless position of victims. Still: an aside and a caveat.)

One tendency in the New Historicism is to resemble old historicisms in taking necessary contextualization to the point of overcontextualization that is construed as explanatory. On this view, an adequate historical interpretation is characterized by a superabundance of information, and there is a tendency to extend Clifford Geertz's valuable stress upon "thick description"[5] into the indiscriminate, unqualified rule: the thicker the description, the better. (The rule may, however, not be substantiated in critical practice, where the historical dimension of an account may at times appear to be rather "thin.") One may also find a relatively weak theoretical overlay in the invocation of the concept of power, which itself threatens to become a universal solvent in explanation and interpretation. It may also be the unmoved mover in a kind of gallows functionalism—a gallows functionalism in which artifacts invariably operate to reinforce a dominant system that co-opts and recycles them as ballast for its power structures.

It is tempting to interpret this frame of reference as a neo-Foucauldian reformulation of the late-sixties idea of the "system" (or even more generally as a delegitimating analogue of systems theory, with Talcott Parsons disguised as Jean Genet). In the wake of the defeat of New Left politics, this reformulation veers from

[5] See Geertz's seminal essay in *The Interpretation of Cultures* (New York, 1972), chap. 1.

the one-sided extreme of finding the greatest (if not the sole) critical potential in artifacts of high culture (à la Adorno) to the other one-sided extreme of seeing these artifacts as mere symptomatic points of symbolic resistance that actually serve as sump pumps for the power of the dominant system. Aside from resulting in an excessively homogeneous model of the way high and dominant culture interact, this frame of reference threatens to deflect attention from more intricate problems of hegemony and authority for which the concept of power is insufficient to account. More generally, at least two crucial issues tend to be obscured in a gallows functionalism and an undifferentiated idea of power (or subversion), the first being the precise nature and context of "transgression," from ordinary crime through contestatory artifacts to outright revolution. The second is the complex configuration of the hegemonic structure in which "power" operates, and that includes both the variable relation between shared ideologies that legitimate institutions and the negative integration not through shared, differentially internalized ideologies but through dissensus and fragmentation that inhibit the formation of oppositional movements, abet the play of interests or divisive ideologies, and facilitate a strategy of divide and rule.

It may be noted that historicism both stimulates and has a relation of mutual reinforcement with a tendency that is often deceptively taken as its alternative: formalism. Historicism and formalism are not genuine alternatives. Indeed the two tendencies arose together historically, feed off one another, and may be combined in the work of the same figure. In its most familiar guise, formalism relegates contexts to a background if not a coffee-table status, and its focus is upon the internal, synchronic functioning of a text (classically, the so-called autotelic text). It may be attended by a presentist perspective in which history is seen as a burdensome legacy, a displaced myth, or a rhetorical mystification—something to which one is condemned and from which one may perhaps be liberated. But formalism—with a New Historicism as its strange bedfellow—may also come in other guises, for example, in an intertextual and multileveled format. Here contexts from popular, commodified, and high culture are reduced to set pieces, and their relations to texts are "negotiated," "thought" or "stitched" together in precious tableaux through relatively facile associationism, juxtaposition, or pastiche. In Walter Benjamin, the technique of crosscultural juxtaposition presumably served as the occasion for a "profane illumination" that was to have a shock effect. But I think that recent uses and abuses of this technique tend to have little shock value, especially insofar as they take the more or less routinized form of finely crafted, decorous stylistic assemblages in which there is little attempt to pause and puzzle over difficult or dubious steps in an argument. The commendable but demanding and problematic ideal of intertextual and cross-cultural analysis thus receives too easy and contemplative a solution—what might be called the pseudosolution of weak montage or, if you prefer, cut-and-paste bricolage.

The appealing element of the New Historicism within literary and art-historical studies is the manifest desire to find connections between levels of culture that are often left in splendid isolation. The difficulty is how to move beyond mere association or montage, each of whose elements may be "interesting" or even fascinating but whose overall shape seems nebulous or random if not at times irresponsibly assembled. In the absence of a cogent, historically differentiated account of connections or of their tenuousness or nonexistence (for seeming nonconnections also pose a historically significant problem), it may be more candid to make explicit one's desire and one's reliance on montage as a marker of desire that has yet to find an acceptably articulated object. In fact this desire for connections may be part of the historical significance of the technique of weak montage itself. (At present we certainly hunger for connections, but it may be better if we leave the stress marks or traces of production evident in our efforts.)

My own critical response to weak montage does not mean that one may draw a distinction between it and, say, strong or effective montage with intellectual ease or apodictic assurance. Nor does it imply a dismissal of all forms of paratactic organization. But it is bound up with two further points: first, the need to be concerned about an excessive reliance on associationism with no other levels or dimensions of discourse that resist and situate it, particularly when the paratactic brings with it juxtapositions and anecdotes (especially exotic, seemingly historicizing inaugural anecdotes) that are at times ingratiating to the point of kitsch; second, the need to supplement and complement the use of paratactic devices with an attempt to develop other modes of articulation, notably with respect to a conception of how society and culture interact at a given time and over time. One such requirement would be an account of the nature and relations of levels of culture and society—of elite, middle-class, and popular cultures; their links with a commodity system; and the manner in which they are embedded in social groups and structures. Such an account need not be identified with totalizing theory or terroristic metanarrative. It may be based upon the kind of self-critical research and argumentative critical theory whose very possibility seems obviated by the polarization of thought into totalizing theory, on the one hand, and more or less random association (or even paralogy), on the other.

I indicated earlier that the New Historicism in literary and art-historical studies is a diverse and changing phenomenon, and my own generalizations about it are particularly precarious and tentative. Indeed some of the problems I have specified have recently been noticed and commented on by avowed New Historicists themselves. Stephen Greenblatt, in the first chapter to *Shakespearean Negotiations*, makes a number of cogent and stimulating observations about the complex and variable interaction between literature and society. One may question whether his own discussions of specific artifacts always agree with his methodological assertions, but those assertions at times embody criticisms of tendencies prevalent in the New Historicism, including (on his generously self-critical admission) Greenblatt's earlier work. For example, he observes:

> I had tried to organize the mixed motives of Tudor and Stuart culture under the rubric *power*, but that term implied a structural unity and stability of command belied by much of what I actually knew about the exercise of authority and force in the period.
>
> If it was important to speak of power in relation to Renaissance literature—not only as the object but as the enabling condition of representation itself—it was equally important to resist the integration of all images and expressions into a single master discourse. For if Renaissance writers themselves often echoed the desire of princes and prelates for just such a discourse, brilliant critical and theoretical work in recent years by a large and diverse group of scholars had

194

demonstrated that this desire was itself constructed out of conflicting and ill-sorted motives. Even those literary texts that sought most ardently to speak for a monolithic power could be shown to be the sites of institutional and ideological contestation.[6]

Historicism as it appears in the discipline of history is also a large and diverse phenomenon about which generalizations must be taken cum grano salis. If one allows for the leavening effect of polemical hyperbole, one may nonetheless hazard a few observations. In the sort of historicism that is still prevalent among professional historians, one attempts to understand the past in its own terms and for its own sake, as if the past simply had its own terms and was there for its own sake. Today it is difficult to escape the idea that values at least affect one's choice of problems and that theoretical assumptions have something to do with the way one construes facts. Although Max Weber's methodological reflections have become common sense in the human sciences and Thomas Kuhn's views have received sufficient currency to approach a similar status, historicism may continue to exist as an ideal, and it may be both approximated in practice and accommodated in established research procedures. In its more empirical variant in description and narration, it requires that each proposition in an account state a fact that may be footnoted, preferably with a reference to an archival source. (Hence the familiar fact/footnote format of historical articles, where there may even be the winsome assumption that footnoting a banality somehow gives it special weight—a little *Sitzfleisch* perhaps. In addition to its legitimate scholarly functions, the ability to footnote may authorize statements one would hesitate to make more directly in one's own voice.) The more permissive possibility is a footnote per paragraph that states in more general terms the sources for a larger segment of discourse. In its analytic and social scientific variant, historicism requires that hypotheses and models be open to testing through an appeal to facts that are established and validated on an empirical level. In other words, descriptive-narrative and analytic approaches are alternative (or at times complementary) ways of coding the same facts or body of data. For

[6] Berkeley and Los Angeles, 1988, pp. 2-3.

certain limited purposes of documentary reconstruction, these procedures are unobjectionable and even necessary. The question is
whether they define the sufficient conditions for acceptable historiography, particularly when they are accompanied by further protocols of proper discourse. What further protocols?

In historiography (at least Anglo-American historiography), a
premium is often set on straightforward prose (the no-jargon rule)
and on assumptions and assertions that illuminate or extend commonsense without contradicting or disorienting it. The commonsense in question is of course that of a relatively restricted elite of
middle-class individuals with a general education. As a colleague
who teaches at Stanford put it in a lecture with specific reference
to intellectual history, the goal of the historian should be to write
on a level and in an idiom that would make his or her work suitable
for publication in the *New York Review of Books*. Of course more
insistently scholarly historians might find this goal too popular, and
a more limited group would be open to at least social science jargon. But the latter would expect more or less good-humored chid-
ing from their colleagues about their inability to use good English,
and the former might be proud and defensive about their puristic
rigor.

In addition, the voice or perspective of the historian in all the
foregoing approaches tends to be that of an invisible or transcendental spectator who looks down upon his or her account from a
detached and at times safely ironic distance and attempts to eliminate all problematic traces of production from his or her own text.
More "subjective" responses tend to be reserved for the preface and
perhaps the conclusion to a book or the introduction and coda to
an article. In any event, "subjectivity" is neatly separated from
"objectivity" and allocated to a discrete sector of discourse in the
manner in which a bathroom is placed vis-à-vis other rooms in a
well-constructed house. There is much to be said in favor of this
organizing principle, especially if one is attached to norms of classical decorum. But it may be attended by an excessively sharp analytic
opposition between objectivity and subjectivity, however one may
subsequently estimate the relative importance of the objective and
the subjective in research. Hence the marked resistance to any
attempt to question the binary opposition between objectivity and

subjectivity as well as to the use of more self-questioning procedures—particularly of so-called blurred genres (or what I would prefer to call liminal and dialogic modes such as free indirect style) in historiography—even when, as they must be in historiography, these procedures are mediated by significant controls. (By the way, I take exception to the notion of blurred genres, which is overly indentured to the idea of clear-cut disciplines or genres. To give an analogy: I have a dog that is a hybrid. To me he does not look like a blurred dog.) Whether the discrete and explicit subjective option is invoked may be left to the discretion of the individual historian, and its use varies over time. The sixties were of course a prime time for show-and-tell sessions in which one's existential preferences or subjective values were revealed to one's readers or audience—a practice I think had largely purgative functions.

Despite the simplification inherent in large-scale generalizations, I do not think that the foregoing represents an unwarranted distortion or caricature of the approach of many "working historians." But it of course does not exhaust the nature of more notable achievements in historiography. The very fact that historians tend to work with concrete exempla as reference points and shy away from theoretical self-reflection as a beguiling invitation to narcissism may enable at least some of them to achieve an intricacy in narration that rivals the novel. My own feeling is that twentieth-century historiography has been more advanced on its social scientific side (where certain achievements have been spectacular). Narrative has remained closer to conventional forms, but at least the richness of the so-called traditional novel may be attained, even when the more risky innovations of the modern novel (as well as its older avatars such as *Don Quixote* or *Tristram Shandy*) are kept at arm's length—if they are deemed relevant at all. For example, E. P. Thompson's *The Making of the English Working Class* is justifiably taken as a modern classic.[7] It is close to the older three-decker *Bildungsroman* in structure. Its massive accumulation of detail—its "thick" description and narration—is agitated by strong empathy, approaching identification, with the working class and marked antipathy for

[7] New York, 1963.

Methodism. This dualism becomes problematic insofar as workers were Methodists; for it is difficult to see in Thompson's account what the real appeal of Methodism might have been for English workers in the nineteenth century. Methodism's power of ideological distortion seems, in Thompson's rendering, too overwhelmingly blatant to be possible among the same people who had so many down-to-earth qualities, including hard-nosed common sense and practical reason. Thompson offers only external reasons for its appeal, reasons of a sort that might apply to any ideology: its indoctrination of workers, its provision of a sense of community, and its role as a spiritual opiate in hard times. And one of his more memorable characterizations of Methodism is as a "ritualized form of psychic masturbation" with a special appeal for women (p. 368). Thompson leaves the reader with an insufficiently explored paradox: the fact that a significant number of workers were Methodists. What is relatively rare in historiography in contrast to the modern novel is the articulation in the same account of both narrative and sophisticated critical theory (for example, with reference to the relations among class, gender, and religion in Thompson's case).[8] When the historian does turn to theory or at least—and more typically—to a more or less theoretically informed attack on certain kinds of theory, he or she tends to do it in a separate book or article (the so-called think piece), as did Thompson himself in his *Poverty of Theory* (with reference to Althusser's structural Marxism, which, whatever its limitations, at least does raise the question of the constitution of the subject through ideology).

---

[8] On the question of the articulation of narrative with critical theory, one might contrast *The Making of the English Working Class* with Thomas Mann's novel *Doctor Faustus*, for example. Thompson certainly relies on certain theoretical assumptions, but he does not sufficiently integrate or relate narrative and critical theory. Indeed his orthodox Marxist axiom that economic revolution should normally lead to political revolution leads him to assume that England was in a "revolutionary situation" in the early nineteenth century and that the absence of revolution may be explained by counterrevolutionary reaction to the French Revolution. This assumption obviates the need for an analysis of structural differences in English and French society and politics that might provide more internal reasons for the absence of revolution in England. More generally, Thompson seems to tell more the story of the unmaking than the making of the English working class—at least as a revolutionary "subject" in history. In this sense, an unexamined narrative subtext jars with his ostensible plot.

In the case of intellectual history, J. G. A. Pocock has attempted to formulate theoretical positions and to put them to work in his specific studies of past discourse. In his earlier work, he relied on Thomas Kuhn's notion of paradigms, and in his more recent contributions he has referred to speech-act theory, especially as it has been accommodated to historiography by Quentin Skinner. But throughout his career Pocock has insisted that the specifically historical task is the objective reconstruction of past discourses in their own contexts of enunciation and reception. His role in the reorientation of intellectual history in accordance with this "ideas-in-context" approach has been quite influential, and even his anxieties over the status of intellectual history have a rather exemplary quality within the subdiscipline. Yet it is important to note that intellectual history in all its forms, including the most conventional and orthodox, tends at present to be relatively marginal to the discipline of history in the West. This position is related to a more general process of marginalization of canons in the recent past, a process that has been more successful in historiography than in literary criticism or art history.

Pocock's contribution to the *Intellectual History Newsletter* of April 1986 is quite interesting in these respects; for it shows both Pocock's willingness to entertain the possibility of approaches to intellectual history other than his own and the manner in which he situates that possibility.[9] His manner of establishing his credibility as a historian indicates that, if intellectual historians share a certain anxiety, it is not that generated by their position within the triangulated field of Marxist, psychoanalytic, and structuralist-poststructuralist forces.[10] For good or ill, this "triangular anxiety" characterizes only a rather small group. The "anxiety" of most intellectual historians is that created by their—our—standing in the eyes of other professional historians, a standing that is especially problematic when one engages in paraprofessional activities such as criticism.

[9] The *Intellectual History Newsletter* is a samizdat publication currently available through the History Department of Boston University; all further references to this piece, abbreviated *IHN*, are included in the text.

[10] See Hans Kellner, "Triangular Anxieties: The Present State of European Intellectual History," in *Modern European Intellectual History: Reappraisals and New Perspectives*, ed. Dominick LaCapra and Steven L. Kaplan (Ithaca, N.Y., 1982), 111-36.

Because of the "confusion, prejudice and hostility" that surround the understanding of intellectual history, Pocock prefers to refer to himself as a "historian of intellectual activity" or even more narrowly as a "historian of political discourse" (*IHN*, p.3). So he changes his name, his identifying label, and he underscores the fact that he is a historian like other historians by dropping the qualifying adjective "intellectual." He asserts, "The business of the historian is to select some human activity and study how it generated a language—or perhaps borrowed some language otherwise generated—in which its practice could be discussed; after that, to show how the use of this language came to be itself discussed, and how theory, philosophy, science, history, or some other sophisticated mode of discussing the use of language, came into being as a result" (p. 5).

Pocock further specifies that the "working historian" will investigate the questions of whether various activities do indeed give rise to theoretical discourses and the extent and nature of interaction among such discourses at a given time and over time. These are certainly important questions. But what is clear is that the primary if not the defining characteristic of the "working" intellectual historian is the reconstruction of intellectual activities and discourses. (This is one important way the concept of "working historian" itself works. "Working historians" reconstruct the past. They do not deconstruct, criticize, or reflect theoretically about their own discourse, however much these undertakings may be related to a critical history of the present or to a more self-critical exchange with the past.)

Pocock expects attacks from two very different quarters. One set of opponents objects to the nature of Pocock's object of study, insisting upon the paramount importance of "realities." This group—what one might label the "more-historical-than-thou" group—sees little value in a study of theoretical discourses unless the question guiding it is the actual effect of past theory upon past practice. Pocock asserts that the intellectual historian will be

accused of failing to relate (they mean subordinate) "ideas" to "realities," as if the sole function of the practice of theory were to denote or reflect other practices in society, and not to explore the terms of its own practice [curious, contemplative shades of Plato and of the early Althusser but without the critical dimension of theory]. . . . You can reply that the relations of theory to practice and speech to action may be very many and various, that you have no general theory of what these relations are, and merely wanted to know what happened in various recorded instances [less curious shades of Ranke]; but a considerable number of your critics will simply not be listening. (*IHN*, pp. 8-9)

The use of the term "working," even though Pocock is careful at first to enclose it in scare quotes, itself creates the impression that a perspective more self-conscious about the role of theory in the writing of history (and not simply in past discourses) is itself less "real" or at least less serious than other perspectives. The result is a reinstatement of the prejudice against theory that Pocock is anxious to attack when it applies to objects, rather than to methods, of study. Apparently, for Pocock, what is good for the observed goose is not good for the observing gander. (The use of gendered terms may not be out of place here.) Thus the professional intellectual historian should beware of becoming an intellectual—something that would approximate a breach of professional ethics (if not effeteness and effeminacy). This point becomes explicit in Pocock's response to the other source of criticism of his approach.

This critical alternative is methodological or even theoretical but apparently not itself historical for Pocock (he thus separates or dissociates history and theory). In his reaction, Pocock threatens to replicate the attitude of the first group of critics toward his own approach. For here Pocock is mildly permissive, massively ironic, and, in his own inimitable way, musingly Anglo:

It is possible to define "intellectual history" as the pursuit by the "intellectual" of an attitude towards "history," and to write it as a series of dialogues between the historian himself, as intellectual, and his probably French or German predecessors, in the attempt to arrive at a "philosophy of history" or something to take the place of one. Such "intellectual history" will be meta-history, meaning that it will be reflection about "history" itself. But it is also possible to imagine a "working historian" who desires to be a historian but not (in this sense) an intellectual, who desires to practise the writing of history but not to arrive at an attitude towards it, and who does not look beyond the construction of those narrative histories of various kinds of intellectual activity which she or he knows how to write.... It is such a working historian of this kind whom I have presupposed in this article. (*IHN*, p. 8)

A cloud passes over the sun when Pocock mentions "meta-history" —the kiss of death for most "working historians," the nefarious Mata Hari of historiography, fickle Fortuna revisited. The shadow cast by the cloud is dissipated somewhat by the edifying image of the humble craftsman relying on tacit knowledge and working in a guild that has miraculously achieved role reversal between the sexes. Finally, Pocock drops the scare quotes around the term "working historian": he has apparently located the *Ding an sich*.

It in fact does not take much imagination to imagine a historian of the type Pocock envisions, since such a historian is prominent if not dominant in the profession even when her or his object of investigation (or evaluation of the relative importance of objects) differs from Pocock's own. Although Pocock's depiction of the "dialogic perspective" is, I think, partly inspired by some of my own writing, it creates the mistaken impression of a simple either/or choice between documentary (or constative) reconstruction of past discourses and a dialogic (or performative) relation to them. One need not see the relation between perspectives in this light. The question is whether there is a supplementary relation between perspectives even in presumably documentary or reconstructive approaches that aspire to be pure history in Pocock's sense—a relation that remains unacknowledged, unthematized, relatively uncontrolled, and perhaps less cognitively responsible to the extent it is covered by what may after all be an ideology of pure historical reconstruction. It would not, I think, be difficult to reveal such tensions—at times fruitful tensions—in Pocock's own masterwork, *The Machiavellian Moment*.[11]

---

[11] Princeton, 1975. These tensions stem in part from the proximity of Pocock's own voice both to civic humanism on a political level and to a rather contemplative, conceptualistic philosophy on a discursive level. The tensions may be related to the problematic status of civic humanism in modern society—a status that fosters a contemplative, conceptualistic rendering of an active political ideal. Pocock thus seems at times to be a strange composite of Plato and Cato.

I maintain, moreover, that crucial aspects of a documentary or reconstructive approach to the past remain important for any attempt to link intellectual history and critical theory, but the larger discursive framework in which they operate may differ in ways that have implications for the way history is written. Norms of accuracy in research and the need to relate artifacts to their contemporary contexts of creation and reception, for example, are crucial aspects of any mode of research that claims to be historical. Of course the very contexts one deems pertinent for understanding, or comes to emphasize as particularly important, are intimately related to the kind of exchange with the past into which one enters. Historicism tends to place a premium on exhaustiveness of contextualization to an extent that may at times seem like overkill or an impediment to responsive understanding from a more critical-theoretical approach. As I intimated earlier, overcontextualization may take the form of documentary empiricism (for example, in accordance with the dictum concerning thick description, which is congenial to both old and new historicists). Or it may take the form of conceptual or type/token determinism (for example, in construing texts only as symptoms or instantiations of epistemes, ideologies, conventions, codes, stages, social formations, modes of production, "the system," or what have you). In both cases, overcontextualization often occludes the problem of the very grounds on which to motivate a selection of pertinent contexts. And it may well furnish an illusory explanatory effect through an uncritical amalgamation of conventional accounts of contexts and equally conventional or at least extremely reductive readings of texts. The incentive of a more discriminating critical strategy is, by contrast, to facilitate an exchange between past and present that seeks a differential analysis of artifacts and recognizes, indeed intensifies, our implication in processes of reading in a manner that may have import for the future.

It is nonetheless true, I think, that the farther back one goes in time, the less obvious the contexts informing discourse tend to become, and the more difficult it may be, at least in a technical, philological sense, to reconstruct them. It may also be the case that accurate reconstruction may itself have a critical function when it both examines processes whereby more or less dominant traditions achieved their status and inquires into forms of thought and life that either represent or suggest possible alternatives. The latter consideration would apply particularly to submerged or repressed dimensions of tradition that are not given due weight in canonical approaches. Reconstruction in this sense is thus part and parcel of an attempt to enter the subdominant sides of the past into a more provocative interaction with traditions that have been more obvious elements of continuity between past and present. Indeed it may bring out internal tensions and contestations in what we at times refer to, in excessively homogeneous fashion, as *the* tradition.

Hence, for example, there is an appeal in Frances Yates's efforts to show the role of Hermeticism in the Renaissance as well as to suggest its later fate, however one may come to estimate its relative importance or value in comparison with humanism and the beginnings of what became orthodox science. Yates's initiative alerts us to, among other things, the problem of displaced hermetic tendencies in later times and in our own day. The same point might be made concerning Mikhail Bakhtin's inquiry into carnival and the carnivalesque, and the two initiatives converge in any investigation of the relations between Hermeticism and the carnivalesque, prominently including the hermetic use of older carnivalesque forms once having a popular dimension. Perhaps to a lesser degree, one might make similar observations about the stress of Pocock and others upon civic humanism in the light of what had been the more dominant emphasis upon traditions of individualism and contractualism, for example, with reference to the ideological origins of the American Revolution.[12] With respect to a phenomenon such as Romanticism, one might inquire into the relation between the canonical emphasis on the high-minded, anxious, at times sublime quest for wholeness, prominent in M. H. Abrams (or, in

---

[12] Yet Pocock, like Bernard Bailyn and others, tends to take the discourse of civic humanism at face value, in good part because of his own affiliation with it. Pocock does not investigate the question of the extent to which civic humanism functioned as an ideology that legitimated and dissimulated hegemonic structures. Here I may mention Anthony Grafton and Lisa Jardine's *From Humanism to the Humanities* (Cambridge, Massachusetts, 1986), with its treatment of gendered elitism in Renaissance humanism as well as its critique of the tendency of commentators to conflate humanist ideals and practice. What Grafton and Jardine nonetheless share with Pocock is a relatively restricted reading of texts; they do not sufficiently explore the possibility that specific texts may not simply illustrate but refine, complicate, or even contest certain of their theses.

inverted form, in his critics) and the role of "lower" contestatory forces including certain carnivalesque and grotesque uses of irony and parody, say in Byron and Carlyle.

In contrast to historicism, old or new, one may thus insist upon the importance of a critical concern with history in which an interest in form need not eventuate in formalism and in which the concept of history becomes neither an empty rhetorical topos nor a pretext for regression to precritical positions (including historicism itself). A crucial problem here would be to attempt to construe the relations between texts and contexts in an exchange with the past having implications for the present and future. What would be taken as problematic and not subject to proleptic solutions or premature foreclosure would be the differential nature of the interaction among symptomatic (or legitimating), critical, and potentially transformative relations in the way texts or artifacts inscribe and possibly rework contexts. This interaction would undoubtedly itself vary, both over time and with respect to different levels or areas of society and culture. It would also vary with respect to given texts and corpuses.

One implication of this view is that one cannot simply conflate high or elite and dominant or hegemonic culture insofar as so-called high or canonical artifacts *may* have critical potentials that are underplayed or even repressed in canonical interpretations and jettisoned or denied in more or less ritualistic, seemingly militant, condemnations of canons. My basic contention here is that there are no intrinsically canonical texts, but there are canonical uses and interpretations of texts, which certain texts may invite more than others. Thus one may assert or reassert the importance of careful study of at least certain significant texts or artifacts formerly having canonical functions, without accepting or defending all of these functions. Indeed the curious thing about Western traditions (at least in the modern period) is that it seems to be typically the case that artifacts posing certain resistances to canonical functions are precisely the ones assimilated to canons and subjected to canonical (or, recently, anticanonical) interpretations that eliminate, domesticate, or radically marginalize their noncanonical or contestatory features. In this sense, the point of a critical appropriation of past artifacts would not be simply to destroy or dismantle canons (to the extent they still exist) but to question their exclusivity and to read items included in them in noncanonical ways. This would require relating them as cogently as possible to artifacts and processes often excluded from canons (for example, black, woman's, and third-world writing) and thus contesting canonical interpretations and uses of them (for example, in providing a common culture—or at least a cultural suntan—for a future corporate elite).

One necessary caveat, however, is that the critique of canons has a different resonance in historiography and in literary criticism. Literary criticism (like art history and philosophy) has tended to be fixated on canonical artifacts even though the canons have recently fragmented or even begun to speak in many polyphonous or even cacophonous voices. In at least partial contrast, historiography has in the recent past been insistently anticanonical but often for methodological, indeed at times narrowly positivistic, rather than political reasons, especially given the orientation of history toward a certain kind of social science. Historians at present do not have a canon (or even competing canons) of shared textual reference points, and the absence of such reference points may even further archival fetishism; a reliance on tacit, craftlike procedures; and a marked resistance to theory. One may even question whether historians as a group have anything approximating a shared "historical culture" in contradistinction to certain limited features of professionalism. Indeed, in historiography there have been viciously paradoxical pretensions to disciplinary hegemony on the part of those who stress the importance of the noncanonical, popular, and nonhegemonic in the past. To put it bluntly, some of the most elitist members of a profession may privilege the study of nonelites. And reductive, sociocentric explanations may provide a false sense of superiority over the figures one treats or even license an anti-intellectual history.

To some extent, there may be more to be said for a critique of canons in literary criticism (as well as in art history and philosophy), at least as a provisional maneuver. But there should, I think, also be the awareness that this kind of critique may have self-defeating consequences, particularly when the New Historicism, in its practical or theoretical reliance on the tacit and the craftlike, seems very close to older historicisms that still have currency in departments of history. A second point is that a principal task of analysis and argument is to attempt to determine the extent to which modern culture has been converted into a reinforcing component of a commodity system and whether, in this form, it retains a significant critical potential. This question concerning commodification is relevant to all forms of modern culture. But one danger, which is particularly evident in a blind populism, is to interpret with a vengeance by simply eliding popular and commodified or mass culture and attributing to the latter the traits traditionally, normatively, or mythically associated with popular culture. The very level of capital investment in commodified "popular" culture and the imperatives in marketing it should make us quite tentative in attributing markedly critical or legitimately utopian potentials to it.

Once one rejects the indiscriminate idea that contexts are ipso facto explanatory, a crucial problem is how to motivate the selection and emphasis of certain contexts or combinations of contexts in the reading of texts. (Here the Dresden approach of saturation bombing has its obvious limitations.) I have suggested that the grounds on which to motivate contextual choices, while of course always open to counterevidence and counterargument, are both intellectual and sociopolitical and that they depend in good part upon the interpretations one is trying to counteract or to reinforce and upon the sociopolitical possibilities one is attempting to disclose. Hence, for example, a stress upon the mutations of the carnivalesque may itself be motivated by a critical concern for the actual and desirable interaction of work and play in culture. It may also be motivated by a judgment about the relative underemphasis of this issue in theories of modern society and culture, including certain variants of Marxism. On a formal level, this stress might direct one to the way in which stylistic features of texts—for example, the use of the so-called free indirect style in modulating irony and empathy in the dialogic reaction of a multiply masked narrator and various characters or objects of narration—may be interpreted in terms of displaced carnivalesque forms as well as in terms of a challenge to concepts of full individual mastery and ownership of discourse. The more general point is that the very motivation of contextual emphases and the attempt to construe the precise manner

*207*

in which texts inscribe contexts, and are in turn reinscribed by contexts, pose historical and critical problems that so-called New Historicisms, like old historicisms, may do more to obscure than to illuminate. In any case, history should not be coded as the antithesis of theory, and the turn toward history should not be made at the expense of either close reading or theoretical sophistication. It should be a way of making both reading and theory more informed and politically viable, especially with reference to our own transferential and dialogic relation to the past, which is bound up with an intellectual and sociopolitical intervention in the present.

What I want to do in conclusion is simply and inadequately to indicate the area in which the intellectual and sociopolitical motivation of the selection of contexts is now most pressing. This is the area in which our own transferential relation to the past is most heavily "cathected," or invested with affect. It is also the area where there is the greatest need to work critically through that relation rather than to deny it—or to remain fixated in compulsively repetitive processes of acting it out. I earlier referred to the triangular anxiety agitating a small group of intellectual historians but perhaps increasingly impinging upon the work of a somewhat larger group: the anxiety marking the relations of psychoanalytic, Marxist, and poststructuralist approaches. Recently this anxiety has been supplemented and even displaced by another set of forces that not only complicate the picture but may disorient or even undo the Oedipal and "phallocentric" notion of triangulation itself. I am referring to modes of investigation sensitive to problems of class, gender, and race. Indeed the three latter terms have at times been run together to form a portmanteau word: class-race-gender—a word the sequence of whose hyphenated parts depends upon the priorities of the analyst.

A portmanteau word signals the danger that an overly formulaic if not stereotyped solution to problems may be emerging. Any overly formulaic solution is misleading, and it should be resisted. But this danger should not be made to downgrade or to obscure the importance of articulating the relations among class, race, and gender in the critical and historical investigation of problems. Indeed a crucial question at present is how to relate psychoanalytic, Marxist (or post-Marxist), and poststructural orientations to one another and to the set of problems bearing on relations of class, race, and gender. It has become clear that an exclusive focus on any one of the latter relations is overly confining, as is an exclusive reliance on any one of the former theoretical orientations. The articulation of all of these relations is no doubt the imposing, problematic current horizon of critical thought.

This critical articulation of relations should of course not come in the purely abstract form of a pseudosolution to a problem set. It should inform investigations that illuminate actual historical and interpretive issues, and it should increasingly become a more or less differentiated theme of reflection in various disciplines. Indeed it is precisely in terms of such a critical articulation that intellectual history itself may be legitimately dissolved into a broader form of inquiry or continue at best as a relatively specific perspective within a larger but still ill-defined mode of historical, cultural, and sociopolitical investigation. My own limited references to gendered, class-based, or ethnic problems, as well as to the significance of inquiry into the formation of levels of culture and society in the modern period, may be taken as indications of the need for a larger critical and self-critical framework. What we call this "framework" or mode of articulation (say, cultural criticism or critical theory) is relatively unimportant. What is important is that we not only recognize the need to elaborate it but actively formulate the problems we investigate in terms that lend our discourse to reformulation in other, at times unpredictable, and perhaps more valid terms.

# Index

Library of Congress Cataloging-in-Publication Data

LaCapra, Dominick, 1939
    Soundings in critical theory / Dominick LaCapra.
       p. cm.
    Includes index.
    ISBN 0-8014-2322-8 (alk. paper).—ISBN 0-8014-9572-5 (pbk. alk
paper)
    1. Criticism—History—20th century. 2. Literature—History and
criticism—Theory, etc. 3. Literature. Modern—20th century—
History and criticism. I. Title.
PN94.L36   1989    801'.95'0904—dc19     89-30080